The Rajiv I Knew

The Rajiv I Knew

And Why He Was India's Most Misunderstood Prime Minister

Mani Shankar Aiyar

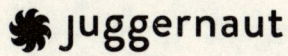

JUGGERNAUT BOOKS
C-I-128, First Floor, Sangam Vihar, Near Holi Chowk,
New Delhi 110080, India

First published by Juggernaut Books 2024

Copyright © Mani Shankar Aiyar 2024
Excerpt from *Memoirs of a Maverick* © Mani Shankar Aiyar 2023

Lok Sabha speeches in the book have been reproduced from Lok Sabha Debates
with the permission of the Hon'ble Speaker, Lok Sabha.
Rajya Sabha speeches in the book have been reproduced from Rajya Sabha Debates
with the permission of the Hon'ble Speaker, Rajya Sabha.

10 9 8 7 6 5 4 3 2 1

P-ISBN: 9789353457525
E-ISBN: 9789353454067

The views and opinions expressed in this book are the author's own.
The facts contained herein were reported to be true as on the date of publication
by the author to the publishers of the book, and the publishers are not
in any way liable for their accuracy or veracity.

All rights reserved. No part of this publication may be reproduced,
transmitted, or stored in a retrieval system in any form or by any means without the
written permission of the publisher.

Typeset in Adobe Caslon Pro by
R. Ajith Kumar, Noida

Printed at Thomson Press India Ltd

Dedicated to my three lionesses:

Suranya, a Gandhian in thought, values and action, who has found amazingly creative ways of bringing Gandhiji's 'My life is my message' to contemporary audiences to show that the Mahatma is as relevant to the India of the twenty-first century as he was to the twentieth. And who, besides, has brought comfort and succour to hundreds of immigrant families, Indian and East European, whose children have been filched from their parents by Western child protection services on the most trivial and culturally biased grounds, for which work she had been made a Laureate of the Nordic Human Rights Council. She is an activist who is often in demonstrations and has even undertaken long fasts to bring injustice to the attention of cruel, uncaring authorities. In fulfillment of Wordsworth's famous lines, she has proved that 'the child is father of the man'.

Yamini, a monument to courage and daring, who was pole-vaulted at the tender age of thirty-eight to preside over one of India's leading think tanks for her astonishing intellectual and administrative abilities, and her work as a columnist of note. With determination and persistence, she has faced persecution aimed at her institution and her personally, but refuses to be cowed down or give up on her principles, or bend her knees before insolent might. An authority on my subject of Panchayati Raj, I have learnt more from her than she ever learnt from me.

Sana, a professor of history at the Massachusetts Institute of Technology at Cambridge, US, to whom I invariably turn when bewildered by some turn of events, especially those of the past, that I don't completely comprehend. Strange as it may sound, I would describe her as my mentor, despite the forty years that separate us, for her reasoning is clear, her knowledge is deep and her analytical powers are profound. My pride in her is as great as my gratitude for leading me out of many a mental trap.

This book was initially an integral part of the first volume of my Memoirs. However, as I was not personally witness to, or personally involved with, much of Rajiv Gandhi's thoughts and actions in the political field, it read more like a political biography than an autobiography, especially as a great deal of the source material for this volume emerged in the public domain after his assassination on 21 May 1991, in some key cases a decade or even longer after his death. This meant the mode of my Memoirs suddenly changed from 'autobiographical' to 'biographical', which my publishers felt – and I agreed with them – wrecked the integrity and consistency of the work. It was, therefore, decided, with my concurrence, that these pages should be separated from the first volume and, after due editing, published as a separate standalone work.

Contents

Introduction	1
1. The Accords	15
2. The Controversies	49
3. Foreign Policy Initiatives	149
4. Innovative Domestic Initiatives	183
5. Panchayat(i) Raj: The Defining Initiative	203
6. Rajiv Gandhi – The Man and His Office: A Brief Evaluation	247
Index	255
Acknowledgements	265
A Note on the Author	267
Excerpt from Mani Shankar Aiyar's Memoirs of a Maverick	269

A note on the QR codes

For each chapter a QR code is given that may be scanned to access detailed footnotes and endnotes.

Introduction

As we were moving on the tarmac to board an Indian Airlines flight in January 1990, soon after his electoral defeat, former Prime Minister Rajiv Gandhi suddenly turned to me and said, 'People say I am arrogant. Am I?'

I replied, 'Well, you were born with a silver spoon in your mouth, sir. And you turned it into gold. Perhaps they don't like that.'

RG never brought up the subject again. I wondered why he had asked. And was he asking me – or just posing the question to himself? He had just lost the election, crashing from over 400 seats to under 200, the biggest defeat in Indian electoral history – after winning by the highest margin ever five years earlier. It had put him in an introspective mood. Where had he gone wrong?

I seek an answer three decades on. It eludes me. But the journey makes me reflect on who he was and how he came to be PM. For although he was the eldest son in India's first political family, with a mother and a grandfather both prime ministers who between them ruled the country for thirty-five years, he himself had so avoided the limelight that when his grandfather came to school to meet him, he simply could not be found anywhere. Until a schoolmate blew the whistle on him, suggesting he might be hiding in one of the large laundry wicker baskets placed in the bathrooms. And, sure enough, it was there that he was found, hiding from public view.

Later, when he was a pilot with Indian Airlines, he always said, 'This is Captain Rajiv speaking from the flight deck', never 'Captain Rajiv *Gandhi*' – partly because he did not want to be mobbed, but mainly because he shied away from public recognition. He had no intention, no desire, no wish to become prime minister himself. And he never would have had his brother, Sanjay, who was avidly grooming himself to take over from his mother, not been killed in a self-inflicted accident performing aerial acrobatics while piloting an aircraft. That was when 'Mummy' asked Rajiv to help her. He was reluctant but answered his mother's insistent pleas.

Little did he imagine that just four years down, Prime Minister Indira Gandhi would be assassinated by her own bodyguards and the party apparatchiks would turn to him, wholly unprepared and just forty years of age, to take over the reins. His wife Sonia says she begged him not to, pointing out they would be killed. Rajiv replied that, in any case, they would all be killed, and stepped forward.

But once in office, he showed little hesitation in rising to his duties. These were immediately overshadowed with the outbreak of mass rioting targeting innocent Sikhs, at least 3,000 of whom were to lose their lives in an orgy of violence not seen since the Partition riots. RG had his mother's most trusted minister, P.V. Narasimha Rao, as his home minister, and in P.G. Gavai, a former Union Home Secretary, a senior, well-respected lieutenant governor of the union territory of Delhi, both of whom he trusted. He thought he might leave the control of the pogrom in their tried-and-trusted hands but discovered within a day that they were not equal to the situation. It was the first and most telling example of misplaced trust that was to play havoc with his innings as PM. Eventually, taking the full responsibility upon himself, he called in the army and went personally in the dead of the night to the worst-affected areas. Calm began to be restored from the next day. It was a bloody blooding.

But he did not sack the additional commissioner of police, New Delhi Range – to whom he was related. That would have rescued his personal reputation but would have failed the test of due process. It was the first example of his scrupulous adherence to the principle of no punishment until the enquiry was over and the person indicted had been given the opportunity to clear his or her name, a commendable principle in private life but often misplaced for a head of government who has to act in the heat of the moment when public opinion is most exercised. It happened again with another relative, Arun Nehru, over the opening of the locks at the Babri Masjid and the Bofors deal; with other friends like Arun Singh; with party colleagues like V.P. Singh and Arif Mohammed Khan; and with officers like General Sundarji, and even RG's closest aide Gopi Arora, who crossed red lines of armed forces and civil service discipline. That harmed them but harmed the prime minister more – and all because he trusted them to the point where they thought they could substitute for him. Rajiv Gandhi's insistence on giving others a fair opportunity to explain themselves (commendable in private persons but often unsuited to those in public office) caused him and his office huge damage. That was the central paradox. What made him a good man – compassionate, diligent, honest, upright, unruffled, bold, truthful – was what felled him as PM. He lacked the guile, deviousness and deceit which may have helped him become a more long-lasting PM.

I had included all this – at somewhat inordinate length – in the first draft of my memoirs, but my arguments and conclusions were based not on personal knowledge but on an earnest pursuit of the record decades after the events. This gave the exercise the air of political biography as against personal reminiscences around which the rest of my memoirs were woven. My publisher, Chiki Sarkar, felt this did not sit well with the tone or theme of my memoirs. I, on the other hand, believe that what makes my life a possible matter of public interest is my six-year association with Rajiv Gandhi. To remove these reflections on what made him India's most misunderstood prime minister would, I felt, mean a disservice to the central catalytic relationship in my public life. I also felt that I should stand up for him and be counted rather than pretend all was hunky-dory during those turbulent times. Chiki and I compromised by removing these pages from the autobiography (with brief mentions or some discussion of the incidents) and publishing these reflections sequentially as a separate, self-contained companion volume. That is how this book came to be.

While all these contretemps were swirling around the Prime Minister's Office (PMO), we, as civil servants working there, were placed in water-tight compartments of sectoral responsibility and kept so busy with workdays that stretched from sixteen to eighteen hours that there was little opportunity – beyond snatched moments of gossip – to discuss them among ourselves. Besides, RG himself kept such a cheerful mien and concentrated with such diligence on the task at hand that newspaper headlines were soon forgotten in the whirl of office work under the benign, ever-smiling aegis of the unfazed and spirited prime minister. Moreover, RG held the lines of work responsibility firmly in place – and woe to him or her who attempted to cross into zones not their own. I was definitely not the PM's confidant on matters political, and apart from passing comments he made and occasionally overhearing his conversations with others, I had little opportunity of discussing these burning issues with him. I was in no sense an 'insider'. I, therefore, knew only as much as any newspaper reader about almost all that is recounted in these pages – and possibly even less because my duties kept me too preoccupied to give more than a cursory glance to the news of the day.

It is only the archival genius of my principal private secretary for thirty years, N. Venkatraman, and the prolonged lockdown over COVID-19 that gave me the opportunity of revisiting the Rajiv Gandhi accords and controversies and filling out my memory of his numerous innovative initiatives, domestic and foreign. I have used all this to bring perspective to events that played out to their conclusion, especially in the courts, decades after Rajiv Gandhi's death. The judgments on highly controversial issues, in particular – such as the Shah Bano and Bofors cases – confirm that Rajiv Gandhi was right. The Supreme Court judgment of 2001 on the Muslim Women (Protection of Rights on Divorce) Act, 1986, passed by the RG government following the Supreme Court's 1985 judgment on the Shah Bano maintenance case, ruled that – far from 'reversing' the 1985 judgment, as is often maliciously claimed even today – Rajiv Gandhi was entirely right in codifying that judgment into the civil law of the country. And, on the so-called Bofors 'scandal', the Delhi High Court in 2004 found not 'a scintilla of evidence'[1] had been unearthed after over 4,000 days of investigation, and the investigation by CBI of all relevant papers from Swiss and Swedish sources, to suggest RG was anything other than totally innocent. In 2018, the Supreme Court in effect endorsed the Delhi High Court finding. Yet, judgments on neither of these issues have adequately entered public and media consciousness, so that even today, some twenty years on, misunderstanding and worse continue to be propagated.

This is what made it imperative, in my considered view, to write at length about these still contested issues where others may want to let sleeping dogs lie. My conscience tells me otherwise.

The question that remains after delving into all these issues is why Rajiv Gandhi as prime minister appears so often to not have been in control of what was happening around him and in his name. For instance, how could he not have known that the Congress government in Uttar Pradesh (UP) was leaning on the judiciary to allow the locks to be opened at the Babri Masjid? How could the defence ministry and the chief of army staff have kept him in the dark about their not cooling down Operation Brasstacks despite stringent orders to do so? How could the PM not have known that AE Services had been recruited to fill the gap after the prime minister-level agreement with the Swedish

---

[1] Kartongen Kemi Och Forvaltning AB . . . vs State Through CBI on 4 February, 2004, Indian Kanoon, https://indiankanoon.org/doc/561739/?type=print.

prime minister not to permit any middlemen in the Bofors deal? Why was the prime minister so woefully misled by all the agencies – army, intelligence, diplomatic – about the downside of accepting Sri Lankan President Jayawardene's request to send in the Indian Peace-Keeping Force (IPKF) to the north and east of Sri Lanka? Was his presentation to the United Nations (UN) of his Action Plan for a Nuclear-Weapons-Free and Non-violent World Order a trick played on the international community to keep their eyes off India's nuclear weapons programme which was given its initial go-ahead by the same PM? These and other questions are answered in the pages that follow but the basic question of whether Rajiv Gandhi was really in charge deserves an answer right at the start. So, here goes.

Prime ministers can either be suspicious, secretive, even paranoiac, like RG's mother was, or transparent and trusting as he was. Even as he would have never betrayed a benefactor, he assumed that others shared his values. Not being duplicitous himself, he did not understand that others might betray him for a host of reasons. Not having striven for power, he did not quite understand what made others power-hungry. Because he trusted those to whom he gave responsibility, he assumed they would not violate his trust. Because he was a good man, he thought others would be the same. Until they gave him cause to remove his trust. Then he acted swiftly. And decisively.

Perhaps the biggest betrayal was by the man who made him PM, his cousin Arun Nehru. So firm was Arun Nehru's hold on the party that Rajiv Gandhi initially outsourced much of his authority as party president to his cousin. This cousin was a different person altogether. He had no time for scruples and wielded power to impose his will on others. He got the relatively obscure Veer Bahadur Singh elected chief minister of UP with the aim of using him to gain firm control of Hindu sentiment over Ram Janmabhoomi/Babri Masjid – an issue that in 1985 was entirely local (the unlocking of the gates at the Babri Masjid) but had the potential to become a partisan national issue, garnering the support of large swathes of the majority community even as it alienated the Muslim minority. Arun Nehru also knew that RG would never play the game this way as he was quintessentially secular and believed deeply in the fundamental principle of unity in diversity to keep the nation together. Moreover, with complete control over the Lok Sabha there was no need for the prime minister to divide to rule, quite apart from his moral repugnance at such majority appeasement. Arun Nehru, on the other hand, saw which way RG's mind was working on the Shah Bano issue and noted that anger was growing in sections of the majority community, especially those who believed a great victory had been scored over the minority and its clerical leaders – the mullahs and maulvis – by the Supreme Court coming down so harshly on Muslim Personal Law. So, keeping the PM well out of the way was essential to Arun Nehru's 'clever' strategy of compensating the majority for Muslim Personal Law being preserved by giving Hindu worshippers access to '*Ram lalla virajman*' (Baby Ram present) within the precincts of the Babri Masjid. That explains RG knowing nothing of the goings-on in the Faizabad sessions court until the fait accompli of the locks being opened, with crowds of devotees surging in.

Rajiv Gandhi did not take this lightly. He ordered a party enquiry into the role of both Nehru and his political adviser Makhan Lal Fotedar. The enquiry showed Fotedar to be blameless but found Arun Nehru responsible for getting the locks opened. So, Fotedar was spared but Nehru was removed from the Council of Ministers; he was downgraded within the party and deprived of all clout and influence before himself quitting the party.

Moreover, Rajiv had also discovered Arun Nehru's shenanigans in the Bofors deal. Feeling cheated (by the prime minister's policy of no middlemen) of his grand strategy of filling the party coffers by creaming funds off overseas defence contracts, Nehru was instrumental in setting up the AE Services deal, as indicated by the diaries of Martin Ardbo, managing director of Bofors, which indicted various personalities by initials. Among the initials was 'N', which either stood for Nehru – or Nobody! AE were promised payment of US$35 million by Ardbo who was convinced the Government of India would otherwise place the order with his French rival, Sofma. When Arun Nehru was sacked from the Council of Ministers in September 1986, only a single instalment of some $7 million had been paid. Mysteriously, no other payment was ever made once Nehru was removed from the scene although the contract stipulated further instalments totalling some $28 million. Most observers, including Chitra Subramaniam, the journalist behind the Bofors 'expose', are agreed that Arun Nehru's desire to hide his own role was the primary reason for the V.P. Singh government dragging its feet on prosecuting the Bofors case once it came to office.

When he was nominated by his party as PM following the assassination of Indira Gandhi, convinced that it was wrong to continue without electoral sanction, Rajiv Gandhi had called an election within a few weeks of his becoming prime minister. Riding a massive sympathy wave, he was sworn in a second time in as many months as prime minister – and with an unprecedented mandate. With the same moral rectitude, when he was defeated in 1989, instead of staking a claim to form a coalition government on the grounds that his was still the largest single party, he preferred to inform the president that he would be content to sit in Parliament as leader of the Opposition. I have recounted in my memoirs how his classmate, Aroon Purie, owner-editor of *India Today*, believed RG would push aside the people's disapproval by resorting to technicalities to try to become PM a third time. On the basis of my knowledge of the man, and without asking him, I replied that he was not proceeding to Rashtrapati Bhavan to seek a third chance but would act on principle to tell the president that his opponent, the National Front, should be given the opportunity to form the government. And so it happened. Of course, the V.P. Singh government collapsed within eleven months – but that is a different story and brought on his own head by the much-vaunted master 'manager of contradictions'.[2] The fact is that instead of adroit political manoeuvring, Rajiv Gandhi preferred the straightforward constitutional way of resigning office when he lost the trust of the electorate. Would Arun Nehru have ever thought that way?

I underline that until his mother's assassination, Rajiv Gandhi was not preparing himself for high office. He inherited from her all those who let him down: Arun Nehru, Arif Mohammed Khan, V.P. Singh, Gopi Arora, et al. Of his own friends whom he inducted into politics he was let down only by Arun Singh. Others like Ghulam Nabi Azad, Oscar Fernandes, Tarun Gogoi, Ahmed Patel and myself held firm. True, he made a bad choice for chief of army staff in General Sundarji – but I know of no PM in history anywhere in the world who has not tripped up on some appointments. What needs further underlining is that apart from a few exceptions, scores of ministers, thousands of party cadres and hundreds of government officers he appointed remained true to him. Picking the wrong man was not a characteristic but a hazard of office. I had wondered until recently whether he had not made a serious mistake in alienating President Giani Zail Singh. K.C. Singh's recent book shows that the PM was quite right in suspecting that the president had not risen to the standards of his high office.[3] He was still little more than a petty provincial politician playing his politics from the presidential palace against all constitutional norms. He did so even when (indeed especially when) this crossed the most important strand of Rajiv Gandhi's political

---

[2] Dipankar Sinha, *Asian Survey*, University of California Press, Vol. 31, no.7, July 1991, pp. 598–612, https://stor/stable/2645379.

[3] K.C. Singh, *The Indian President: An Insider's Account of the Zail Singh Years*, HarperCollins, Gurugram, May 2023, pp. 204–23. It provides a view from inside Rashtrapati Bhavan of shenanigans that reveal a president deeply involved in hatching conspiracies with politicians, journalists and jurists to unseat a democratically elected prime minister by pushing presidential powers to the outer limit. The Constitution blocked him. The prime minister was fully informed of these sinister plots and stratagems.

policy – tackling Punjab by forging an agreement with moderate elements of the Akali Dal and its leadership.

On matters of policy, it was Rajiv Gandhi's exceptionalism that temporarily did him down but he stands vindicated by subsequent history. Thus, on Shah Bano, the easiest way out was perhaps the one commended to him by his desk officer for minority affairs, Wajahat Habibullah: that the highest court in the land had spoken and it was best to leave matters at that.[4] Moreover, given the huge adverse reaction of large sections of the majority community and the intellectual, public opinion-moulding, left-liberal class, to intervene politically after the highest echelon of the judiciary had spoken was politically suicidal. Yet RG persisted because he felt that as PM he could not but listen to the anguish of the minorities – as expressed in Parliament and elsewhere – over the threat to their Personal Law, which they had been promised at the outset of independence would be protected. To betray that pledge would amount to endorsing the widely bruited view that Muslims as a community and their Islamic law was antediluvian, discriminatory, anti-women and oppressive. Rajiv Gandhi believed that as PM it was for him to understand, not condemn. He, therefore, carefully followed the seven-month-long debate in Parliament and interacted intensively with all concerned (as testified to on the floor of the House by the leader of the Opposition, Madhu Dandavate).[5]

It was only after thoroughly acquainting himself with all aspects of Muslim divorce law and practice that he concluded the answer lay in making Muslim law on divorce justiciable in our civil courts, so that abuse could be ended without giving offence to or betraying promises made to

---

[4] Wajahat Habibullah, *My Years with Rajiv: Triumph and Tragedy*, Westland, Chennai, 2020, p. 98.

[5] See Columns 378–79 of Lok Sabha Debates on 5 May 1986, where Dandavate cited the PM as saying: 'I am studying the entire situation and unless we take you into confidence no new legislation shall be brought.'

the minority. His numerous opponents seized on this to proclaim that Muslims were being 'appeased' by protecting Muslim Personal Law, while Hindus were being 'appeased' by opening the locks at the makeshift Ram Lalla temple built on the premises of the Babri Masjid, completely ignoring the larger context in which the decision was taken. Moreover, fifteen years later (and ten after Rajiv Gandhi was assassinated) the very Supreme Court that had passed the 1985 Shah Bano judgment ruled in 2001 that far from 'reversing' that judgment, the 1986 Muslim Women's (Protection of Rights on Divorce) Act, 1986, actually 'codified' the judgment and made it integral to our civil law. And all this was achieved with the approbation of the Muslim community. For the past two decades, it is this codification in Indian civil law, wrought by the combined genius of Rajiv Gandhi and his law minister, Asoke Sen, that has governed all divorce cases, thus ensuring fair play for Muslim divorcees under the stern gaze of the local magistrate and the availability of the higher judiciary, if necessary, to divorced Muslim women. It is highly significant that for twenty years and more the Act has worked so well that little or no recourse has been had by any affected Muslim woman to the higher judiciary.

He was politically damned by Bofors. That too was a lie. In 2004, the Delhi High Court dismissed all charges of corruption against 'public officials', that is, the then PM, Rajiv Gandhi, and Defence Secretary S.K. Bhatnagar. The Modi government went in appeal but in November 2018 the Supreme Court snuffed that out by pointing to an investigation lasting over 4,000 days having yielded nothing. Yet Rajiv Gandhi continues to be pilloried. In this case too, he could have taken the easy way out, as recommended by Arun Singh and General Sundarji, of getting Bofors to name the recipients of the post-contract payouts and the reasons for these, subject to the PM pledging himself in advance to *not* acting on the information provided. Singh and Sundarji simply brushed off that condition. But RG would not let the prime minister of India's word be played with in such a cavalier manner. Note that all papers relating to the payouts have been in the public domain and the courts since at least the latter half of the 1990s. They unequivocally show that, as RG had asserted, the payments were indeed 'winding up charges' and contractual payments, not bribes to secure the contract for Bofors.[6] True to his word in Parliament, neither Rajiv Gandhi nor any member of his family was involved in any dubious financial transaction. And the Bofors gun, despite all the doubts raised about its military effectiveness, has proved its worth in the Kargil conflict. Yet general public opinion and a motivated press continue to castigate the innocent.

Rajiv Gandhi's first full year in office – 1985 – was a golden year. But from the beginning of 1986 to the end of his term in November 1989, it was largely downhill all the way. He saw many of his initiatives, such as in Punjab, which had seemed magical at first, unravelling and found himself simultaneously caught in swirling controversies ranging from the Shah Bano affair to the Babri Masjid, from the very ugly public spat with the president, Giani Zail Singh, to the IPKF expedition to Sri Lanka and, above all, the Bofors deal. These wrecked his public standing, leading to a humiliating defeat at the hustings. Had he the guile and amorality of Arun Nehru; the deviousness of V.P. Singh; the hypocrisy of Arif Mohammed Khan; the viciousness of Arun Shourie; and the opportunism of lesser fry, he might have lasted longer as PM, but would not have been the decent, compassionate, deeply caring, hard-working, constructive and imaginative human being he was.

These qualities of head and heart were manifest in his other initiatives: the accord that moderated violence-filled discord in Punjab, Assam, Mizoram, Jammu and Kashmir (J&K) and Darjeeling; the constitutional amendments on Panchayati Raj; his bold opening to China that gave us thirty-five years of peace and tranquillity on the borders; his reaching

---

[6] See Justice R.S. Sodhi's judgment of 31 May 2005 reported at 2005 SCC online Del 676, which may be accessed at http://indiankanoon.org.

out to Pakistan; the push he gave to ending apartheid, colonialism and external invasion in Africa; his Action Plan for a Nuclear-Weapons-Free and Non-violent World Order, which, after all these decades remains the only ever practical plan presented to the UN by a head of government for time-bound, phased and verifiable disarmament of nuclear and other weapons of mass destruction; his Technology Missions aimed at harnessing high-tech to the urgent felt needs of the poorest of the poor; his attention to drought-proofing and flood control; his giving India its highest ever annual growth rate – 10.67 per cent in 1989–90 – never before achieved and not exceeded so far; his conception of the performing arts as a principal instrument for promoting the emotional integration of our culturally very diverse country; his drawing to the mainstream the social and geographical periphery of the nation; and his overarching aim of restoring India to the vanguard of the advancement of human civilization – a position India (and China) had held until the advent of European imperialism. All this, in the media's view as transmitted to general opinion, and as aggravated by incompetent press briefing in the PMO, was overtaken by V.P. Singh pulling out of his pocket a piece of paper on which he made the patently false claim that written on it was the number of the Swiss bank account into which the Bofors bribe of Rs 64 crore had been paid to Rajiv Gandhi. A total lie.

Ultimately, V.P. Singh proved to be not only one of the most transient prime ministers in the history of our democracy but also the one who restored respectability to the saffron forces that are now undoing our democracy. In the eighteen months he served as leader of the Opposition Rajiv Gandhi was arguably on his way to being restored as PM after having intensely reflected and introspected on ways that might have made him a less misunderstood and more long-lasting prime minister. But that was not to be. An assassin's bomb – the tragic outcome of his ill-advised decision to send the IPKF to Sri Lanka – blew all that away to the realm of speculation.

This book – a companion volume to the author's *Memoirs of a Maverick*, published by Juggernaut in August 2023 – is an attempt by an observer and sometime participant, but hardly an 'insider', to fairly assess the high and low points of Rajiv Gandhi's prime ministership.

Mani Shankar Aiyar
30 May 2023/7 November 2023

22, Atherton Road
Brookline, Boston, US
and
G-43, Jangura Extension,
New Delhi 10014, India

See detailed footnotes and endnotes by
scanning the QR code above.

1

The Accords

Punjab, Assam, Mizoram, Rajiv–Farooq: J&K, Darjeeling

Punjab

The Punjab Accord,[1] signed by Prime Minister Rajiv Gandhi with Sant Harchand Singh Longowal in July 1985, started unravelling from the end of January 1986. According to the accord, Chandigarh was to be transferred to Punjab on Republic Day, 26 January. Haryana, which was sharing the city with Punjab, was to be compensated by transferring an appropriate slice of Punjab to Haryana, based on specific criteria that were set out in the terms of reference of a commission set up under retired Justice K.K. Mathew to decide the issue. These criteria included: 'village as a unit'; 'linguistic affinity'; and 'contiguity'.[2] The tehsils of Fazilka and Abohar had been identified as possible areas to be transferred, provided the three criteria were met. The problem was that

---

[1] 'Rajiv–Longowal Memorandum of Settlement (Accord), July 24, 1985', *The Sikh Times*, http://www.sikhtimes.com/doc_072485a.html.

[2] See paras 1 and 4.12 of the Annual Report 1986–87 of the Ministry of Home Affairs, Departments of Internal Security, States and Home, Ministry of Home Affairs. Also see P. Shiv Shankar, then law minister, at p. 9 of *Rajiv Gandhi's India*, Vol. I, elaborated in footnote 3 of this chapter.

the overwhelming majority of Punjabi speakers in Kandu Khera came in the way of contiguity. This became the bone of contention. It was only if Kandu Khera and another smaller village were found to have a Hindi-speaking majority, however slight, that the contiguity of Fazilka–Abohar with Haryana could be established. Recognizing the crucial role of these two villages, both sides attempted to infiltrate speakers of their respective languages to create the requisite marginal majority. Amarinder Singh, a personal schoolfriend of Rajiv Gandhi's, played a crucial role in mobilizing the Punjabi speakers to sabotage the implementation of the accord. (So much for the 'Doon School mafia'!)

The situation deteriorated so rapidly that the home ministry flew in the Central Reserve Police Force (CRPF) to Fazilka–Abohar. When the Punjab government objected that the CRPF was biased towards Haryana, Punjab chief minister Barnala suggested that the more neutral Assam Rifles be brought in. This was accepted by the PM and acted upon overnight. All this lent considerable drama to the evolving events.

But late at night on 25 January, on the very eve of Republic Day, Justice Mathew threw in the towel, reporting that his commission had not been able to make a determination on which compensatory areas should be transferred to Haryana by Republic Day, the optimistically set deadline. In consequence, temperatures were raised in both states. A last-minute effort to get a decision from another former judge, Justice D.A. Desai, also failed to resolve the deadlock. Republic Day passed. The issue was later remitted to another learned retired justice, E.S. Venkataramiah, but the moment he calculated that Haryana deserved 70,000 acres in compensation for losing its place in Chandigarh, Punjab saw red. Thus, did good intentions melt into thin air and no one came away satisfied.

Rajiv Gandhi was right in seeing that Chandigarh could not be transferred without Haryana being compensated. What he had not or perhaps could not have foreseen was the difficulty in doing so. Not even three Supreme Court ex-judges could help him break the impasse. Some thirty-five years later, the issue has been rendered irrelevant with both states having settled down to rationally sharing the city. The Corbusier buildings in the heart of Chandigarh are with Punjab, and the Panchkula suburb with Haryana, obviating the need to transfer any land. The two states have now been coexisting harmoniously for so long that one might well wonder what the fuss was about. However, since the Aam Aadmi Party government came to office in March 2022, there has been some idle talk of reviving the issue. It would only revive the violent troubles that Rajiv Gandhi thankfully ended.

There was another element of the accord that made it a package deal: the building of a link canal that would carry surplus Sutlej waters to the Yamuna which flowed past Haryana and thence through the Indira Gandhi Canal to irrigate parched northern Rajasthan. The prime minister had expected that both states would rationally see the advantage to *India* of the Sutlej–Yamuna Link Canal. Neither did. Their interest was confined to state interest and did not include any larger national interest. Hence, the efforts of yet another judge, Justice Balakrishna Eradi, and his commission to determine the fair shares of the three states concerned came to nought. That link too was to be completed by Republic Day, 1986, and inaugurated along with the transfer of Chandigarh to Haryana. But the project was barely begun by that date and remains a paper plan to date.

The only beneficiary of the unravelling of the accord and its non-implementation over the last three decades has been Pakistan. Under the Indus Waters Treaty of 1960, Pakistan was entitled to the full flow from the Indus, Jhelum and Chenab rivers. India was entitled to all the waters of the Ravi, Beas and Sutlej. But we failed to implement enough projects to fully utilize our share of the waters. Thus, the surplus waters flowed into Pakistan.

Rajiv Gandhi had not anticipated that Punjab and Haryana, both then under Congress control, would hold out in the manner they did. He seemed to have believed that they, like him, would place national interest above narrow state interest and the chief ministers' personal political interests. It could be said that he was naïve to imagine that they would be as large-hearted as he himself was. While the accord had generated considerable euphoria, the failure to ensure sustained follow-up action and the insistence on unrealistic target dates ruined both the accord and the reputation of the prime minister.

Before I close my remarks on the Punjab Accord, I must take note of a fallout of the crisis that could have shaken the constitutional foundations of our democracy. When the deadline of 26 January passed without the transfer of Chandigarh to Punjab, the Barnala government was threatened with the defection of some of its members of the legislative assembly (MLAs). To save the elected Akali Dal government, the PM decided that praise might be bestowed on the chief minister in the traditional President's Address to the joint Houses of Parliament in February 1986, notwithstanding Zail Singh having been a long-time rival of the Akali Dal in Punjab state politics. As he now held the highest national position, that of rashtrapati, and as everyone knew the President's Address is written by the government of the day and not the president personally, the PM hoped Zail Singh would rise above personal prejudices to serve the national interest. The rashtrapati initially refused to do so and returned the draft for reconsideration. He had to be reminded that his office constitutionally required him to act on the advice of the government if the proposal was put to him a second time. He eventually swallowed this bitter pill but his resentment spilled over in sometimes bizarre ways.[3]

---

[3] I would urge interested readers to look at https//www.rajivmisunderstood.com (by scanning the QR code at the end of the chapter) where I have compiled extracts from an oral history of Rajiv Gandhi's premiership, including the Punjab issue, voiced by leading players of the time, including Chief Minister S.S. Barnala and P. Chidambaram, then minister of state for internal security in the home ministry. These are from Vol. 1 of *Rajiv Gandhi's India* (UBSPD, New Delhi, 1997) subtitled *Politics: Nationhood, Ethnicity, Pluralism and Conflict Resolution*. The four-volume publication is a faithful record of all discussions

Ritu Sarin reported in the *Indian Express* later that President Zail Singh told her he was attempting to collect Rs 40 crore (a huge sum in those days) to topple Rajiv Gandhi.

Relations between the PM and the president having already soured, this incident at the start of 1986 marked the beginning of open warfare between Rashtrapati Bhavan and Race Course Road. At the peak of this unseemly controversy, I got Vir Sanghvi, editor of *Sunday* magazine, to accompany the PM and me on a visit to Mizoram. Although the PM had never before met Sanghvi, he opened up a broadside aimed at Giani Zail Singh. I was so taken aback that after I had escorted Sanghvi to his seat, I went back into the PM's cabin and asked him whether he had really intended to disclose all he had to an unknown journalist. Sounding surprised at the question, the PM said he had not really disclosed the 'awful personal goings on at Rashtrapati Bhawan'. I held my peace but, inevitably, Sanghvi, on returning to Delhi spilled it all out to the president, giving Zail Singh the golden opportunity to join issue publicly with the PM on their differences. Interestingly, the entire incident made Vir Sanghvi one of the PM's most favourite journalists!

Perhaps RG should have tried to mollify the president, or Zail Singh should have reconciled his views to those of the government, as behoved his constitutional post, or resigned. As none of this happened, and others, particularly Arun Shourie, then editor of *Indian Express*, started taking political advantage of the breach by egging on the president, the atmosphere got charged with animosity, to the benefit of neither. Indeed, I got caught in the crossfire when, unaccompanied by the PM, I went to

---

at 'A Golden Jubilee Retrospective' organized at the Rajiv Gandhi Foundation on the fiftieth anniversary of RG's birth. Many of the principal personalities of the Rajiv Gandhi period were still alive and active then, and their reminiscences were recorded, transcribed, edited (by me) for ready comprehension and then published under the overall supervision of Ashok Chopra, now with Hay House Publishers. Please also see Ambassador K.C. Singh's *The Indian President* (HarperCollins, 2023) for an authentic insider's account of the shenanigans that preoccupied Rashtrapati Bhavan.

a function in May that year addressed by the president and Shourie put him up to bait me, catching me on the horns of an agonizing dilemma to either talk back to the holder of the highest office in the land or just take it on the chin. It was typical of Shourie's bullying that he should have impaled me on these horns. Fortunately, with the intervention of R.K. Dhawan in early 1989, a reconciliation of sorts was effected between the PM and ex-President Zail Singh by RG inviting Zail Singh to break bread with him in the PM's house.

However, RG's endeavours on Barnala's behalf notwithstanding, the Barnala government could not long be sustained. The state government was dismissed, President's Rule imposed, 'supercop' K.P.S. Gill turned full blast on the Khalistani terrorists, and Operation Black Thunder II launched which cleared the Golden Temple complex of terrorists and thus broke the back of Khalistani terrorism in the state. Although Gill has been much praised for having rid Punjab of terrorism by the expedient of killing every known or suspected terrorist, one has to note the criticism of the best-informed critics like the very competent, law- and rule-abiding deputy commissioner of Amritsar at the time (and later chief secretary of Punjab), Ramesh Inder Singh, that Gill's policemen were 'war cops', 'lawless police-at war'. In consequence of the depredations on both sides, the victims killed, including the victims of terrorism, amounted to 'about 21,660 people, including nearly 11,787 innocent civilians' as against 'around 8,112' terrorists killed.[4] He concludes that 'the cost of war was 'calamitous' and the strategy adopted 'inflicted a long-lasting scar on the Sikh psyche'.

Ramesh Inder Singh cites Gill's defence that 'there was at no stage in the Punjab operations, a state policy based on arbitrary violence, intimidation, human rights violations or the lawless elimination of alleged terrorism by the police'. Ramesh Inder then adds, 'The de facto reality,

---

[4] Ramesh Inder Singh, *Turmoil in Punjab*, HarperCollins, 2022, particularly chapter 35 ('The War Cops'), pp. 371–92.

though, was quite different from the de jure stand.' His telling last line is: 'The Punjab Police eliminated militancy – it won the undeclared war for the nation, but in the process disabled many citizens and the State alike.'

It needs to be highlighted that notwithstanding the unravelling of the Punjab Accord, there was a huge contrast between the Punjab that Rajiv Gandhi inherited and the Punjab he left. The political atmosphere in Punjab had been so altered by the mere fact of the accord that, implemented or not, the prime minister was able to unleash K.P.S. Gill on the terrorists and crush the Sikh separatist movement in the state. Hence, by the time the Rajiv Gandhi era ended, 47 per cent of police stations in Punjab reported no terrorist incidents in their thana areas in the previous year.

Taking a longer view of the Punjab Accord in the third decade of the twenty-first century than had been possible in 1986, we see that following RG's initiative, peace and democracy have been restored to the state. In contrast to the vicious violence and communal tensions that had overtaken the state during the Janata regime (1977–79) and stretched into Indira Gandhi's second coming, leading to her assassination at the hands of her Sikh guards in 1984 and the dreadful Sikh pogrom that followed, Punjab today is a picture of communal harmony, well integrated with the rest of the country. The awful late seventies and early eighties have been relegated to the past. Rajiv Gandhi may not have succeeded in implementing the Punjab Accord, but his consistent actions – from releasing Sant Harchand Singh Longowal in January 1985 to visiting Hussainiwala in March 1985; preventing vengeance killings with an iron hand when eleven transistor bombs went off in Delhi in May 1985; signing the accord in July 1985; holding elections in September 1985; setting tight deadlines for the implementation of the accord; then conceiving and supervising Operation Black Thunder II – are what moved the state towards the normalcy that now prevails. Above all, it was his fearless tours of all parts of Punjab in 1988–89, travelling everywhere by road (I organized the tours and travelled in the front open jeep), that reassured the people that it was the government, not the Khalistanis, who were with them. That is achievement enough.[5]

Assam

Less than a month after the Punjab Accord, the prime minister scored his next important political goal: the Assam Accord. R.D. Pradhan, Rajiv Gandhi's home secretary, has described in detail in his *Working with Rajiv Gandhi*[6] how he fulfilled the PM's mandate to bring the All-Assam Students Union (AASU) to the negotiating table. The origins of their often vicious and violence-filled agitation (as in the case of Punjab) lay in the dying days of the previous Janata government (1977–79). It had been aggravated by Indira Gandhi insisting on going ahead with the state assembly elections in February 1983 which brought in Hiteswar Saikia of the Congress as the chief minister. The awful massacre of hundreds (sometimes estimated at 'thousands') of innocent Muslims in and around the village of Nellie during the elections had, fairly or unfairly, stained her reputation as she was seen as putting political advantage before common humanity, delegitimizing both the elections and their outcome.

The brutality and violence in the Brahmaputra valley were part and parcel of Rajiv Gandhi's political heritage. He had charged Home Secretary Pradhan with the responsibility of getting the student leaders to put their demands down in writing against the assurance that any agreement with them would be put to the test in free and fair elections – even if that resulted in a premature end to the Congress's Saikia government and the ushering in of an Asom Gana Parishad (AGP)

---

[5] See Rajiv Gandhi's address on 3 March 1989 to the Lok Sabha in his *Selected Speeches and Writings*, Vol. 5, pp. 94–96, reproduced on this book's website that can be accessed by scanning the QR code at the end of the chapter.

[6] Indus (HarperCollins), 1995, pp. 93–112.

government under the leadership of the student leader Prafulla Mahanta. It was a bargain that Mahanta and his colleagues could not refuse,[7] although Rajiv Gandhi would pay a heavy price within the party for the Congress losing the states of Punjab and Assam in quick succession in 1985. That was typical of the man, putting national interest above party interest, knowing full well that it was only a matter of time before the Congress was back in office. It was a sacrifice never popular with the rest of the Congress leadership – although it went down extraordinarily well with the chattering classes.

As the student leaders took control of the state government, the violence they had engendered petered out. The north-east returned to the national fold, and while there were glitches, including the Bodoland agitation and United Liberation Front of Asam (ULFA) terrorist violence that needed to be tackled and ironed out after RG was no longer on the scene, the accord has held these last four decades. Assam is back to being part and parcel of the democratic ethos of India but is now being threatened by a Bharatiya Janta Party (BJP) Union home minister who has referred to immigrants from Bangladesh (mostly Muslims) as 'termites'. To go into all that, however, would be to take the Assam tangle to well beyond RG's premiership.

---

[7] In an otherwise critical account of the events that followed over close to four decades of the Assam Accord, Sangeeta Barooah Pisharoty in her *Assam: The Accord, The Discord* (Penguin/Ebury, 2019) admits, 'The mood was buoyant. Brij Sharma recalled, "It was akin to the moment of [India] gaining independence; as if we got for the Assamese people freedom and rights over their homeland when they were sleeping beyond the midnight hour"' (p. 7). The allusion to Jawaharlal Nehru's address on Independence Day is unmistakable: 'At the stroke of the midnight hour, while the world sleeps, India awakes to life and freedom.' She adds on the next page (p. 8): 'The prime minister's mention of the Accord (at his Independence Day address) as a significant agreement from the pan-Indian point of view helped the AASU and AAGSP leaders remain confident about their decision to sign it.'

Mizoram Peace Accord

Although I am jumping the timeline, it seems to me to be appropriate to deal with the Mizoram Peace Accord of 30 June 1986 at this point to round off the story of how Rajiv Gandhi defused the three major hotspots – Punjab, Assam, Mizoram – he inherited when he was sworn in as PM.

One of the longest insurgencies in India, of twenty years standing beginning 1966, was in Mizoram. While the even longer insurgency in Nagaland had in a sense petered out several decades earlier after Jawaharlal Nehru had persuaded the Naga dissidents to participate in the democratic process, the insurgency in Mizoram had proved much more difficult to squelch since Mizoram's western border ran along the East Pakistan frontier, making it easy for the Mizo insurgents to slip across the border into the welcoming arms of the Pakistan army, who became their chief suppliers of military equipment and other military stores. Also, the eastern borders of Mizoram ran along the virtually unadministered border areas of Burma (Myanmar), making Burma too an easy place of refuge, a sanctuary for the insurgents, especially since there were ethnic and tribal bonds with those living in Burma. Most important of all, infrastructure development in this part of India was so poor that the Indian government had immense logistical difficulties in rushing emergency relief supplies to this distant corner of the country.

In consequence, when severe food shortages struck Mizoram in 1966, there was little the Government of India could or did do to keep the people from going hungry. The root cause of the food shortage was the 'flowering' of the bamboo, the most abundant plant in the hills of Mizoram. 'Bamboo flowering', which occurs on a wide scale around once every forty years, brings out rats in large numbers. Having eaten the bamboo flowers, the rats then gorge themselves on stored foodgrains and rapidly reproduce. This, in turn, brings about severe shortages of basic foodstuff for the people. The virtual famine of 1966 had sparked insurgency under the leadership of Laldenga, a militant rebel leader of considerable political talent. While attempts had been made by Indira Gandhi's two governments (1966–77 and 1980–84), as well as by the Janata government (1977–79), to bring an end to the insurgency, it was only when Rajiv Gandhi took decisive steps to find a political settlement that finally brought the insurgents out of the maquis.

The crux of Rajiv Gandhi's political settlement lay in inducing Laldenga's Mizo National Front (MNF) to lay down their arms in return for the Centre handing over the post of chief minister to the insurgents' leader and getting the Congress party's duly elected CM, Lalthanhawla, to step down to become deputy CM.[8] Elections followed; Laldenga was confirmed as CM in alliance with Brigadier Sailo; the two had a falling out shortly thereafter; another election followed in 1988 and the Congress party's Lalthanhawla triumphantly returned to the chief minister's post.

Since then, the Congress and the MNF have alternated in power every ten years. (The Big Question in Mizoram is whether this pattern will change in the 2023 state general elections. However, whatever the outcome, the Rajiv–Laldenga Accord will hold firm.) The former insurgents have, for the best part of four decades, wholeheartedly accepted the democratic electoral order in which the people decide by ballot, not bullet, who will rule and for how long.

The transformation of Mizoram from the most insurgency-ridden state for two decades, 1966–86, into the most peaceful state in the India over the next four decades has everything to do with Rajiv Gandhi's large-hearted, humane, and sensitive statesmanship in temporarily sacrificing his party's power to persuade the other side to give up arms and become

---

[8] Mizoram figures so little in the consciousness of most Indians that I would refer the interested reader to https://www.rajivmisunderstood.com (or scan the QR code at the end of the chapter) for a more intensive explanation by Mizo participants and others to get the full flavour of the negotiations and their consequences, which were set out in Vol. 1 of Rajiv Gandhi's *India: A Golden Jubilee Retrospective, op.cit.*

a part of the normal democratic process. This is what he did in Punjab; this is what he did in Assam; and this is what he did in Mizoram.

I have vivid memories of the three-day tour of Mizoram that Rajiv and Sonia Gandhi took in the wake of the accord. We landed at Silchar, and drove to Aizawl via Vairengte and Kolasib. After a night halt at Aizawl, where the CM had arranged a concert by Van Lal Ruati, Mizoram's international singing sensation (I've never met a Mizo who does not sing beautifully), we continued through Serchip and Champhai to stop for the night at Lunglei. From there, we took a helicopter to Saiha.

It was a dizzying experience. Thousands lined the road chanting, '*Pu Rajiv Gandhi, Pi Sonia Gandhi*,' strewing the road with flowers and petals, 'welcome' written not only on their banners but on their faces wreathed in smiles. They shouted out 'We love you' as the jeep sped past. I must have been on a hundred road journeys with Rajiv Gandhi, but none was as uplifting. There was not one dissident voice, not one frown. The geographic periphery of the country, it's very edge, was opening its heart to the prime minister.

We had with us a brilliant photographer, Aloke Mitra of the *Telegraph*, to capture all this for posterity. At the end of the trip, he gently mocked me in his Bengali Hindi: '*Tum kuchch nahi ho. Tum Bharat shorkar ke liye kaam karta hain. Mein Aubheek Shorkar ke liye kaam karta hoon.*' (You are nothing. You work for Bharat sarkar.[9] I work for Aveek Sarkar [the *Telegraph* editor/proprietor].) Aveek Sarkar has not stopped dining out on that story.

At Tlabung at the extreme south-west edge of the state, almost tipping into Bangladesh, the athletic Rajiv Gandhi climbed to the plateau on which our helicopter awaited us. I was straggling along well behind when a local villager caught up with me and asked who was the person ahead. I told him, 'The prime minister.' Shaking his head disbelievingly, the man said, 'Doesn't look like him. He doesn't have a moustache.'

---

[9] For the Non-Hindi-speaking reader, I am taking the liberty of translating 'sarkar' into 'government'.

With a shock I realized the man thought his prime minister was General H.M. Ershad of Bangladesh. As our chopper took off, I recounted the incident to the PM. He ordered me immediately on return to tell Ajit Panja, the junior information and broadcasting (I&B) minister, to put up one of the first television towers on that plateau. And that is how TV came to Mizoram!

Although it is little remembered, I would regard the Mizoram Accord as the high point of Rajiv Gandhi's stewardship of the country. This was not a long-term view shared by many in the Congress party leadership. It, therefore, contributed in no small measure to the split in the party in 1987 and the defection of his cousin, the once-powerful Arun Nehru, as well as Arif Mohammed Khan and several other senior Congresspersons to the V.P. Singh camp. Practitioners of realpolitik may consider it foolish to surrender three Congress state governments to a nebulous future but my assessment is different. Morality and national interest triumphed.

It was not blindness that marked the Rajiv era. He was so confident that the Congress would ultimately triumph that he willingly surrendered power for a while in the full recognition of his party's inherent resilience to fight its way back. Punjab was to see several Congress governments after the Punjab Accord; the Congress, after a short five-year absence following the Assam Accord, returned to office in Guwahati/Dispur; and, as we have just seen, the Congress has been in office every ten years since the MNF was persuaded to end its insurgency in return for Laldenga being sworn in as CM even before contesting elections. The litmus test is whether ending rebellion and the threat to national integrity in Punjab, Assam and Mizoram was worth giving up, for a few years, the CM's seat to the other side.

Of course, the question was asked – and remains thirty-five years on – as to whether Rajiv Gandhi was not being naïve in turning over power to his opponents to the chagrin of his own supporters, some of whom turned against him. The answer depends on how politics is viewed. If the point of politics is power by hook or by crook, then Rajiv Gandhi got the comeuppance he deserved. If, however, being prime minister means putting the national interest over petty partisan interest, then Rajiv Gandhi emerges in a different light. It was this different light that gave Rajiv Gandhi his 'golden year'; it was the revenge of the old politicos that spelt his nemesis. That downfall was temporary. Within eighteen months, he was riding back – when an assassin struck.

Mizoram stands integrated with India, transformed into the most peaceful state of the Union, indeed showing the way to the country how refugees fleeing the junta in Myanmar ought to be humanely welcomed. There are few problems of law and order, no problem of majority–minority clan clashes, and a large number of its brightest young men and women are joining the civil services and the armed forces. My private secretary as Minister, DoNER, was Vanlalvawna, Indian Foreign Service (IFS), a Mizo, who has just returned as Joint Secretary to Headquarters after serving as our ambassador to Azerbaijan. He was a superb choice, loyal to a fault, very hard-working and hugely knowledgeable about the region. Mizos, like other north-easterners, are spread across the country, prominent in the airlines and the hospitality industry. In the course of several visits to the state, in my capacity as Congress observer for the hill regions of the north-east (2000–02) and later as Union minister for the development of the north-eastern region (2006–09), I have learned that the people and all party leaders give the credit for the peace and harmony and opportunities for education, employment and development they enjoy to Rajiv Gandhi and his peace accord.

Tragically, in the last few months since this section was written, Mizoram has been swamped with some 40,000 refugees from Myanmar. There is commendable humanism in the manner these refugees have been welcomed in Myanmar, in sharp contrast to the political convulsions, emotional disintegration and ruthless violence that has overtaken the neighbouring state of Manipur. Nothing illustrates more vividly the difference in approach to national integrity between the Rajiv and Modi governments as the virtual paralysis we have witnessed in Manipur.

Rajiv–Farooq Accord: J&K

The alliance between Farooq Abdullah of the National Conference (NC) and Rajiv Gandhi on behalf of the Indian National Congress was signed in November 1986 and the next month Rajiv decided to first visit Jammu and then Kashmir. I was on the trip. When we reached Udhampur, the army base, the weather turned so bad that his Air Force plane could not take off. Rajiv Gandhi then decided to drive up to Srinagar. We reached there in blinding snow. The following cars (which carried our baggage) got cut off by a landslide. We arrived in Srinagar six hours later, chilled to the bone and went straight to a meeting in the Centaur Hotel.

For the next two days, we were stuck in the snow-bound city but travelled around the Valley. Rajiv greeted and spoke to knots of Kashmiris gathered along the road. At one point, a Special Protection Group (SPG) personnel ran up to me in the front jeep and said the PM wanted me. I ran back to his jeep, and he simply pointed to the feet of the young women gathered around his vehicle. None of them had any footwear! They were walking and running on the snow and ice on their naked soles.

The visit, at one level, was a huge success in that it signalled the firming up of the alliance, and was underpinned by an unprecedented thrust to economic and infrastructure development, including bringing railways to the Valley, taking up huge hydroelectric projects and cleaning the Dal Lake. The downside was that the fundamentalist and separatist Muslim outfits made use of the Rajiv–Farooq Accord as a weapon in their vitriolic campaign against the secular forces.

When the promised elections to the state assembly got under way, the Muslim United Front's (MUF) campaign theme was that a victory for the party in the elections would be a victory for Islam. There was no doubt that although the MUF might not win a majority of seats, it would make its presence felt as an effective and powerful opposition.[10] In the event, thirty-eight seats went to the NC and twenty-six to the Congress (giving the alliance a total of sixty-four); the MUF won only four seats. However, the victory of the Farooq–Rajiv alliance in the J&K elections was somewhat pyrrhic because it presaged unprecedented turmoil in the Valley. Although the MUF lost the election, it received a lot of public sympathy.

Wajahat Habibullah cites the egregious example of rigging in the Amira Kadal constituency in Srinagar contested by a senior minister in Dr Farooq Abdullah's government, Ghulam Mohiuddin Shah, against the MUF's Mohammad Yusuf Shah. Drawing on Sumantra Bose's detailed study of the election, Habibullah concludes the Abdullah family simply got the returning officer to switch votes from the MUF to the NC to give their candidate a majority. This so incensed the 'losing' candidate that he and his polling agents joined the Hizb-ul-Mujahideen or the Jammu and Kashmir Liberation Front (JKLF), preferring the bullet to the ballot.[11]

Did Farooq Abdullah go in for selective rigging because he wished to retain his independence without having to rely exclusively on Congress party support? This intriguing thought is put forward by Wajahat Habibullah who concludes that there was clear evidence of malpractice in only ten constituencies, primarily in Srinagar, where the support base of the NC had been tenuous.[12] If Habibullah is right about the rigging of ten seats, that would have brought the NC score down to twenty-eight, a whisker above the Congress's twenty-six. The election would have gone

---

[10] Khem Lata and O.N. Wakhlu, *Kashmir: Behind the White Curtain, 1972–91*, Konark, New Delhi, 1992, p. 321.

[11] *Ibid.*, pp. 176–81 and other occasional writings, and Wajahat Habibullah, *My Kashmir: The Dying of the Light*, Penguin/Viking, Gurugram, 2011, pp. 72–75.

[12] Habibullah, *op. cit.*, pp. 178–79.

to the alliance but left the NC dependent on the Congress. This analysis implicitly holds that Rajiv Gandhi had nothing to do with the rigging; whatever rigging took place was undertaken only by the NC.

Habibullah believes that had rigging not occurred, the MUF – a potent though not dominant force – might have won fourteen seats. Perhaps this would have helped integrate Kashmir's politically conflicting forces but given the MUF's determination to undermine the integration process, such an outcome was unlikely.

While discontent may indeed have simmered in the Valley in the period between the state assembly elections of March 1987 and the general elections of November 1989, there was little outward manifestation of this discontent. As the government was in control of the situation, RG could make a number of very successful visits to Jammu, Kashmir and Ladakh, marked by peace, tranquillity and bonhomie, through the remaining years of his premiership. I was witness to all these visits.

One of the most remarkable of these was to the very remote village of Padam in the Zanskar valley of Ladakh that had been hit by a bad avalanche in the winter of early 1989. RG and Farooq Abdullah, accompanied by me, flew by helicopter from Leh to Padam, but could not land because the rotating wings would whip up the soft snow into a storm. This obliged the pilot to proceed to Kargil. At Kargil, I received a message from the advance SPG unit at Padam that it had stopped snowing and we could try now to land. After confabulations, it was decided that I should go back to Padam, and if I succeeded in landing, the chopper would return to Kargil and pick up the PM and CM.

I landed successfully. While I went around telling the waiting crowd that a second landing was being attempted, the two leaders returned, but the snowstorm caused by the rotors persisted. So, the chopper hovered a few inches above the ground while the PM and CM leaped off, went among the waiting crowd, and then jumped back on the hovering aircraft. I was a fitter and of course younger than I am now, and our athletic PM was, of course, fit as a fiddle. The same could not quite be said of Farooq but he was game for this bit of gymnastics. The point I am trying to make was that there was no fear of public disorder disrupting the tour.

At a more personal level, Governor Jagmohan invited me and my family to spend a holiday in Srinagar as his guests in May 1989. We travelled to all the tourist spots from Gulmarg to Pahalgam, and all over the city and the gorgeous Dal Lake, with no security protection and no fear of any kind. The governor clearly felt that his guests were in no danger.

Added to all this was the massive tourist influx in October–November 1989 to see the leaves of the chinar turn golden. Nothing untoward happened to any of them. All of this goes to show that, at least on the surface, there was a measure of normalcy. The ensuing chaos after V.P. Singh became PM, and particularly after he nominated Jagmohan to the governorship, were rooted in the misjudgments of the V.P. Singh government and the blind prejudices of Governor Jagmohan.

Apart from the rumours of rigging that stoked the militancy of the nineties, the winding down of the jihad in Afghanistan brought in hordes of well-trained, well-financed and heavily armed jihadis, sponsored by Pakistan, into the Valley. A series of other adverse events also contributed to the deterioration of the political environment in the state: the utterly incompetent handling by V.P. Singh of the crisis over the kidnapping of his home minister's daughter; the needlessly meretricious release of captured terrorists who went on to wreak mayhem; the irresponsible appointment as governor of Jagmohan aka 'Halaku Khan';[13] the resignation of the duly elected Farooq Abdullah on Jagmohan's appointment; the subsequent dissolution of the J&K

---

[13] A thirteenth-century marauder, grandson of Genghis Khan, who conquered large parts of central and west Asia, and notoriously wrecked the famous library in Baghdad while laying the city to waste. At his instance, havoc was wreaked on the Delhi sultanate. In popular language, Halaku (also spelt Hulagu) has become synonymous with mindless inhuman destruction.

elected assembly by governor's fiat; selective targeted assassinations that were answered by the panic mass evacuation of Kashmiri Pandits; and the progressive weakening and eventual overthrow of the government of Benazir Bhutto, with whom Rajiv Gandhi had attempted to open a new chapter in India–Pakistan relations.

It was the election of the V.P. Singh government in December 1989 that shattered the calm. V.P. Singh appointed as his home minister Mufti Mohammad Sayeed, the Kashmiri Congress dissident who had resigned from the Congress in protest against the Farooq–Rajiv Accord and joined the dissident Congressmen whom VP had succeeded in gathering around himself in the National Front (which Rajiv Gandhi had famously mocked as the 'National Affront'.[14] That it was, indeed, a National Affront is evident in how it legitimized the Hindutvist Bharatiya Janata Party – BJP – by making them partners in their war against Rajiv Gandhi, and that it took less than a year for the Front to collapse under its inherent contradictions).

Within days of Mufti taking over as the Union home minister, his daughter Rubaiya was kidnapped and held for several days. While Rajiv Gandhi, as leader of the Opposition, was attempting through his sources, particularly a Kashmiri judge in the Allahabad High Court, to get Rubaiya released without a stain, particularly on the grounds that Islamic law and practice prohibited the kidnapping of single adult women, the V.P. Singh government went on a completely different track. It decided to secure Rubaiya's release in exchange for the release of several dreaded terrorists being held in Kashmiri jails, who have since waged a proxy terrorist war against India in the Kashmir Valley.

In the middle of this maelstrom, the government announced the re-appointment of Jagmohan as governor. Jagmohan had kept a low profile

---

[14] 'It is National Affront, Not a National Front: Rajiv Gandhi', *India Today*, 13 November 2013, https://www.indiatoday.in/magazine/indiascope/voices/story/19881231-it-is-national-affront-not-national-front-says-rajiv-gandhi-798106-1988-12-30.

while the Congress government of Rajiv Gandhi was in power at the Centre, only privately complaining to the PM about the J&K CM, but brought his hostility towards Farooq Abdullah into the open as soon as it was announced that he would be replacing General K.V. Krishna Rao as J&K governor. Farooq, in protest, also tendered his resignation as CM. This put Jagmohan in complete and unfettered charge of the state under the J&K Constitution. Targeted killings rose, communal provocations were blared from mosques on loudspeaker, and Kashmiri Pandits started their exodus; Jagmohan seemed completely incapable of controlling the situation.

While all this was happening, I was in my ancestral village of Kargudi trying to get myself registered as a voter with a view to standing from Tamil Nadu for election to the Rajya Sabha. In late January 1990, Rajiv Gandhi's private secretary, Vincent George, rang me at RG's instance to summon me back to Delhi post-haste. I arrived, found RG very concerned at developments in the Valley, especially the ability of militants to pick up and individually assassinate police informers, showing that they had access to secret lists. He tasked me to inform myself on the subject as fully as I could. I spent a month boning up on the subject and listening to RG sharing his views on developments in the Valley, partly with me but mostly with others. So, when the V.P. Singh government decided to send an all-party parliamentary delegation to Kashmir in March 1990, RG asked me to accompany him as a note taker. It turned out to be a searing personal introduction to the reality of J&K, and I dwell on it below in some detail because in my six years of working with RG, this was the first time I had occasion to watch him in combative action in a confidential discussion. (As things turned out, it was also the last.)

Despite the deputy prime minister, Devi Lal, heading the delegation, Governor Jagmohan was not at the airport to receive him or the delegation. On the way into town from the airport, Devi Lal loudly remarked on the complete absence of anyone on the roads. Everyone bar

Jaswant Singh of the BJP agreed with him. Not even George Fernandes spoke up for Jagmohan. Clearly, Jagmohan was just a BJP choice, not the consensus candidate of the ruling coalition.

So, when Rajiv Gandhi spotted that we were being driven to the Raj Bhavan and not to our hotel, the Centaur, he insisted that the bus driver reverse and take us first to the hotel. The governor arrived there panting but received little sympathy from any member of the delegation, except, perhaps, Jaswant, who was silently sulking in his corner. When RG objected to the discourtesy of the deputy PM being seated to the left of the governor instead of his right, Jaswant blew up like an untamed volcano and accused Rajiv Gandhi of being needlessly disruptive with minor points of protocol instead of coming to grips with the grave issues that had brought us to Srinagar. Meanwhile, I started taking down the proceedings almost word for word and I could see intrigued looks being darted in my direction as my pen flew over the pages of my notebook.[15]

The proceedings began placidly enough with the governor saying that the situation in the Valley was very grave, with not just a 'collapse' of the administration but a 'take over', leaving no civil administration worth the name. He asserted that 'every component' of the previous power structure had been taken over and the atmosphere was one of 'fear and indifference'. He laid the blame for this squarely at the doorstep of the previous Farooq Abdullah government. He went on to inform the meeting that the whereabouts of officers of the Intelligence Bureau (IB) and the police were being supplied to the local militants; station house officers were receiving instructions from the terrorists; and everyone had been imprisoned in 'a cage of terror'.

He went on to claim that on Friday, 26 January – Republic Day – plans had been afoot to gather 10 lakh people under the guise of

---

[15] Interested readers are requested to look up the virtually verbatim record of the discussion and related documents on this book's website: https://www.rajivmisunderstood.com/ or by scanning the QR code at the end of the chapter.

conducting namaz with the aim of proclaiming independence through the captured stations of Doordarshan and All India Radio. He had, therefore, imposed a curfew and taken other stern measures to forestall the designs of the militants.

The governor then turned to the JKLF whose 'writ', he said, 'ran everywhere, with flags flying, terrorists converting hospitals into sanctuaries, and storing arms and ammunitions there. Even the doctors are in league with these terrorists.' He said calls to mass violence came from hundreds of mosques fitted with loudspeakers with extensions into the streets that made an 'unbearable noise' and were principally used to make 'political proclamations, in extreme language, using fundamentalist expressions'. He claimed he had sought to rectify 'this terrible situation' by rebuilding the administration. Moreover, he had stopped Maqbool Butt Day from being exploited by the militants. After he had come to Srinagar, there had been 'substantial progress'. He bemoaned the fact that 'the nation does not understand the gravity of the situation … The situation is very, very grim.'

At this point, there occurred the first flare-up of interjections when Rajiv Gandhi asked on which dates these killings of IB and police officers had started. As the governor vaguely replied, 'November … December …', P.L. Handoo (NC) asserted that the first assassination was in Anantnag (south Kashmir) on 2 January and we should 'stick to facts'. The governor said investigations into the killing of these officers had not even begun, claiming this was because of a collapse of the administration with a large number of government servants absenting themselves and being involved in subversive activities. He had had to start afresh.

The governor then turned to the action taken by him to deal with 'a local festival, Meeraaj-e-Aalam, which is just like our Dussehra'. This sparked further interjections and when the commotion died down, Rajiv Gandhi asked whether the terrorists had sophisticated weapons. The governor replied, 'In burst, they can fire sixty rounds.' At this, RG, who was something of an expert on ballistics, expressed astonishment and the governor's adviser, Ved Marwah, had to clarify that the correct figure was not 'sixty rounds' but 'thirty rounds – Kalashnikovs'.

The meeting then turned to the vexed question of the governor unilaterally dissolving the state assembly. His explanation was that 'it was a totally unrepresentative assembly'. Instead of answering RG's question, 'How do you measure unrepresentativeness?', the rattled governor said that it was his constitutional right. 'The Constitution empowers me to make this determination in my own discretion.' (He was not referring to the Indian Constitution but to the J&K Constitution.) He categorically stated, 'Under the J&K Constitution, I have the right to decide this without consulting anybody.' He rejected the argument put forward by a CPI(M) member of the delegation that he should not have acted independently but consulted the Central government as the dissolution of the assembly is not an administrative matter but 'a political question'.

While the governor spiritedly maintained that 'by dissolving the assembly, I have shown the young men that they can elect whom they want', he refuted Rajiv Gandhi's point that the constitutional process could have been restored by asking the state assembly to elect its leader. Jagmohan's point was that the J&K Constitution did not require this matter to be decided 'at the satisfaction of the president but of the governor'. He had taken the decision to dissolve the assembly, because, in his view, what was needed was 'a new beginning to wean away the youngsters from terrorism'. The delegation did not accept the governor's argument, saying such a political decision required the governor to have gone in for 'wide-ranging consultations'. Rajiv Gandhi remarked, *'Yeh ajeeb baat hai . . .'* (This is weird talk) and Devi Lal concurred: *'Hai toh!'* (Yes, indeed it is!)

In the face of the governor's claim that he was 'establishing links with the people', RG asked him to realize that he was now 'completely isolated from the masses, with no control over the police, none over the officers, and no proper information network'. Supplementing another CPI(M) member's remark that the governor's actions 'were only leading to anarchy', RG provoked the governor into asserting that, in his judgement, both the NC and Congress, which together held a clear majority in the assembly, 'had become irrelevant'. He cited by way of proof the complaint of youth that 'the 1987 elections were rigged'. He also cited the statement of Shabbir Shah, the People's League leader, that 'if the Farooq government is removed, the problem will be solved'. I saw Handoo's eyebrows rise in astonishment.

The governor then made the extraordinary suggestion that the answer to the political conundrum lay with the JKLF as it is 'based on the catholic, eclectic, and accommodating local version of Islam . . . If we give JKLF youth the opportunity to elect their representatives, they will fall in line.' This evoked derisive laughter from most members of the delegation.

Rajiv Gandhi then moved to the crux of the matter. He asked, of the seventy-six seats (plus two nominated) in the assembly, how many, in the governor's opinion, were rigged? Instead of answering this straight question, the governor offered the unbelievable assertion that 'Shabbir will fall in line after the hard core is pushed out by administrative action. We will demolish the Jama'at-e-Islami and Hizb-e-Islam.' He went on: 'In my judgement, if the terrorists are arrested, we will be able to hold elections.' The governor then added that Farooq Abdullah, on 15 February, had accused him of 'turning Kashmir into a Nazi concentration camp, compared me to Halaku and threatened an international inquiry . . . In the face of such inflammatory statements by the former CM', the governor claimed he was left with 'no alternative but to dissolve the assembly'. Rajiv Gandhi's riposte was succinct: 'The plan is clear. Finish the Congress and NC. And bring in the JKLF!'

RG then returned to his question of how many seats, in the governor's view, were rigged. Forced into a corner, the governor replied, 'Not less than sixteen or seventeen.' Rajiv Gandhi responded, 'The governor says sixteen seats were rigged. That means the NC–Congress won a clear fifty out of seventy-six seats.'

P. Shiv Shankar of the Congress, former law minister, then enquired what were the numbers of 'infiltrators, terrorists, fighters'. The governor replied, 'between 2,000 and 5,000'. To combat them, the governor said he would 'rebuild the administrative structure', to which Rajiv Gandhi responded: 'First, you destroyed the political process and now you are destroying the administration.'

Responding to a question from Biplab Dasgupta of the CPI(M), the governor said that as the success of their programme depended 'on the balance we strike', his instructions were 'to use the minimum of force'. 'Neither our paramilitary nor BSF [Border Security Force] are permitted to use their sten guns.' To which Rajiv Gandhi retorted: 'The BSF does not have sten guns. They have carbines. Can we be more precise, Governor?'

P.L. Handoo of the NC – he whose eyebrows had shot up – then turned to the importance the governor was attaching to Shabbir Shah. He remarked that Shabbir Shah, the leader of the People's League, had been in prison since 1983. 'After his release, he went underground. He was caught and had been jailed again.' How could such a person be relied on? Handoo observed that Doordarshan had shown the militants celebrating the release of five hardcore terrorists on 13 December 1989. 'That,' he asserted, 'was the start of the trouble.'

The debate then moved to the troubling question of the exodus of the minorities. Handoo asserted, 'We have always been a secular people. The Kashmiri Pandits have always been protected by the Muslims.' The governor replied that the terrorists were looking for soft targets like the Kashmiri Pandits and he had acted on the request of the Kashmiri Pandits Association.

When he was asked how many Kashmiri Pandits had left, the governor replied, '6,000 to 7,000 families'. But Kedar Nath Sahni of the BJP said,

'14,000 families, amounting to about 80,000 individuals, were registered in Gita Bhavan [New Delhi] alone'. At which Rajiv Gandhi pointed out, 'Out of one and a quarter lakh [KPs], 80,000 have left the Valley. 70 per cent! Why is the governor's information on the exodus wrong? How then can he be right about the numbers killed?'

On RG asking the governor to arrange for the delegation to go into town and meet the people, including the associations for which he had a ready list, the governor declined, said he had 'no contact with local associations and would not arrange for the delegation to meet anyone'. At this point, Deputy PM Devi Lal concluded the meeting, exclaiming: '*Governor sahib, aap hame airport tak pahunchayen toh ganimat hogi*' (Governor sahib, if you could but reach us to the airport, it would be a great mercy).

During this meeting, RG was clearly better prepared than his interlocutor and was adept at assessing the governor's performance. The meeting remains in my memory as one of the most memorable exchanges I have witnessed. I am glad I recorded it virtually verbatim.

In the afternoon a 'Joint Statement by the Leaders of the Political Parties' was prepared for release to the press. Asserting that 'the identity of Jammu and Kashmir has been maintained within the framework of the Constitution and this shall be maintained', the leaders 'firmly' declared that 'no sinister designs against the unity and territorial integrity of India shall be permitted to succeed'. Affirming their conviction that 'political activity in Jammu and Kashmir must be revived', they said, 'All our efforts will be unitedly directed to this national goal.'

While this statement was being drafted, RG met with some fifty-four Kashmiris representing diverse political and business interests, as well as intellectuals from academia and the media, who were rounded up at short notice by the J&K Congress leaders in the face of the governor's refusal to cooperate. This gave RG a broad-spectrum picture of the ground position, aided by the summaries of these conversations that I was able to furnish him. He also attempted to meet the staff of the hotel, but that encounter was disrupted as slogans of 'Azadi' rent the air.

Following the press release, a statement was made by the official spokesman at the meeting that it was 'recommended that the Government of India appoint a Cabinet Minister for Jammu and Kashmir Affairs who will associate with his work an Advisory Committee which would include representatives of political parties participating in the meeting' to 'examine ways and means of reviving political activity, mobilizing people and involving them in the fight against the forces of secessionism'.

On returning to Delhi, RG drafted a letter to Prime Minister V.P. Singh dated 12 March, to which I contributed as well. I then personally delivered it to the PM's residence. Pointing out that neither Doordarshan nor Akashvani had broadcast the crucial paragraph relating to the Advisory Committee required 'to revive the political process and look into the genuine problems and grievances of the people', the letter said that while almost all newspapers had led with this paragraph, this information could not reach the people of the Valley because 'newspapers from rest of India are not reaching the Valley'. While noting the appointment of a Cabinet Minister for J&K Affairs had been announced, RG urged the government to end the delay in naming the minister and nominating the Advisory Committee.

RG then called on President Venkataraman, with me and others, to confidentially brief him on what we had seen and heard. He subsequently told the Congress Parliamentary Party that while matters had been under control during the tenure of the previous government, the governor himself had described the present position as not the 'collapse' of the administration but its total 'take over'. RG asserted that 'no one agrees with what the governor is doing', with the steps he had taken 'only result[ing] in a total alienation of the local civil service and the local police'. RG then went on to charge the governor with 'simply playing into Pakistan hands' by making irresponsible allegations of rigging in the March 1987 elections.

The Congress president then explained that 'the governor's administration was seen as a totally communal government' and the governor himself had admitted to his lack of contact 'with any local association or body of people'. He further underlined that as a result of the 'total isolation of the governor from the people' the local Kashmiri people were describing him as 'Turkman Gate commander', 'Hitler' and 'General Dyer' (he did not mention the most popular appellation: 'Halaku'). The Congress president then underlined the revival of political activity in the state as the 'basic requirement', given that 'normal life in the Valley had been totally disrupted', with Indian Airlines accepting no cargo, post offices accepting no packets, telephone lines down, communication and transport links with the rest of India virtually snapped, and even the Kashmiri language newscast on Doordarshan coming from Delhi, not from Srinagar.[16]

While George Fernandes was named minister for J&K affairs, the all-party advisory committee was never set up. But soon after the delegation's visit, Jagmohan was prematurely recalled in May, and another more sensitive and sensible governor sent in his place.

Whether the mass exodus of Kashmiri Pandits was the consequence of genuine fear or the incompetence of the governor in not providing them with adequate assurances of safety or adequate physical security is a battle that still rages in the politics of the state, in think tanks and discussion groups, in Parliament and the media, but there is no getting away from Jagmohan's own statement in his memoirs that his additional director general of police had informed him that from 'December 1989 to May 15, 1990, 134 innocent persons were killed by the militants', the number of Hindu victims being seventy-two.[17] The governor did not do the simple arithmetic required here: this meant sixty-three of

---

[16] All India Congress Committee (AICC) press release extracts.
[17] Jagmohan, *My Frozen Turbulence in Kashmir*, Allied Publishers Ltd, New Delhi, 1991, p. 478.

the 134 victims were Muslims! This, in turn, meant that the number of assassinations of Muslims and Hindus were substantially comparable, from which the conclusion may be drawn that while the terrorist killings seriously impacted the Kashmiri Pandit community, it affected Kashmiri Muslims almost as much and eventually much more. Yet the governor was complicit in abetting or acquiescing in the mass departure of the Kashmiri Pandits. They have never since been enticed back or settled in the Valley, bar stray individuals or groups (and now non-Kashmiri retired armed and security forces personnel), although all political elements, including the Hurriyat, have declared that Kashmir without the Kashmiri Pandits is not the Kashmir they want. The efforts of the BJP government since the abrogation of Article 370 and removal of statehood on 5 August 2019 have signally failed to resettle the community in Kashmir, and many of the thousands of Pandits recruited into government service have fled their posts in the Valley in the face of the administration's gross failure to afford them adequate security with several Kashmiri Pandit officers being the target of terrorist attacks.

Recently, Ram Puniyani of *Secular Perspectives* has circulated a Right to Information Act (RTI) response from the deputy superintendent of police, Srinagar, which affirms that the total number of Kashmiri Pandits killed since 'the inception of militancy in 1990' is eighty-nine, compared to the killing of people of other faiths (principally Muslim) that stands at 1,635.[18] These official figures demonstrate that starting from V.P. Singh's time, there has been chaos and anarchy in the Valley fuelled by terrorism but that the communal colour being given to the troubles by films like *The Kashmir Files* (2020) is, to put it mildly, 'unhistorical'.

I had my final word when Jagmohan wrote a personal account of

---

[18] The response was to P.P. Kapoor of Samalkha, Panipat, Haryana, dated 27 November 2021, No. HQR's/RTI/S-91/2021/108-09. A facsimile of the RTI response is reproduced on my website https://www.rajivmisunderstood.com/ (or scan the QR code at the end of the chapter).

his tenure under the curious title *My Frozen Turbulence in Kashmir*. The opening sentence of my review for *Sunday* magazine read: 'My Frozen Turbulence, is not, as you might imagine, the autobiography of a stud bull. It is Governor Jagmohan's exculpation of himself.'

Jagmohan never thereafter spoke to me. I was not surprised.

Darjeeling

The naming, establishment and operationalizing of the Darjeeling Gorkha Hills Council was the only political issue where I was directly instructed by the PM to involve myself. I have refreshed my memory by reading the proceedings on Darjeeling at the 1994 Rajiv Gandhi Golden Jubilee Retrospective.[19] It was a session I chaired.

Subhash Ghisingh (his name is variously spelt in English) served as a Junior Commissioned Officer (JCO) in the Indian Army and on retirement started a little-noticed agitation for 'Gorkhaland' in 1979, forming the Gorkha National Liberation Front (GNLF) in 1980. The demand reverberated in the hearts and minds of the Darjeeling Gorkha population. Over the next few years, Ghisingh succeeded in harnessing the trade unions of the tea plantations. Soon, the Darjeeling Hills appeared to have become the political fiefdom of Subhas Ghisingh.

It was as his personal popularity rose and rose that Ghisingh made his cardinal error. Not finding a willing ear to listen to him in either Calcutta or Delhi, he unleashed a spate of violence and arson to draw attention to the cause. Even more dangerously, he visited the king of Nepal in Kathmandu (on 23 December 1983) to persuade him to denounce the 1835 treaty under which Nepal had ceded the Darjeeling Hills tract to British India to serve as a 'sanatorium' for British soldiers of the East India Company. The following year, Ghisingh also petitioned the UN

---

[19] See the text of the proceedings at https://www.rajivmisunderstood.com or by scanning the QR code at the end of the chapter.

for the restitution of the rights of the Darjeeling Gorkhas. As a result, he was labelled an 'anti-national' by the Marxist government of West Bengal and in general Indian opinion.

The crux of the issue was the question of ethnic identity; overlaying this was the issue of discrimination. The inhabitants of the hill areas of Darjeeling were not Bengalis but Gorkhas; they did not speak Bengali but Gorkhali/Nepali. Frustrated at not being heard and desperately seeking some way to articulate his grievances, Ghisingh gave his opponents the chance to denounce him as 'anti-national' – and that closed the door to further discussion.

It was at this point that PM Rajiv Gandhi stepped into the breach. He sent for Inderjit, a well-known journalist, who, at the invitation of the West Bengal Governor Uma Shankar Dikshit, had gone to Darjeeling in May 1986 with his family on a short vacation. When the governor had asked Inderjit whether, as a newsman, he wanted to meet Ghisingh, Inderjit demurred. But his daughter, who had just started at the *Times of India*, insisted she would like to go with her father to meet Ghisingh. The meeting launched Inderjit as Delhi's principal interlocutor with the GNLF. Inderjit told the prime minister that all Ghisingh wanted was a separate state, not a separate nation. India had conceded such states as Nagaland and Mizoram, and Ghisingh accordingly felt it was the Gorkhas' due.

On 18 December 1986, Rajiv Gandhi drove into Darjeeling at the end of a long road journey that had taken him along the spine of West Bengal in what was clearly the opening shot of his election campaign for the West Bengal assembly elections of March 1987. On the road journey over several days and several visits, he had been mobbed by the most ardent crowds, to the delight of the local Congress leaders and workers who thought (as I did) that this spectacular welcome betokened a comeback for the Congress in Bengal from the political wilderness. (We were wrong!)

I had expected a similar welcome at Darjeeling. So, I was stunned by the embarrassingly thin gathering at the St Paul's grounds when the PM arrived to address his first public meeting in Darjeeling. There was not a Gorkha face to be seen. Ghisingh had ordered a boycott of the prime minister and his orders had been obeyed. I was further utterly confused to see Rajiv Gandhi mount the podium, quite unfazed, and deliver himself of a full speech to almost nobody. I asked him later why he had bothered to speak at such length to nobody, and he replied: 'I knew Ghisingh had ordered his people to not turn up but I also knew he had posted his people all around the ground to hear what I said. So, I spoke at length knowing that every word I uttered would be transmitted within minutes to Subhas Ghisingh.'

After the West Bengal assembly elections of March 1987, Rajiv Gandhi resumed his efforts at effecting a tripartite agreement among Ghising's GNLF, the West Bengal state government and the Centre. These negotiations bore fruit in August 1988 with the creation of a semi-autonomous council to look after the district of Darjeeling. It was proposed to include Ghisingh's party in the council, with him at its head. One last hurdle was the name of the hill council. Home Minister Buta Singh called me to say the PM had asked him to discuss this with me.

I replied, 'Surely Darjeeling Hill Council should do?'

'Ghisingh,' said the home minister, 'is insisting that Gorkhaland should figure in the name. Jyoti Basu says, "Nothing doing." What do you suggest?'

'How about Gorkha, not Gorkhaland?' I suggested.

The compromise – Darjeeling Gorkha Hill Council – was accepted by all.

Funds were provided for a secretariat to house the council. The PM travelled to Darjeeling in May 1989 to inaugurate the building. Ghisingh made up for his discourtesy of December 1986 by organizing a truly massive public reception on the same St Paul's grounds.

The Darjeeling Accord was the final feather in Rajiv Gandhi's cap, vindicating his policy of not regarding dissidents as enemies, but partners in nation-building whose concerns should be heard, understood, and accommodated. Another key principle: always ensure that national interest takes precedence over party interest, if the two are in conflict. It is a lesson the present establishment (2023) needs to learn or relearn.

Having examined the accords that brought peace to various hotspots around the country, we now turn to the controversies through which he waded from the beginning of 1986 to his defeat in the general elections of November 1989.

See detailed footnotes and endnotes by scanning the QR code above.

2

The Controversies

Shah Bano, Babri Masjid, Operation Brasstacks, IPKF, Bofors

Shah Bano

At the start of 1986, Prime Minister Rajiv Gandhi visited the Vainu Bappu Observatory in Kavalur, Tamil Nadu, with me in his party, to see Halley's Comet, which in mythology is supposed to presage great danger. A Tamil reporter had sought and secured an interview with the PM. The thrust of his questions appeared to be to ascertain the PM's views on the Shah Bano issue: the Supreme Court's award of maintenance to a divorced Muslim woman, Shah Bano, in April 1985 under the vagrancy provisions of the Criminal Procedure Code, overruling the processes of divorce settlement set out in the sharia, or Muslim Personal Law. The draft answers I supplied were the usual bland and banal comments on what appeared to me to be an open-and-shut matter: that the Supreme Court (SC) had spoken, and it was now everybody's duty to carry out the court's directives. So, I could barely believe my ears when RG cast aside my draft and answered the questions in an entirely unexpected way – that there was a valid complaint in that the SC judgment did impinge on the Personal Law guaranteed to the Muslim community, and that he was trying to find an answer in consultation with the best jurisprudential advice available.

When the interview was over and the journalist had departed, he smiled at the stunned expression on my face and said, 'That's what I believe.'

It was only in due course that I came to understand the logic and imperative of the stand he took. I had only vaguely been aware of a long debate on a Private Member's motion moved by an Indian Union Muslim League veteran of long standing, G.M. Banatwala, in May 1986 seeking the reversal of the Supreme Court judgment by Parliament. The debate was spread over several Friday afternoons stretching more than six months from May to December 1985, in which the issues raised had been thrashed out.[1] The media covered the debate extensively, if in a manner biased against Banatwala and his colleagues, who included virtually all the Muslim Members of Parliament (MPs) in the Lok Sabha, other than Arif Mohammed Khan and Saifuddin Chowdhury of the CPI(M) (who in any case regarded 'religion as the opium of the masses', as Karl Marx had said).

---

[1] For the interested reader, I have compiled extracts from the debate, including the principal antagonists, Arif Mohammed Khan and Z.R. Ansari, both ministers of state in Rajiv Gandhi's government, and placed them on my website https://www.rajivmisunderstood.com. They can be accessed by scanning the QR code at the end of the chapter. The extracts include not only the debate on the Private Member's motion but also the subsequent discussions in the Lok Sabha and Rajya Sabha on the draft Muslim Women (Protection of Rights on Divorce) Bill, 1986, in which there were participants from virtually every political party represented in Parliament, many at a high level in their respective parties, such as L.K. Advani and Somnath Chatterjee, besides Madhu Dandavate for the Opposition and, for the treasury benches, Home Minister P.V. Narasimha Rao, Law Minister Sen and the minister of state for home, Ram Niwas Mirdha, who, in 1973, had first assured the house that Section 125 of the revised Criminal Procedure Code, the bone of contention in *Shah Bano*, did not impinge on Muslim Personal Law. In addition, Arif's perspective on the matter has been extracted from a very detailed interview he gave to Scroll in 2015.

The Muslim MPs also found remarks in the *obiter dicta* at the end of the judgment offensive to sanctified Muslim practice in matters of marriage, divorce, and maintenance, and deeply disturbing in its call for the enactment of a common civil code irrespective of Muslim or other minority opinion. They, however, ceased pressing the point as Rajiv Gandhi reassured them early in the controversy that his government had no intention of enacting a Uniform Civil Code (UCC).

Rajiv Gandhi had kept himself fully informed of these deliberations. He had been struck by the fact that there was near unanimity among the Muslim members that the judgment impinged adversely on their Personal Law. This was not widely understood or appreciated in the majority community and left-liberal opinion, probably because few Hindus and other non-Muslims have attended a Muslim wedding ceremony and closely followed its rites and rituals. Perhaps earlier this was not the case, but after Partition sundered social ties between the two communities, even the most secular of Hindus hardly attend or pay attention to the reading of the *nikah* (the wedding vows that include detailed provisions for the maintenance of the divorcee and her children); they tend to concentrate instead on devouring the delectable kababs, kormas and meat curries on offer, not the process of solemnization of vows.

RG's style of open-minded consultations without being taken in by the views of any one faction is well illustrated by an episode that Salman Khurshid has related in a recent book. Seeking to hear the views of young, highly educated, modern-minded Muslims – who, it was generally believed, found a role model in Arif Mohammed Khan – Salman says Rajiv Gandhi came over to his house to meet with a group of Aligarh Muslim University (AMU) students who wanted to discuss with the PM issues arising out of the 1985 Supreme Court judgment in *Shah Bano*. The PM, says Khurshid, listened patiently to the points cited one by one by the students. At the end, he stood up and said: 'I understand that all of our many communities have their own way of life, and we must take that into consideration to preserve our unity in diversity.'[2] I think that one sentence sums up why Rajiv Gandhi overruled not only the official advice he received from his key official in the PMO,[3] but also the vast mobilization of public opinion by both the BJP and the left-liberals against his stand to take the principled view that he did.

The AMU students introduced to the PM by Salman Khurshid were by no means theologians or clerics or political leaders. They were representative of thinking, educated, 'modern-minded', secular Indian Muslims, the cream of their generation, who were concerned with their identity and dignity as a progressive minority in contemporary India. Should their views have been run over roughshod? If, on the other hand, they were not representative of Muslim opinion, how is it that in the three and two-thirds decades that have passed since his halcyon days with the Congress, Arif Mohammed Khan has wandered from party to party failing to get elected and now finds himself in the embrace, as their anointed governor in Kerala, of the very party, the BJP, he had set out to combat as a young, highly regarded president of the AMU Students Union and a formidable youth leader of not just the minority community but the youth of India? Pique has never had worse consequences.

While I was not personally consulted about this highly controversial issue by the prime minister, who ran an extremely compartmentalized PMO, I did sit in on a most informative conversation the PM had with M.J. Akbar on a long flight – from Dibrugarh to Delhi – in March 1986. It was then that I began to appreciate RG's rationale in interesting himself in this matter, discarding the easy route of unquestioningly accepting the 1985 Supreme Court judgment.

The PM spoke in detail of what he had learned of Muslim law on the subject of the maintenance of divorced Muslim women. His point of

---

[2] Salman Khurshid, *Triple Talaq: Examining Faith*, Oxford University Press, New Delhi, 2018, p. 156.

[3] Habibullah, *op. cit.* pp. 97–100.

departure was that Muslim marriages were not a sacrament so much as a contract, premised on the understanding that the marriage might not last. If that happened, Muslim Personal Law spelt out the terms on which the marriage might be dissolved. He observed that, unlike the practice in some other Indian religious communities, a bride is never 'given away'. Under Muslim law she retains a lien on her family of birth which is obliged to look after her if the marriage turns sour. This is a point often overlooked by those who regard the Shah Bano case as essentially one of 'women's rights' in a patriarchal society under patriarchal religious laws. RG was behind none when it came to championing women's rights,[4] but he had to take account of whether the Muslim male MPs were right in claiming that Muslim law not only respected but privileged women's rights, especially when it came to women in distress. As a responsible, secular PM who respected all communities, he could not, like many others, dismiss Muslim Personal Law as a barbaric holdover from the deserts of seventh-century Arabia.

The PM went on that under Islamic law, on deciding on divorce, the couple are required to have no marital relations for three months (*iddat*), after which the dower (*mehar*) is to be returned to the wife and a full settlement of the financial terms for maintenance made in accordance with the stipulations set out in the *nikah nama* (marriage agreement). It is also provided that once the divorce is finalized, there shall be no further contact between the divorced couple. There is also provision for financial compensation if the wife initiates the divorce process.

After divorce and settlement, responsibility for the woman becomes that of the father, and, failing him, other close male relatives, such as

---

[4] This was most evident in the PM's pioneering work in constitutionally reserving positions for women in Panchayati Raj Institutions (PRIs). As we go to press, there are well over 14 lakh women elected to our PRIs. Indeed, *there are more elected women in India alone than in the rest of the world put together*. The details are in Chapter 5 of this volume. I regard this as India's greatest achievement since the proclamation of the Constitution. Could this achievement possibly be the handiwork of a male chauvinist?

brothers or uncles or adult sons. If, for any reason, these close male members of the family do not discharge their financial obligations to the divorced woman and her children, the Waqf is required *by Quranic injunction* to arrange for the financial upkeep of the divorced woman – at least until she gets married again. Additionally, law, custom, and usage in the Muslim community not only allow but even encourage remarriage after divorce. No social stigma is attached to women finding another husband as soon as possible after divorce.

Later, I found that nothing illustrates better the perfect acceptability of remarriage among Muslims than a sample survey of 3,811 Muslim women divorcees carried out by Abusaleh Shariff and Syed Khan under the aegis of the Centre for Research and Debate on Development Policy.[5] The survey found that fully 78 per cent of divorced Muslim women had found other husbands within two years of divorce. Such astonishingly high remarriage rates are simply unthinkable in most other communities in India, including especially the majority Hindu community. Traditional Muslim social practice has long been that if one marriage ends for whatever reason, another marriage may be contracted as soon as possible. It gives a completely different perspective to the question of the maintenance of Muslim women divorcees.

The PM concluded his exposition with the observation that in terms of invoking the powers of the Waqf Boards and ensuring that the funds they provide the divorcee are fair and reasonable, the only problem is of how to make the clerics rise above patriarchy and privilege to ensure the Waqf does its duty. Could the answer lie in making Waqf Boards answerable to magistrates under the civil laws of the country?

After patiently listening to what the Muslim MPs had to say, and widely consulting others – both Muslims and non-Muslims interested in

---

[5] 'Unimportance of Triple Talaq', *Indian Express*, 29 May 2017.

this question of vital importance to the fundamentals of our Constitution – RG appears to have concluded that far from being the atavistic divorce code it was made out to be, sanctified Muslim practice on divorce-related matters had much to commend itself. But it was widely misunderstood in India as there were huge differences in approach and content to questions of marriage and separation between the Hindu practice and the Muslim practice. The crux of the problem, it seemed to the PM, was that if the men in her family and the local Waqf failed to provide her with justice, as was often the case, especially with poor, unempowered Muslim women, the only recourse available was the local qazi, mullah or imam. Many of these shared the patriarchal and prejudiced views of men in general regarding women's rights and were, therefore, frequently incapable of rendering justice.

So, what could be done if all the men in her family and then the Waqf authority were to fail the divorced woman? RG decided that the answer to that conundrum lay in codifying the Personal Law provision, that is, bringing into the ambit of Indian civil law the rights of Muslim women on divorce. *Thus, Muslim Personal Law would be preserved and yet made justiciable in a civil court of law.* In this manner, the arguments of almost all Muslim MPs might be reconciled with the essential injunctions of the ill-worded 1985 SC judgment. It was a brilliant piece of legal legerdemain, the essence of which lay in Law Minister Asoke Sen inserting sections 3 and 4 into the Muslim Women (Protection of Rights on Divorce) Bill, 1986, that provided for due compensation to be paid '*within*' the three-month period of *iddat*, not '*for*' the period of *iddat*, as the Muslim clergy had often held.[6]

---

[6] The provisions in sections 3 and 4 of the Muslim Women (Protection of Rights on Divorce) Act, 1986, may be accessed at the website of this book: www://rajivmisunderstood.com which may be accessed by scanning the QR code at the of the chapter .The text of the Act may be seen at: www.indiacode.nic.in/bitstream/123456789/15353/1/muslim_women_%28protection_of_rights_on_divorce%29_act%2C_1986.pdf.

I revert to Arif Mohammed Khan's interview to the Scroll news and commentary website.[7] According to Arif himself, given Arif's strong views on the matter, the PM's Political Secretary, Makhan Lal Fotedar, confidentially called Arif (on the PM's instructions) and asked him to call on Law Minister Asoke Sen. Sen pulled out the draft bill and had Arif take a look. Being the very bright and astute man he is, Arif quickly noted the significance of the language that said 'fair and reasonable settlement' had to be made 'during' the period of *iddat* but not 'for' the *iddat* period. Arif asked if the Law Minister had shown his draft to Banatwala and others. Sen confirmed that he had done so, and no one had objected. He requested Arif to not comment on the draft in public.[8] The bill was introduced in the Lok Sabha in May 1986 and taken up thereafter in the Rajya Sabha. It passed muster in both Houses. But Arif chose to resign and emerged as a hero of those opposed to the measure.

Dissatisfied with the passage of the Muslim Women (Protection of Rights on Divorce) Act, 1986, a very well-known jurist, Danial Latifi (himself a nominal Muslim, nominal because of his pronounced Marxist views) filed a Special Writ Petition in the Supreme Court in September 1986. In its usual manner, the Supreme Court took all of fifteen years to give its judgment. The judgment was pronounced by a five-judge bench on 19 September 2001.[9] The learned bench unanimously held that the

---

[7] Ajaz Ashraf, 'Arif Mohammed Khan on Shah Bano Case: "Najma Heptullah Was Key Influence on Rajiv Gandhi"', Scroll, 30 May 2015. Extracts of the interview may be found on my website https://www.rajivmisunderstood.com/ or by scanning the QR code at the end of the chapter.

[8] *Ibid.*

[9] 'Danial Latifi & Anr vs Union of India on 28 September 2001', https://indiankanoon.org/doc/410660/.

Act does *not* reverse the 1985 judgment, as is often alleged; 'the Act actually and in reality codifies what was stated in the Shah Bano case'.[10]

The judgment further clarified that as per the Act, the 'liability of a Muslim husband to his divorced wife' to 'pay maintenance is not confined to the *iddat* period' as 'reasonable and fair provisions extending *beyond* the *iddat* period must be made by the husband *within* the *iddat* period' (emphasis added). Thus, the divorced wife was guaranteed reasonable and fair maintenance under Indian civil law while scrupulously respecting the Islamic injunction against any transaction between the divorced couple after the divorce was through. But what if male relatives are unable or unwilling to maintain her? The Supreme Court authoritatively interpreted the Act to allow the injured woman to 'proceed against her relatives who are unable to maintain her' and for 'the Magistrate to direct the State Waqf Board established under the Act to pay such maintenance' direct to the party concerned.

Perhaps the most significant part of the 2001 SC judgment on the 1986 Act was its finding that 'the provisions of the Act do not offend Articles 14, 15 and 21 of the Constitution of India'. These are the articles included in the section on 'Fundamental Rights'. It had been alleged by Latifi in his Special Writ Petition (and continues to be alleged by the commentariat to this day) that whereas the 1985 SC judgment had vindicated the fundamental rights guaranteed to Shah Bano and all women, Muslim and non-Muslim, the 1986 Act had deprived divorced Muslim women of this right. The heart of the Supreme Court judgment in 2001, after careful consideration of the issue for fifteen years, held such allegations to be misplaced. Shah Bano's 'right to equality before law', guaranteed by Article 14, had not been abridged; 'prohibition of discrimination on grounds of religion or sex', under Article 15, had not been violated; her 'Overall right to protection of life and personal liberty',

---

[10] 'Danial Latifi & Anr vs Union of India on 28 September 2001', https://indiankanoon.org/doc/410660/.

under Article 21, had not been transgressed. The Act was declared to be in conformity with the Constitution of India.

And that explains why Rajiv Gandhi's Muslim Women (Protection of Rights on Divorce) Act, 1986, remains on the statute books despite India having seen at least twelve governments since then, most of them led by prime ministers who had spoken against the bill, inside or outside Parliament, while it was under deliberation and subsequently. RG's final decision, embodied in the Act of 1986, not only ensured that under no circumstances would a divorced Muslim woman be 'thrown on to the streets' but also spelled out her rights on divorce and prescribed in detail the measures for the implementation of her rights that would be undertaken under the aegis of a magistrate. Indeed, the legislation reinforced national integration by preserving the identity of our single biggest minority, while ensuring through law, as legislated by Parliament, that a Muslim woman's rights on divorce were justiciable and enforceable at the judicial level, as incorporated in the civil law of the land.

It is hence clear that the late Rajiv Gandhi had been quite unfairly accused of Muslim 'appeasement' – a favourite concoction of both the Sangh Parivar and the left-liberal intelligentsia in their attacks against Rajiv Gandhi. In fact, the continued criticism of the Act, especially after the Supreme Court's judgment of 2001, is an egregious example of 'appeasing' extremist sections of the majority community. It also gave the lie to the media assertion then made and subsequently reiterated *ad infinitum* that the 1986 Act was meant to balance the opening of the locks at the Babri Masjid in a failed attempt to cater to religious sentiment on both sides for illicit political gain.

The Supreme Court's 2001 judgment certainly redeemed Rajiv Gandhi's moral reputation but, alas, he had been assassinated ten years earlier. Justice delayed is indeed justice denied.

I wonder why those who are so insistent on the implementation of the 1985 Supreme Court judgment choose most often to disregard the

Supreme Court's 2001 judgment on the same question. If SC 1985 must be upheld, then all judgments of the Supreme Court on the same question, including SC 2001, must be upheld too. The reason such consistency is often not displayed is that the nefarious alliance between the left-liberals and the communalists sparked in 1986 over Shah Bano marked the resurrection of the BJP,[11] and has now resulted in the present political dominance of the advocates of Hindutva. Unprincipled political alliances between followers of ideologies that are the polar opposites of each other – as was the case in 1986–87 – led in the 1989 election to V.P. Singh's unstable National Front government dependent for survival on two unequal crutches, the secular left-liberals, on the one hand, and the communalists, on the other. Such opportunistic alliances often have such unforeseen and deleterious consequences in the long run. Yet, the 'liberal' view survives by ignoring the 2001 Supreme Court judgment in *Danial Latifi*.[12]

There is another matter – that of the UCC – raised by the 1985 Supreme Court judgment although it was no part of the Supreme Court's remit in the Shah Bano case. The court had taken upon itself the task of reprimanding the government for not acting on Article 44 of the Directive Principles of State Policy to bring in a UCC for the country. The government itself was not represented in this private case, so it could not tender its views on the subject in court. The Supreme Court could have itself impleaded the Union government if it really wanted to hear the rationale of the Union government's view but chose not to. Worse,

---

[11] The BJP then held just two seats. The unprincipled alliance between the National Front and the BJP raised the number of BJP seats to eighty-eight, rendering the V.P. Singh government desperately dependent on BJP approval. When that support was withdrawn in October 1990, the V.P. Singh government ignominiously collapsed on the floor of the House a week later.

[12] An egregious example of wilful neglect of the 2001 Supreme Court judgment is to be found in Neerja Chowdhury's, *How Prime Ministers Decide* (Aleph, New Delhi), August 2023.

the kind of language resorted to by the court in urging the enactment of the UCC to the detriment of the sanctified, institutionalized Personal Law, followed for over a millennium by the community, was offensive to most Muslim ears (and ought to have been to secular ears but was apparently not).

The *obiter dicta* pronounced by the court sparked a needless social and political controversy. On the one hand, members of the Opposition, especially from the BJP, took their expected position that it was most regrettable that the minorities had been allowed an unreformed Personal Law; others took the left-liberal position that even if the hidebound clerics had their theological objections, they should simply be overruled and compelled to accept a more 'humanitarian' order.

It was particularly significant in the eyes of the commentariat that one Muslim member, Arif Mohammed Khan, minister of state (MoS) for home, had been invited by the prime minister to participate in the debate on a Private Member's motion, although this was unprecedented, and encouraged to speak his mind. He had indeed done so over a speech, studded with quotations from the Quran and other holy texts, that lasted the better part of two hours. Indeed, RG had written him a congratulatory letter that was mistakenly supposed to have endorsed Arif's view.

Inevitably, another minister of the government, Ziaur Rahman Ansari, sought and obtained the permission of the prime minister to intervene – but while 'left-liberal' opinion applauded the decision to allow the 'modern-minded' Arif to intercede, it hypocritically criticized the same facility being offered to another allegedly 'reactionary' and 'backward-looking' minister of the community. Ansari rubbished Arif, gently mocking him by repeatedly referring to him as a 'nephew' who had taken a wrong turn.[13] Yet, ultimately, it was Ansari who brought

---

[13] Even as this manuscript was being finalized, Z.R. Ansari's son, Fasihur Rahman, sent me his biography of his father, *Wings of Destiny* (Highbrow Scribes Publications, New Delhi, 2019) that examines in detail Ansari's views on the 1985 Shah Bano judgment and the

the debate to an end by persuading the mover, Banatwala, to withdraw his motion as the government had assured Ansari, through the prime minister, that they were working on a formula to meet all objections. Otherwise, all Muslim members were clear that the Supreme Court judgment had transgressed Muslim Personal Law and offended Muslim sentiment. In particular, objection was taken to the judgment having focused on Article 44, 'Uniform civil code for the citizens', to attack the government for 'wanting the Muslim community to take the lead and Muslim public opinion to crystallize the reforms in their personal law'.

Thankfully, early on in the controversy, the prime minister had stilled concerns in regard to a UCC by reiterating the forty-year-old Congress position that reform had to come from within the community; until that happened, the constitutional guarantee given to the minority communities that their Personal Laws would be safeguarded would continue. A massive rally held in Bihar of the Muslim community upholding their Personal Law added strength to the government position.

I have often wondered how a parliament that has but 4 per cent Muslim members is going to legislate amendments to Muslim Personal Law, especially considering that it was a House of close to 85 per cent Hindus who had to be dragooned by Jawaharlal Nehru in the mid-fifties to pass the Bills arising from the original Hindu Code Bill drafted by Babasaheb Ambedkar. Are 96 per cent non-Muslim MPs going to decide for the entire community of nearly 200 million Muslims the intimate details of Personal Law for the Muslims? It took a Dr Ambedkar to challenge Hindu orthodoxy, and Ambedkar was so disillusioned by it that about the same time that the Hindu reform Bills were being passed, he left the Hindu religion to become a Buddhist. For Muslim Personal Law to be drastically reformed, they would first need to produce their own Dr Ambedkar.

---

subsequent 2001 judgment of the Supreme Court on the 1986 legislation. Unfortunately, I received the book too late to refer to it here *in extenso* but would urge the reader to do so.

Some 'modern-minded' Muslims were of the view that the 1985 Supreme Court judgment in *Shah Bano* should not be interfered with even to protect Muslim Personal Law. There was a large body of middle-class opinion, especially non-Muslims and liberals and feminists, who strongly supported this view. It is for them to find and raise a reformer of Muslim personal law of the stature and ability of Dr Ambedkar. Until that happens, if ever it happens, it behooves us as a pluralist nation to accept that a jurisprudence whose origins go back a millennium and more should not be so casually and insultingly dismissed. If, indeed, there is any considerable body of Muslims seeking reform, it is for the Muslims to influence change, instead of urging them to ally themselves, as some former National Front types are suggesting,[14] with those who have neither sympathy nor empathy with the Muslim community. The community is neither so barbaric nor so inhuman nor so wanting in the milk of human kindness as to require being instructed from outside as to where they might have gone wrong.

And they might indeed find such an Ambedkar. For, after all, Islam has seen many jurist-reformers in its 1,400-year history.[15] Muslim jurisprudence is as much the contribution of orthodox belief as it is of the jurisprudentially sanctified concepts of *masalaha* (public welfare), *shura* (consultation), and *ijtihad* (individual reasoning).[16] So, the day when the Indian Muslim community itself desires reform of their

---

[14] Notably Arif Mohammed Khan, the current BJP-nominated governor.

[15] I was amazed to discover in Nicholas B. Dirks' *The Scandal of Empire* (Harvard University Press, Paperback edition, 2008, p. 109), Edmund Burke's description of 'Mahometan Law' as a 'A Law interwoven with the wisest, the most learned and most enlightened jurisprudence that perhaps ever existed in the world'. This was stated in his impeachment of Warren Hastings, February 1788.

[16] I recall the line from Omar Khayyam, 'The two and seventy jarring sects confute'. Even by the twelfth century when Khayyam wrote, there were seventy-two schools of Islamic jurisprudence! The community is well versed in arguing the finer points of its jurisprudence. It is best to leave it to their scholars to suggest reform of Muslim Personal Law.

Personal Law may yet come, but that will never happen so long as the Muslim community feel themselves under siege. In these circumstances, for other communities to impose their views on this minority (or any other minority) is not compatible with the inclusive, secular conception of nationhood and citizenship that constitutes the bulwark of our Constitution.

Indeed, the only way an element of uniformity can be introduced in our personal laws is by doing what Rajiv Gandhi did: incorporate the Personal Law into civil law and then make the judiciary responsible for ensuring its implementation, especially in terms of gender equality in a society where religious dogma, is dominated by patriarchy. Has our present generation of politicians the statesmanship that Rajiv Gandhi displayed to do so?

Another angle to the case that greatly agitated Rajiv Gandhi, to go by comments made by him to me or in my hearing, was that the Supreme Court had not raised beyond Rs 179.20, the pathetic monthly payment to Shah Bano, to keep her from straying into 'vagrancy', the prim Victorian euphemism for beggary or prostitution. The 'sensitive minds' on the 1985 SC bench saw no need to enhance Shah Bano's maintenance beyond this paltry sum that was to end her 'palpable suffering'. Yet the onus for such suffering was placed entirely on the Muslim community, denigrating the sanctified institutional arrangements made in Muslim Personal Law for 'indigent' women to be looked after by their male relatives and, failing that, by the community Waqf Boards.

In actual fact, although this is little known and less commented on, Shah Bano never collected the amount deposited in court (she died a few years later). Was she a 'vagrant' or in danger of 'vagrancy', which was the sole criterion to be applied under the relevant sections (125/127) of the Criminal Procedure Code? RG not only brought the quantum of compensation within the ambit of Indian civil law, he did so with the consent of the Muslim community. It was also RG who raised the minimum amount payable to Rs 500 per month, an amount in need of further enhancement now in view of raging inflation over the last four decades.

RG's handling of the Shah Bano controversy typified his style of working, that of carefully listening to all points of view and only then rising to his responsibility as PM to make a final decision. It was a decision that was endorsed by the Supreme Court's judgment in 2001. That ought to have been the end of the matter. Unfortunately, however, sections of public opinion, in particular those that consider Muslim Personal Law to be callous and the 1985 SC judgment to be 'enlightened', continue to assert this judgment was 'reversed' by the Rajiv Gandhi government; that Muslim women were deprived of the rights they secured through the judgment; and that Muslim clerics were 'appeased'.

The question remains: why did Rajiv Gandhi rush into the controversy instead of ignoring it and going by the advice of the director of minority affairs in his PMO, Wajahat Habibullah, that as the Supreme Court had spoken there was no need for government to involve itself further in the matter? (Indeed, the PM had whispered to me, 'Even Sonia does not agree with me.') Only because the long controversy and the long debate had convinced him that it was his first duty as the PM to hold the country together. He fully realized that the charge of Muslim 'appeasement' and 'vote-bank' politics would be levelled against him, but he would face this. He asked me, rhetorically, one day:

> Where was the electoral advantage for me in all this? I knew I would be losing many of those who had supported me till then and giving an impetus to those who opposed me, but still went ahead to preserve the secular ethos of our nation. According to my opponents, half the electorate – women, whether they are Muslim or non-Muslim – will vote against me. So will men of all other faiths along with those who regard themselves as 'modern' or 'liberal' Muslims. That leaves only the Muslim clerics on my side with me. So, who am I appeasing?

I agreed with his assessment then – and still do. His stand on Shah Bano was in keeping with his overall approach to politics: do the right thing; it is more important to insist on principles than to compromise principles for passing opportunistic advantage. He preferred being ultimately exonerated rather than allowing or encouraging any alienation of any section of Indian citizens, even if this meant sacrificing party interest. He was confident, in controversies and in the accords into which he entered, that the Congress would bounce back. Some Congress leaders did not agree with him. These included Arun Nehru, Arif Mohammed Khan and a number of lesser-known Congresspersons, whose names would mean nothing to readers of the present generation. They were the ones who drifted towards V.P. Singh – and were rewarded with ministerial posts during his eleven-month reign before drifting into the wilderness or, in the case of Arif Mohammed Khan, even into the warm embrace of the Muslim-loathing saffron lot.

Writing as I am more than thirty-five years after these events, I have the advantage of hindsight that Rajiv Gandhi in 1986 did not have. Yet he spotted that ignoring or surrendering on this issue would promote precisely the kind of majoritarianism that has now overtaken the country, ending, perhaps forever, the secular India that was the quintessence of Mahatma Gandhi's and Nehru's vision of a pluralistic nation, celebrating its diversity instead of being imprisoned in revenge and revanchism, as has turned out to be the case. After years of reflection as a citizen of my country on the Hindu majoritarianism that has overwhelmed our country in recent years, I have come to believe that it was the unholy alliance struck between the liberal-left and the hitherto 'untouchable' BJP in 1986–90 on *Shah Bano* and the subsequent Babri Masjid issue that has brought us to the present pass. So upset were the left-liberals by the huge majority Rajiv Gandhi had garnered in the 1984 election that toppling him, come hell or high water, became their sole objective, with no regard for the consequences in this endeavour of restoring the Sangh

Parivar to the mainstream of Indian politics. It was this that sparked the conflagration of communalism that has since been consuming our country. And unless the BJP is defeated in the general elections of 2024, it seems they are bent on introducing a UCC that will bring civil strife on to our streets. As it is, the BJP government at the Centre is working on getting their state governments to draft UCCs for their respective states.

Babri Masjid–Ram Janmabhoomi

In December 1949, a group of about fifty people entered the Babri Masjid in Ayodhya, UP, and placed an idol of Ram Lalla (Ram the infant) in the premises. Fearing communal tensions, the UP government locked its gate. The Pandora's box was opened nearly forty years later when, in February 1986, by the order of a district sessions court in Faizabad, the gates of the Babri Masjid were unlocked. That is the origin of the dispute that was eventually laid to rest thirty-three years later by the Supreme Court judgment of 9 September 2019.

The background to the opening of the locks has been explained in detail by Deoki Nandan Agarwal of the Vishwa Hindu Parishad (VHP).[17] He says that Chief Minister Veer Bahadur Singh visited Ayodhya on 19 December 1985. A VHP delegation led by retired Justice Shiv Nath Katju met the CM to argue that the locks on the gates of the inner courtyard had not been put under the orders of any court or magistrate. This 'interfered with the free exercise of the Constitutional rights to worship Bhagwan Sri Rama'. While the chief minister 'quietly listened' to the delegation, he appears to have ordered 'a close search of the records.'

---

[17] See 'Sri Ramjanmabhoomi: A Legal and Historical Perspective', in A.G. Noorani, ed., *The Babri Masjid, 1528 to 2003: A Matter of National Honour*, Vol. 1, Tulika Books, New Delhi, 2003, p. 301. Extracts from the article may be seen at https://www.rajivmisunderstood.com by scanning the QR code at the end of the chapter.

When the matter was thereafter agitated before the district sessions judge of Faizabad on 1 February 1986, the district magistrate (DM)[18] 'candidly admitted' that 'there was no order of any court or magistrate for locking of the premises'. Then, the DM and senior superintendent of police affirmed respectively that 'the locks were not necessary for preserving the public peace' and that 'law and order' at Sri Ram Janmabhoomi could be maintained 'whether the locks were there or not'. At which the district sessions judge allowed the appeal and ordered the removal of the locks. The locks were dismantled within a few minutes of the order being given, and a storm of Hindu worshippers surged in. There was something clearly orchestrated about this sequence of events.

Of course, since it was in power, the Congress was responsible for the unlocking of the gates. But who in the Congress? The Congress chief minister of UP, or the Congress president and prime minister, Rajiv Gandhi? Stray remarks to me by the PM indicated he had nothing to do with this tragic farce and was deeply disturbed. Another PMO officer, Wajahat Habibullah, handled minority affairs; I was neither asked nor consulted by the PM on the matter.

Wajahat Habibullah writes in his memoirs[19] that he 'put to PM the question of the unlocking of the gates'. Rajiv Gandhi answered, 'I knew nothing of this development until I was told of this after the orders had been passed and executed.' He regretted that 'he had not been informed of this action' but suspected it was MoS for home affairs, Arun Nehru, and his political secretary, Makhan Lal Fotedar, who were responsible. He added that he was 'having this verified. If it [is] true, I will have to consider action.'

---

[18] 'DM' is the designation used in some states, including UP, for the executive head of the district administration. In other states, the head of the district administration is called the 'Deputy Commissioner' (DC) and in yet others as 'Collector'.
[19] Habibullah, *op. cit.*, p. 108.

The political problem he faced in taking action against Arun Nehru was well illustrated by a profile of Arun Nehru in *India Today* of 31 October 1985, on the occasion of Arun Nehru's elevation as the junior minister in charge of internal security.[20] Describing Arun Nehru as the 'fastest rising star in the firmament of Rajiv Gandhi's government', the authors heaped cliche after cliche upon him, describing Nehru as being 'in his element' where he 'exudes a sense of power', with a voice that 'will be heard loud and clear'; as 'the fulcrum on which many key central policies will now turn' and 'will undoubtedly leave his impress on the way the Rajiv administration consolidates its base'.

Yet, in October 1986, just a year after *India Today*'s fawning encomium, Arun Nehru was dropped from the Council of Ministers. The internal party enquiry RG had ordered as Congress president revealed that while Arun Nehru was behind the conspiracy to open the gates at Ayodhya, Fotedar was not. So, Arun Nehru was dropped but not Fotedar. Thus did Rajiv approach this matter with the utmost rectitude: punishing the one and sparing the other, although much the easier path would have been to spare the politically powerful Arun Nehru and punish the party apparatchik, M.L. Fotedar.

The question remains: could Arun Nehru have acted so decisively in such a manner without informing the prime minister? Of course, such impudence would have been out of the question in the normal course, but as the same issue of *India Today* wrote, there was an 'awed realization' within the party of Arun Nehru's clout which was 'in evidence when the Party legislators in UP unanimously chose Veer Bahadur Singh, *his nominee,* as the new Chief Minister' (emphasis added). The evidence on record appears to indicate that the hitherto obscure Veer Bahadur Singh had been chosen to fulfil Arun Nehru's ulterior aim of getting the locks opened to consolidate the party's base by pandering to Hindu

---

[20] The article was authored by Prabhu Chawla and Sumit Mitra.

sentiment. Rajiv Gandhi was not consulted because he would never have agreed to such an unprincipled step. So, the 'formidable cousin' decided to present the prime minister with a fait accompli, unmindful (or, perhaps, conscious) that this would stir the cauldron of communalism.

And another question: could the prime minister have restored the locks after they had been unlocked by judicial order? Only the courts could have reversed the district judge's order on an issue that would undoubtedly have gone to the Supreme Court, taking years and years along the way while religious tension simmered. Besides, the Faizabad session court's judgment had already been challenged in the Lucknow bench of the Allahabad High Court by a Sunni Muslim, Mohammed Hashim, and this was followed by the Sunni Waqf Board filing its own petition and the state government of UP also intervening. Any attempt at reversing the session court's order by executive fiat would have only added fuel to the fire.

Therefore, RG set about trying to see whether a political settlement was possible. To this end, he deputed Home Minister Buta Singh to visit the town in August–September 1989 to explore the possibility of a site in the immediate vicinity of the mosque where a Ram temple could be built without demolishing the masjid. Buta Singh succeeded, in concert with the disputants, in identifying a possible location for the Ram temple but either did not know or deliberately suppressed the fact that part of this site lay within the disputed area. When my former IFS colleague, then a distinguished MP, Syed Shahabuddin, approached me to allege that the home minister was misleading the PM, I told him I could do nothing as PMO work was compartmentalized but recommended that as an MP he was entitled to seek an appointment with the PM to explain matters directly to him. I do not know whether Shahabuddin took my advice, but the country was soon caught in the flurry of general elections, in which the foundation-stone-laying ceremony of the temple, the *shilanyas,* became the single most important cause for Rajiv Gandhi's defeat.[21]

Through most of the year following his defeat, Rajiv Gandhi was preoccupied with finding an answer to this temple/masjid crisis. He closeted himself with a well-chosen cabal of advisers to work out an alternative plan for dealing with the crisis. I was not part of the cabal and only came in when it was time to draft RG's recommendation to the then PM, Chandra Shekhar.

Siddhartha Shankar Ray, the statesman-jurist, was in the forefront of making the argument that the crux of the issue lay in determining whether Babar's general, Mir Baqi, had in fact destroyed an extant Ram temple to erect the Babri Masjid or whether he had only built the mosque on unused land that was now being claimed as the birthplace of Lord Ram. He suggested that it be left to the Supreme Court to pronounce its view on this limited but telling question after hearing the historical and archaeological evidence from respected experts. Ray argued that there were two ways of securing a definitive Supreme Court view on the 'key question'[22]: either by a judgment under Article 142 or by an advisory opinion under Article 143 of the Constitution. Under Article 142, the Supreme Court view would be expressed as an order that 'shall be enforceable throughout the territory of India'. If raised before the Supreme Court as a presidential reference under Article 143, the court's finding would be a non-binding 'opinion' expressed to the president. Ray preferred raising the issue in the Supreme Court under Article 142 as that would result in a 'binding' order.

Another alternative was to request the Supreme Court to convoke a commission of inquiry under Section 3 of the Commission of Inquiry Act,

---

[21] This has been dealt with in detail in my book *Memoirs of a Maverick* (Juggernaut, August 2023), pp. 297–301 and 326–27, and, therefore, need not be repeated here.

[22] Gathered from conversations at the time with RG and Siddhartha Shankar Ray when I was tasked with drafting the letter from RG to PM Chandra Shekhar.

1952, comprising five sitting judges of the Supreme Court, selected by the chief justice of India, to determine the question of fact as to whether, at the site of the dispute, a Ram mandir was in fact destroyed to build a masjid in its place. If it was held that such a commission could not be established owing to the same question pending before the Allahabad High Court, an ordinance or law might be passed under Article 138 enlarging the jurisdiction of the Supreme Court. In any case, the saffron argument was that Lord Ram's birthplace was not a matter of 'fact' but of 'faith' (*aasthaa*).

Some of these alternatives were put to PM Chandra Shekhar by Rajiv Gandhi in writing and others conveyed orally. Chandra Shekhar finally decided on Article 143, a non-binding opinion on a presidential reference. That could not, by definition, have definitively ended the matter. This caused RG considerable annoyance and contributed to his withdrawing support to the Chandra Shekhar government. Had RG lived to become prime minister in the election that followed, I believe he would have followed the Article 142 route. But fate decided otherwise.

Operation Brasstacks

With PM Rajiv Gandhi's approval in principle and under his overall supervision, Arun Singh, the MoS in the defence ministry (Rajya Raksha Mantri – RRM) and the chief of army staff (CoAS), General Krishnaswamy Sundarji, developed plans for the largest military exercise the Indian Army had ever undertaken. Code-named 'Operation Brasstacks', the exercise was designed to take place on a massive, unprecedented scale in the vicinity of the Pakistan border, involving half a million troops – half the Indian Army within a hundred miles of Pakistani territory – and the deployment of Indian naval forces for an amphibious naval trial assault in the Korangi creek that led from the sea to Pakistan's commercial capital, Karachi.

Alarmed at the possibility of the exercise being a feint for the ulterior aim of invading Pakistan, and possibly an Israel-like strike at the Pakistani nuclear plant at Kahuta, the Pakistan PM, Muhammad Khan Junejo, raised the issue with RG at their meeting on the sidelines of the second SAARC (South Asian Association for Regional Cooperation) summit in Bangalore (now Bengaluru) in November 1986.

The Indian PM assured his Pakistani counterpart that he would ensure the scaling down of the exercise and its marginal relocation so as to give the Pakistanis no cause for alarm. He then instructed Arun Singh and the CoAS accordingly, and fully expected them to obey. They didn't – and he discovered to his horror in January 1987, from a casual conversation at the Army Day reception with the field commander, Western Command, Lieutenant General P.N. Hoon, that there had been no change in the dispositions for Operation Brasstacks, an operation 'bigger than any NATO exercise – and the biggest since World War II'.[23]

General Hoon was to later describe it as 'a mobilization of the entire Army of India'.[24] He also says General Sundarji did not inform PM Rajiv Gandhi about the 'scale of the operation' and 'such details were hidden from him'. This was because while the PM was searching for ways to make peace, the RRM and CoAS were searching for ways of making war. When the PM discovered what was going on despite his orders, he put an immediate stop to it and, in fact, got the diplomatic corps and military attaches to watch the final phase of the operation to see for themselves that the Government of India had no intention of launching war against Pakistan. Of course, much of this was at the time top secret. It was only after he ceased being PM that Rajiv Gandhi gave some hint of how he had tackled the situation.

---

[23] 'Brass Tacks', globalsecurity.org, https://www.globalsecurity.org/military/world/war/brass-tacks.htm.

[24] P.N. Hoon, *Unmasking Secrets of Turbulence: Midnight Freedom to Nuclear Dawn*, Manas Publications, New Delhi, 2000, cited by Habibullah, *op. cit.*, pp. 134–41.

This was in an interview that RG gave to Vir Sanghvi and Aveek Sarkar of *Sunday* magazine in August 1990.[25] He said his policy towards Pakistan was the result of the six meetings he had had with the Pakistan president, General Zia-ul-Haq, at various locations around the world in his first year of office (1985). The outcome was a 'time-bound, phased agreement' that he and Zia signed in New Delhi on 19 December 1986 to normalize relations between the two countries, so much so that 'in January 1987, when we were on the brink of shooting each other, I could pick up the phone' and speak to Zia. It was thus that 'we were able to defuse the situation and not go to war'.

I had a small role to play from the margins. One day in mid-January 1987, I went into the PM's South Block office on some official work. As I sat down, he completely threw me with the remark, 'You know, Mani, we're almost at war with Pakistan.' 'What?' I cried. 'Why?' He explained the situation and said he must talk to the Pakistan President, Zia-ul-Haq, but was not sure how to do it. He asked for my suggestions. I replied there were four options: either he could ask Zia to come over to Delhi (problem: Zia had already made five or six unreciprocated visits and might resent being sent for); or RG could go over for a brief visit to Islamabad (problem: how would the nation react?); or he could demonstrate that this was not a state visit but an emergency meeting by popping over to Lahore, not the capital, Islamabad, for a short lunch discussion with Zia without frills; or, fourth option, he might invite Zia to Amritsar.

The PM replied that he had to go to Parliament House, but would I keep myself in readiness to receive a call from him? A few minutes later he called to announce triumphantly that Zia had agreed to come to India. Subsequently, after a further telephone conversation between RG and Junejo, a meeting of the foreign secretaries was scheduled to prevent the pot from boiling over. The crisis was so successfully defused by Rajiv

---

[25] *Sunday*, 19–25 August 1990.

Gandhi's initiative that when Zia came to India in mid-February 1987, according to the note taker, Pakistan Ambassador Humayun Khan,[26] there remained little for the two prime ministers to talk about Brasstacks. The exercise was successfully terminated in March, in the presence of military attaches of foreign missions in New Delhi, without any war clouds on the horizon.

Meanwhile, the renowned Indian journalist Kuldip Nayar was invited to interview the 'father of the Pakistani bomb', Dr A.Q. Khan, at the latter's high-security residence in Kahuta on 28 January 1987. I suspect this was deliberately done for Pakistan to alert hawks in India to the claim that Pakistan already had the bomb, as Khan boasted. Nayar revealed this claim to the Indian ambassador in Islamabad the same evening. However, Nayar's interview was not published in the London paper till 1 March, when India–Pakistan tensions had already been sharply reduced.

In a most perceptive paper, published by the Carnegie Endowment for International Peace on 14 November 2013,[27] a quarter-century after the events just described, P.R. Chari of the Institute of Peace and Conflict Studies, New Delhi, says Nayar met the chairman of the Indian Atomic Energy Commission, Dr Homi Nusserwanji Sethna, in Bombay before proceeding to Pakistan. Sethna had scoffed that Pakistan had 'neither the men nor the materials to make such a weapon'. Chari continues that 'Sundarji [whom he also interviewed] was wholly dismissive of Pakistan's nuclear capability . . . [He believed] Pakistan was far from acquiring a deliverable nuclear weapon.'

War with Pakistan may have been averted, but the PM's relations with his old school friend Roon [Arun Singh] and General Sundarji were so badly damaged as to have the most profound consequences. It injected

---

[26] In conversation with me on the telephone. Unfortunately, Ambassador Humayun Khan passed away on 22 September 2022.
[27] 'Nuclear Signaling in South Asia: Revisiting A. Q. Khan's 1987 Threat', carnegieendowment.org.

the bad blood that was to have the most deleterious consequences when the Bofors issue broke within a few weeks.[28]

The Sacking of the Foreign Secretary

In the midst of the Operation Brasstacks crisis, on 27 January 1987, the PM held a press conference in Vigyan Bhawan. About an hour before the conference began, all officers of the PMO were directed by the PM's Principal Secretary, Sarla Grewal, to gather at the PM's South Block office for a final briefing. The meeting was moving along in a humdrum manner when RG dropped the bombshell that he intended to announce Foreign Secretary A.P. Venkateswaran's dismissal at the press conference.

Everyone present, led by Principal Secretary Sarla Grewal, begged the prime minister to desist. The opposition from his own officers to his proposed announcement was so vocal and so unanimous that the PM was swayed, and we congratulated ourselves on having deflected him from such a disastrous course. At the presser, RG held back until the last question, which came from a Pakistani correspondent:

Q: What about your visit to Pakistan?
A: At the moment, I have got no fixed plans for visiting Pakistan.
Q: The foreign secretary said you will be visiting Pakistan as the SAARC chairman.
A: You will talk to the new foreign secretary soon.

The press conference ended in pandemonium. I returned to my office dazed and disturbed. My colleague, R. Vasudevan, fetched up a few

---

[28] While General Sundarji is no more, I have tried to talk to Arun Singh about these matters in connection with this book. To my intense regret, he has declined to do so, saying he has decided not to talk to anyone about Rajiv Gandhi or his relationship with him. If some enterprising editor could persuade Arun Singh to write his memoirs, they would have a bestseller in their hands!

minutes later. 'What's happened,' he said, 'is bad for the foreign service, worse for the foreign secretary, but worst of all for the PM.'

I do not know why or how Venkateswaran got it into his head that I was responsible for his dismissal. I had noticed him looking at me quizzically when I was in easy banter with Rajiv Gandhi. Maybe that gave him the wholly erroneous idea that I was an adviser to the PM. When Pritish Nandy interviewed him for the *Illustrated Weekly of India,* AP let fly at me by name, warning, 'Let him remember that those whom he passes on his way up are going to be there when he slides down.' I have, therefore, had for long enough reason to understand the circumstances of Venkateswaran's dismissal. These are my conclusions.

As explained earlier, at the Bangalore meeting of SAARC on 16–17 November 1986, Pakistan Prime Minister Muhammad Khan Junejo had shared with his Indian counterpart the growing alarm in Pakistan over the upcoming Operation Brasstacks. RG had replied that he would ensure the intensity and locale of the exercise would be reduced. But this had not happened, and the tension had been ratcheted up instead of being reduced.

Hence, tensions were at a high pitch when Venkateswaran visited Islamabad in December 1986. There, without any authorization from the PM, the foreign secretary announced the first visit to Pakistan by an Indian PM in twenty-five years – albeit in his capacity as chairman of SAARC. Venkateswaran should have known much better than to unauthorizedly make such a momentous announcement in the middle of a serious military crisis. This explains, even if it does not justify, the prime minister expelling such a highly placed official publicly at a widely televised press conference, and also why the PM could not explain the full background and rationale for his decision.

Should he have also sacked Sundarji and Arun Singh for disobedience? Perhaps he should have sacked them, but I imagine he would have preferred to rein them in rather than provoke yet another public scandal on the PM being disobeyed, indeed betrayed, by his own minister of state and army chief. Besides, while much of what was happening around Operation Brasstacks was highly confidential, Venkateswaran's was a highly public issue.

India–Sri Lanka (Rajiv–Jayawardene) Accord and IPKF

Rajiv Gandhi proceeded to Sri Lanka on 29 July 1987. It was the only official visit abroad from which I was summarily dropped. I did not know then, nor later, why I was removed from the delegation. At the final briefing, I even passed to the PM a note asking whether I could be included but RG crumpled the paper without saying anything. While the PM was away, I struggled to remember what slight, or error, or act of moral turpitude I had committed, and being unable to find one, reconciled myself to the thought that I would be sacked when he returned. But immediately thereafter, I was reinstated on all other trips, domestic and international, with no explanation forthcoming for that one exclusion. I was to learn the painful lesson in later life that the Gandhi family never explain why they say yes, or why they say no.

I was not then or later consulted or informed about the steps he undertook in Sri Lanka. Decades later, in January 2017, when I was commissioned by the TV news channel NewsX to do a multi-part TV series on Sri Lanka from distant times to the present, I learned something of the inside story on a long visit to Sri Lanka that included the Tamil-majority areas of Jaffna and Trincomalee and the last battlefields in the east. I spoke to, and filmed a large number of Sri Lankan personalities, starting with an old friend, Chandrika Bandaranaike Kumaratunga, former PM and president of Sri Lanka, and several Sinhala and Tamil politicians (Sampantham, the Tamil MP was the most impressive), a range of journalists and political scientists (Pakiasothy Saravanamuttu proved to be an intellectual giant). In Jaffna and Trincomalee I met a number of former and current Liberation Tigers of Tamil Eelam (LTTE) cadres, sympathizers (Anandi, who lost her husband in the last awful week of the war, was the most fiery) and activists (gathered by Ahilan Kadirgamar, the most well-informed and helpful Sri Lankan Tamil I met). I also met representatives of the small but significant Muslim minority who had been very badly treated by Prabhakaran's LTTE. I also read widely on the subject.[29] It will take another book to recount all that I gleaned from these conversations and readings, so let me sum up.

When Rajiv Gandhi visited Colombo on 29 July 1987, the conflict between the Sri Lanka government and the Tamil militants had reached an impasse. We were clear, as we had been since the earliest beginnings, that, whatever the popular sentiment in Tamil Nadu, it was not in India's interest to abet the splitting of Sri Lanka by encouraging the idea of a Tamil homeland, Tamizh Eelam. It was also accepted and stated policy from the start of the troubles in the late seventies/early eighties, and particularly after the targeted mass killings of Tamil speakers in Colombo

---

[29] My bibliography included Sri Lankan Tamil analyst Ketheeswaran Loganathan's scholarly study, *Sri Lanka: Lost Opportunities* (Centre for Policy Research and Analysis, Colombo, 1996); and *Triumph of Truth – The Rajiv Gandhi Assassination: The Investigation* (New Dawn Press Group, Slough/Chicago/New Delhi, 2004) by the principal investigator of Rajiv Gandhi's assassination, D.R. Kaarthikeyan, IPS, and his collaborator, Radhavinod Raju. I have also drawn substantially on J.N. 'Mani' Dixit's *Assignment Colombo* (Konark, New Delhi, 1998), as also on M.R. Narayan Swamy, *Inside an Elusive Mind: Prabhakaran* (Konark, New Delhi, 2003), arguably the most thorough and perceptive account of the 'troubles'. Anita Pratap's remarkable memoir, *Island of Blood* (Penguin/Viking, New Delhi, 2001) has also been invaluable to penetrate Prabhakaran's 'elusive mind'. For an insider's view on the IPKF's military operations, I am beholden to Major General Ashok Mehta, General Officer Commanding IPKF South and Commander 57 Division, for his brutally frank account, 'India's Counterinsurgency Campaign in Sri Lanka', in Ganguly and Fidler (eds), *India and Counterinsurgency: Lessons Learned* (Routledge, New York, 2009, pp. 155–72). I have also benefited from conversations with General A.S. Kalkat, who commanded the IPKF from late October 1987 to the end of the mission; as also with Ronen Sen and Meera Shankar, then with the PMO; and Kuldip Sahdev, then divisional head (joint secretary), Sri Lanka desk. My grateful thanks to all of them.

in July 1983, that no Indian military intervention would be allowed; the only concession was that the Tamil militant groups (including the LTTE) who had sought refuge in India would be given some training, some weaponry and modest financial resources. The principal political/ diplomatic tool deployed on the Sri Lankan authorities would be gentle persuasion. It was made abundantly clear from the start that India had no interest whatever in fostering or encouraging the partition of the island into a Tamil-majority Eelam and a Sinhala-speaking rump.

Indira Gandhi had come to the conclusion that the only way to safeguard the unity and integrity of the island nation was by the Sri Lanka government devolving a meaningful measure of self-government to the Tamil-majority north and east regions, perhaps by constituting the two distinct areas into a single province. To this end, Indira Gandhi's principal adviser on foreign policy, the venerable G. Parthasarathi, had taken on his team an Indian constitutional expert in the Indian home ministry, Dr Balakrishnan, to draft, in consultation with the Sri Lankans, Annexure C to the agreement negotiated during G. Parthasarathi's 'mediation' under Indira Gandhi's prime ministership. Rajiv Gandhi took up the thread at this point.

The same Balakrishnan was pressed into service to join the group of civil servants charged by RG to prepare, in consultation with the island nation's experts, an amendment to the Sri Lankan Constitution that would ensure effective devolution to a democratically elected provincial council in the Tamil-majority areas (and other provinces of Sri Lanka), incorporating 'land' and 'law and order' in the subjects for devolution; this was called the 13th amendment (it became the predecessor to the amendments RG was to introduce into our Constitution to ensure Panchayati Raj, that is, constitutional status for local self-government in rural and urban India). It was for the Sri Lankan government to accept or reject the proposed amendment; there was no question of India forcing this down the gullet of the elected government of Sri Lanka.

In the light of subsequent developments, it needs to be noted that whereas the external affairs minister, P.V. Narasimha Rao, was reportedly of the view that the signatories to any agreement should be Prabhakaran and Sri Lankan President Jayawardene, in accordance with the earlier Indira–Parthasarathi line, Rajiv Gandhi switched India from a 'mediatory' role to that of a 'guarantor', as Jayawardene wished. Of course, if Rao's line had been followed, there would have been no settlement as Jayawardene would never have agreed to sign an accord with Prabhakaran and Prabhakaran would never have agreed to affix his signature alongside Jayawardene's.

Also, had the volcanic situation obtaining in July 1987 been allowed to blow up, there might well have been a military and political debacle in which India would have lost all its objectives: a united Sri Lanka; devolution to the 'north and east province' as the answer to Eelam; forestalling the real possibility of a Marxist regime in Colombo with close ties to China; as also, forestalling, very possibly, an American naval base in Trincomalee; and allowing a vicious civil war to rage in our immediate neighbourhood with no solution in sight.

President Jayawardene had been pushed into a corner by the outbreak of a Marxist uprising in the Sinhala-majority south and south-west of the island even while the north and east were in turmoil. He overruled the hawks in his cabinet, led by Prime Minister Premadasa and the defence minister, the formidable ex-president of the Oxford Union, Lalith Athulathmudali,[30] to enter into an agreement with the Indian PM to incorporate in the Sri Lankan Constitution the 13th Amendment (which would guarantee self-government within a united Sri Lanka to

---

[30] It is a curious factoid that all three Sri Lankans (Ceylonese) elected to high office in the Oxford Union – S.W.R.D. Bandaranaike as Treasurer in 1927, followed by Lalith Athulathmudali and Lakshman Kadirgamar as President in the late 1950s – were assassinated. A bloody tale. Portraits of Bandaranaike and Kadirgamar adorn the walls of the Oxford Union building.

the regions with a Tamil-speaking majority; this did not include the so-called 'Indian Tamils' who were the bulwark of Sri Lanka's tea plantations in the central highlands).

Immediately after the signing of the Rajiv–Jayawardene Accord, Jayawardene drew RG aside into an adjacent room. There he confided that Sri Lanka's limited armed forces were unable to confront two simultaneous internal armed uprisings at opposite ends of their country; indeed, it could not overcome even the spreading violence in the capital, Colombo. Therefore, would the Indian PM please agree on the spot – *as there was no time to lose* – to dispatch a peacekeeping force to insulate the Sri Lankan army from the Tamil armed rebels as the quid pro quo for Jayawardene having agreed to the proposed amendment to the Sri Lankan Constitution, even in the face of opposition from many (most?) of his senior ministers?

Without seeking time to consult his experts, all of whom were in the hall outside, the PM immediately agreed that an IPKF would be shipped out to act as a buffer between Tamil insurgents and the Sri Lankan army to enable the Sri Lankan government to concentrate its armed forces against the threatened Marxist takeover in the south and south-west of the island. It needs to be emphasized, in the light of subsequent developments, that it was at the instance of the Sri Lankan president, and not at the initiative of the Indian PM, that the IPKF was inducted; and that the peacekeeping force was just that: a unit strictly for ensuring peace between warring factions, not an armed combat force.

Moreover, provision for responding to such a request from Sri Lanka, primarily at President Jayawardene's instance, had been incorporated in the accord just signed (Articles 2.14 and 2.16(c) read with para 6 of the Annexure). This inclusion had been worked out by consensus in Delhi after a conscious revision of the principled position held by Indira Gandhi's government that under no circumstances would India intervene militarily even if the Sri Lankan government were to press for such assistance, as she did not want Indian soldiers shooting at either Tamil militants or Sri Lankan soldiers. In the light of the strategic need to not let Great Power rivalry enter the island just offshore India, Indira Gandhi's successor government had worked out an internal consensus that in the event of the Sri Lankans seeking such assistance, India must be prepared, in our own national interest, to do our duty. That is how the relevant provisions were drafted and decided.

The experts were somewhat stunned when they heard about the PM's extramural decision. They had not anticipated that these provisions would by invoked with such urgency in the immediate aftermath of the signing. Of course, Rajiv Gandhi had known this. Which is probably why he did not waste time consulting his advisers who, in any case, knew that this contingency was written into the accord. He acted decisively – and took on his chin the consequences.

It was in keeping with his character. He paid the price within minutes of his accepting Jayawardene's post-accord proposal. A Sri Lankan Sinhala naval rating, standing in the ranks of the Guard of Honour for the visiting prime minister, attacked his nation's distinguished guest with the butt of his rifle. He would have smashed Rajiv Gandhi's head, possibly killing him on the spot, but the young and extremely physically fit prime minister ducked, sensing the blow coming. The rifle butt missed its target and grazed only his shoulder.

In Delhi, even before news of this had trickled in, Meera Shankar, then a relatively junior IFS officer in the PMO (and later ambassador to the US), who had earlier been closely associated with the 1983–84 G. Parthasarathi mediation effort, went to a colleague and asked, presciently, 'Why are they putting the young man's head on the chopping-block?' (as told to me in a telephone conversation in the summer of 2020). When the PM's party landed in Delhi a few hours later, internal security secretary T.N. Seshan stepped off the plane and, in his usual hyper-hysterical and self-important manner – magnified now by the attack that had been averted – handed me a video of the incident and asked me to rush with it to Doordarshan. I did, as instructed, and spent the next hour looking again and again at reruns of the scene.

The IPKF expedition was a disaster. Military incompetence ruined it at the start and military competence later never retrieved the initial damage. This was compounded by a total misreading by our intelligence/diplomatic/political establishment of the LTTE and its dedication to its inflexible goal of setting up an independent, sovereign Tamil state by force of arms.

Initially, on arrival, the IPKF was given a rousing reception as 'liberators' by the people of Jaffna. A critical reason was that LTTE cadres and supporters joined the welcome in the expectation that the arrival of the IPKF presaged the imminent return to Jaffna of Prabhakaran under Indian Army protection, with the Sri Lanka military kept firmly at bay. Ironically, the welcome was also a reflection of the awfulness of the LTTE's temporary capture of administrative power in Jaffna for large sections of Jaffna Tamils. Numerous non-LTTE activists – a veritable alphabet soup of militants and terrorist groups, EPRLF, PLOTE, TELO, EROS, ENDLF – joined in the warm reception at the prospect of being able to return to the Jaffna peninsula and parts of the east, from where they had been driven out by the LTTE at gunpoint with huge loss of life. The enthusiastic mass welcome extended beyond Jaffna town to all points on the north and east of the island where IPKF troops landed. The general belief in Indian circles was that the people's welcome indicated that Indian diplomacy had pulled off a diplomatic coup that established New Delhi as a benevolent hegemon in South Asia, using its might for 'peacekeeping', not armed aggression.

High Commissioner Dixit confesses in *Assignment Colombo*[31] that

---

[31] Dixit, *op. cit.*

there had been no briefing of the troops, or even commanders, of the ground situation. He attributes this to the absence of time between decision and action (under twenty-four hours). But what was brewing politically (and militarily) provided ample time – two months – for political and diplomatic reflection, and military and intelligence preparation, before armed conflict broke out between the IPKF and the LTTE. The seven weeks or so after the first arrival of IPKF troops were full of portents about what was seriously wrong with the assumptions on which the accord was based. Unfortunately, this window of opportunity was not used. These wrong assumptions would result in converting the IPKF from a peacekeeping force holding the ring between the Eelam partisans and the Sri Lankan army into a regular army taking on Sri Lankan Tamil guerrillas, making north-east Sri Lanka akin to an Indian Vietnam.

The LTTE chief, Velupillai Prabhakaran, had been escorted to New Delhi in the week of the accord. The first signs of trouble arose when he received a copy of the draft accord. Prabhakaran, the chief Tiger, was growling in captivity in Delhi's Ashoka Hotel. He sought time to read the document and discuss it with his colleagues. He then let it be known that the accord was completely unacceptable to him for the following reasons: 'Tamils were not recognized as a distinct nationality; they were being treated on par with insignificant minorities; the north-east region was not reserved for the Tamils; and the long-standing demand for the merger of the northern and eastern provinces was left to the will of the Sri Lankan president.' Also, making it obligatory for the LTTE and other Tamil groups to put down their weapons within seventy-two hours of the pact was *'unrealistic* and *unfair'* (emphasis added).[32]

The enterprising journalist Anita Pratap, of *Sunday* magazine, took a room at the hotel where Prabhakaran was being held as a virtual

---

[32] Narayan Swamy, *op. cit.*, pp. 160–61.

prisoner. Pretending to be from housekeeping, she succeeded in entering Prabhakaran's 'small suite'. He had met her earlier. She recollects:

> I was completely taken aback by Pirabhakaran's[33] tone. All of us had been to varying extents influenced by the optimism emanating from Rajiv Gandhi's office, but Pirabhakaran looked and sounded bleak. He didn't think the accord would settle the problem. He also said if the Indian troops that were to be sent down to keep peace in Tamil areas did not protect the rights of the Tamils, he would fight them. Warning bells began clanging in my ears.

Tragically, no warning bells started clanging in the heads of the Indian establishment: neither our intelligence, nor our officers concerned in the PMO and Minister of External Affairs (MEA), nor our diplomats (including High Commissioner Dixit and First Secretary Hardeep Singh Puri, now the BJP's minister of urban development, who had accompanied Prabhakaran to Delhi as our high commission's liaison officer), nor security nor the defence forces. They all thought the personal charm of Rajiv Gandhi had made Prabhakaran relent when in fact Prabhakaran was only plotting his escape from custody. After a tough meeting with the PM, he was invited to join RG's family at dinner. After their cordial dinner, 'Gandhi called his son Rahul and asked him to fetch his [Gandhi's] bulletproof jacket. He put the jacket on Prabhakaran's back and remarked with his usual charming smile, "Take care of yourself."'

To the few who sounded a note of warning, the PM replied: 'Prabhakaran has agreed, I trust him.'[34] Never were words more misspoken.

The deception continued when Prabhakaran landed in Madras (now Chennai). Narayan Swamy says that when Prabhakaran met the Indian

---

[33] This is how Prabhakaran spelt his name in English, transliterating from the Tamil script that cannot put 'p' and 'r' together without a linking 'i'.

[34] Narayan Swamy, *op. cit.*, p. 164.

general officer commanding-in-chief (GOC-in-C), Southern Command, General Depinder Singh, he 'smiled affably' and offered to hand over to the general personally 'the heaviest gun in the LTTE's armoury'.[35]

Prabhakaran had apparently signalled his willingness to try to work the accord in return for financial assistance of Rs 5 crore. The sum was given. But, in fact, Prabhakaran remained determined to fulfil his overarching goal of achieving Eelam as an independent, sovereign nation. This, the Indians – diplomatic, military, intelligence and political – discovered only as he slowly and deliberately revealed his hand over the two months following the IPKF's landing.

Prabhakaran showed signs of dissidence in the very first speech he delivered on 4 August at Suthumalai in Jaffna. True, he had words of praise and, indeed, 'love' for India, but there was a sting in the tail: 'We love India. We love the people of India. But let me make it clear to you here, beyond the shadow of a doubt, that I will continue to fight for the objective of attaining Tamil Eelam.'[36] Resuscitating an insistence on Tamil Eelam was, of course, to undermine the most important underpinning of the accord – which was the guarantee of the unity and territorial integrity of Sri Lanka.

Worse still, the 'surrender of arms was only symbolic'.[37] When Prabhakaran did not personally attend the arms surrender ceremony, 'his absence at the ceremony was also a political gesture of reservation and withdrawal'.[38] A 'farce'[39] was then enacted with the LTTE putting down only 'a small quantity of mostly obsolete weapons ... The weapons included mortar shells, AK-47s, German-made G-3 rifles, RPGs, .303

---

[35] *Ibid.*, p. 167.
[36] *Ibid.*, p. 132.
[37] Dixit, *op. cit.*, p. 192.
[38] *Ibid.*, p. 191.
[39] *Ibid.*, p. 192.

rifles, machine guns, rocket launchers, mortars.'[40] A final cocking of the snook at the Indians was that 'some of the weapons had been seized by Indian authorities from other militant groups in Tamil Nadu in November 1986 and quietly passed on to the LTTE'.[41] A few days later, the LTTE announced 'that the Tigers had no intention of giving up all its weaponry'.

The confusion this caused is well illustrated by Dixit through his conversation with the commander of the IPKF, Major General Harkirat Singh, and Harkirat's boss, GOC-in-C, Southern Command, General Depinder Singh: 'When I [Depinder Singh] mentioned that the IPKF could have the additional responsibility of ensuring that the Agreement was implemented, his [Harkirat Singh's] response was, "That is all very well, sir, but I do hope we do not get involved in a shooting match."'

Yet, 'getting involved in a shooting war' is exactly what happened.

The need to trust Prabhakaran overwhelmed the imperative to be prepared for the worst. At first, the IPKF and the LTTE entertained cordial relations and the general population continued to smile. Indeed, relations between the IPKF jawans and the LTTE cadres were so friendly that, despite the language barrier, the soldiers were escorted everywhere for shopping and sightseeing. Moreover, the LTTE was even given the radio frequencies over which they could speak to the IPKF base whenever they wanted. This was to have the most catastrophic consequences when fighting broke out.

The LTTE was now intent on buying time to hide their arsenal, accumulate more weapons, politically discredit the accord, engage the IPKF in a guerrilla war, and start a global public relations exercise to discredit India and bring pressure to withdraw the IPKF. The militant organization attained many of these goals. (Tragically, this was to lead eventually to a

---

[40] Narayan Swamy, *op. cit.*, p. 162.
[41] *Ibid.*

gotterdämmerung of horrific proportions in May 2009 when the LTTE and tens of thousands of innocent Sri Lankan Tamil civilians were wiped out.)

Dixit met Prabhakaran thrice in the second half of September 1987 to discuss a list of demands the LTTE had sent in a memorandum. At the meetings, Prabhakaran complained that despite assurances from Rajiv Gandhi on all of them, these were yet to be fulfilled. The LTTE leader Thileepan, who was on a fast unto death protesting the accord, expired halfway through the discussions. Thileepan's 'martyrdom' was a turning point that worked in favour of the LTTE.[42] It was seen by the people as a sign of India's impotence as the guarantor of the accord.

Dixit describes another incident which brought the accord closer to breakpoint.[43] The LTTE leader Pulendran was apprehended by the Sri Lankan navy in the Palk Straits with a boatload of arms and ammunition in violation of the accord. Pulendran and sixteen other members of the LTTE were kept in military custody by the Sri Lankan forces. Dixit asked the IPKF commander to take all appropriate steps to safeguard the LTTE cadres, but General Harkirat's Singh's reply was that he did not figure in the high commissioner's chain of command and, as a soldier, he could only accept orders from proper channels. Thus, the LTTE was permitted to visit the detainees to give them food and medicines. The cadres availed of the opportunity to also pass on cyanide capsules; all seventeen swallowed these and died.

When the coffins arrived at Prabhakaran's birthplace VVT (Velvattithurai), there was widespread anger. LTTE cadres went on a killing spree, slaughtering Sinhalese civilians. Generals Depinder Singh and Harkirat Singh flew by helicopter to the LTTE's main office in Jaffna University to try all means to avoid a showdown. But Prabhakaran had

---

[42] Dixit, *op. cit.*, p. 202.
[43] *Ibid.*, pp. 209–11.

gone underground, and the Indian generals could not meet him. And then, on 8 October, the LTTE ambushed an Indian patrol and shot dead five commandos. Hostilities had commenced.

CoAS General Sundarji reached Jaffna on 5 October and ordered Operation Pawan on 6 October 1987, which was to be a limited operation to neutralize the LTTE. Sundarji, says the high commissioner, told the prime minister: 'The Indian armed forces can neutralize the LTTE in a fortnight or three to four weeks.'[44] That was a fatal miscalculation. Operation Pawan, 'conceived', says Dixit, as 'a limited operation to neutralize the LTTE . . . commenced somewhat disastrously'. That was the understatement of the year. Prabhakaran was 'fully aware of our operational plans . . . nearly four hours before it was launched'. This was principally because 'the radio frequencies of our communications were not changed' when hostilities broke out. These were the very same 'frequencies used for talking to the LTTE'.

The plan was to capture the LTTE headquarters by 'a heliborne attack'. But as it was 'a moonlit night', the paratroopers were clearly visible as they slowly floated down in their 'white parachutes' – 'sitting ducks'.[45] Prabhakaran and other leaders had escaped two hours before the heliborne attack commenced. The IPKF's operation to capture the entire leadership ended in a shambles.

Major General Harkirat Singh was removed from command by the end of October and Lieutenant General Amarjit Singh Kalkat took over.

Major General Ashok Mehta offers a view from inside the IPKF.[46] The token IPKF was expanded into a four-division force but the switch of the LTTE from ally to enemy was disorienting, and exacerbated the problems faced by the ill-equipped and unprepared IPKF. The troops were not prepared for counterinsurgency operations and the LTTE

---
[44] *Ibid.*, p. 337.
[45] *Ibid.*
[46] Mehta, *op. cit.*, pp. 158–67.

pursued a strategy of outlasting the IPKF, bleeding it to undermine political support. Mehta points out that the 54 Infantry Division arrived without even a map and deployed without its heavy equipment or weapons. Other units also arrived at half strength. Even so, 'Indian Army command believed that the LTTE could be rounded up in as little as 72 hours or, at the longer end, between 7 and 15 days.'

The IPKF never 'rounded up' the LTTE. Indeed, the LTTE outlasted the IPKF by twenty years!

However, the IPKF did succeed in pushing the LTTE out of Jaffna peninsula, but at great cost of life, both to itself and to the LTTE, as well as, most tragically, to the civilian population. After they were driven out of Jaffna, they regrouped in the Wanni jungles south of Jaffna and fought from there until the end. The Tigers excelled in the imaginative use of mines, especially improvised explosive devices (IEDs) and used boats along the coastline while running an excellent intelligence network.

Mehta concedes that as time progressed Indian military and political efforts improved. So, he holds, the story of the IPKF is 'not entirely a sordid tale of bumbling failure and remorse'. True, but there is no doubt that the IPKF was outwitted militarily and the Indian commanders at the top failed the nation with their bombast instead of serious evaluation. The only commanders to emerge from the episode with any credit were General A.S. Kalkat and the commander in Batticaloa, my schooldays friend, the late Lieutenant General Jamil Mehmood.

Dixit offers a ruthlessly honest introspection, recorded with utter integrity.[47] He pulls no punches, especially those that land on himself, hides nothing, covers up nothing, as he avers:

The criticism [that it] . . . was a foreign policy failure, is valid . . . Prabhakaran discovered that Rajiv Gandhi's motivations as manifested

---

[47] Dixit, *op. cit.*, pp. 326–50.

in the Indo-Sri Lankan agreement were genuine and sincere and that India had no plans of clandestinely helping him create a separate Tamil state... One miscalculation was our under-estimating Prabhakaran's passionate, even obsessive commitment to the cause of Tamil Eelam, his authoritarian and single-minded nature, his tactical cleverness and his resilience in adversity...

The IPKF was itself handicapped in terms of the brief given to them ... I over-estimated the sincerity and political will of Jayawardene to come to a genuine compromise with the Tamils... My expectation that the LTTE could be successfully isolated from Sri Lankan Tamils also proved to be wrong.

Building on this litany of self-criticism, High Commissioner 'Mani' Dixit turns to Rajiv Gandhi's handling of the issue:

Rajiv Gandhi was given inaccurate advice about the political, military, and intelligence factors... History will judge Rajiv Gandhi's Sri Lankan involvement with greater precision and objectivity. In my perception, his motive was fair, just and as practicable as he could be in his policies. He was courageous in taking on responsibilities to safeguard Indian interests and the well-being of a small neighbouring country. He took upon himself a thankless job for the well-being of the peoples of India and Sri Lanka, and paid for it with his life.

I have nothing to add.

Bofors

The Bofors scandal erupted on 16 April 1987 when Swedish radio announced that many payments (apparently bribes) had been paid into diverse Swiss bank accounts by the arms manufacturer Bofors. They had chanced on this information while a Swedish parliamentary committee was investigating other charges against the firm involving bribery for defence contracts in the Middle East. The Bofors allegation against Rajiv Gandhi's government was an offshoot or sideshow in this Swedish parliamentary investigation into corruption in Bofors involving their managing director, Martin Ardbo. As arms exports to war regions were prohibited under Swedish law, Bofors had allegedly used Singapore as an entrepot for arms shipments to the Middle East, run by 'Bob' Wilson, heading AE Services of Guildford, Surrey, UK. He was often Bofors' agent in these illegal shipments. This needs underlining as Wilson and AE were to play a major role in the so-called 'scandal'.

Rajiv Gandhi was travelling, with me in attendance, when the news broke. The Congress Working Committee (CWC) had been summoned to meet on our return. As I had been tasked with doing much of Rajiv Gandhi's drafting work, I was readying myself to prepare the rough draft of a resolution when I found on landing that Additional Secretary Gopi Arora had already undertaken the job. It contained three words that were to make the resolution notorious: 'false, baseless and mischievous'.

As a huge controversy overwhelmed the media and the political class, RG asked that the Swedish authorities investigate the allegations. In turn, the Swedish government entrusted the Swedish National Audit Bureau (SNAB) with the probe. It bears underlining that the Swedish investigation was not undertaken suo moto by the Swedish government nor at the behest of the media nor at the asking of the Indian Opposition. It was the Rajiv Gandhi government, none other, that requested the Swedish authorities, through proper diplomatic channels, to undertake the probe. Why, I wondered then and thereafter, would RG, of his own volition, put matters in the hands of a foreign investigation agency over which he would have no control – unless he knew he was innocent of any wrongdoing?

The next domestic trip RG undertook in the second half of April

1987, soon after the Swedish radio broadcast hit the headlines, was to the Neyveli lignite mines in Tamil Nadu. As usual, I travelled with him and drafted the notes for his remarks at Neyveli. I included the three words 'false, baseless, mischievous' in a reference to the Swedish radio broadcast. On the helicopter from Trichy to Neyveli, the PM called me and asked what was this 'nonsense' I had written. I feebly protested that I had only paraphrased the CWC resolution. 'I have not even read it,' was his astonishing reply. He spoke at Neyveli without referring to the Swedish radio broadcast, and in no subsequent speech did I include any reference to Bofors. This means there is little on record I can quote from his words but some that I can use from a few interviews he gave and plenty that I can infer from his actions.

The Neyveli incident was my first and last interaction with Rajiv Gandhi on Bofors. His principal aide in the matter was Gopi Arora. I picked up the twists and turns of the tale from newspapers and journals and, subsequently, much documentation that I read specifically for this book. This, therefore, is not a ringside view of events but reflections born out of wondering how a man of Rajiv Gandhi's manifest values and character could have got himself entangled in matters which utterly ruined his reputation and his prime ministership.

The Bofors Papers

Let me begin my tale from the middle of my story, that is, from when I wandered into the visitors' gallery of Parliament on 28 December 1989 – after the general elections of the previous month had ousted RG from his premiership – to listen to an exchange between the former and current prime ministers. This was the debate on the motion of thanks to the president for his address to both Houses of Parliament, held about a month to the day since V.P. Singh won the election. Just weeks earlier, I had sought and obtained voluntary retirement from the IFS to take up an alternative career in politics and media. I was at leisure to delve into anything that interested me – such as this debate.

I sat riveted to my seat as the following exchange on Bofors took place between the former and new prime ministers late at night (I am reproducing only the portions relevant to the demand made and pressed by Rajiv Gandhi for placing all the Bofors papers and files on the Table of the House):[48]

SHRI RAJIV GANDHI: ...We would like you to find the people who have taken the money because we know when you find the people, all the accusations that you have made during these years will turn out to be false [Interruptions] ...I think you have been grossly unfair. If you read my notings, my notings relate very clearly to the security perception, the cost of cancellation. About 7 or 8 points have been made. Those records are still in your office. They are not available to me. Please read my notings to this House ... [Interruptions]

SHRI VISHWANATH PRATAP SINGH: Yes, I will read it. Tomorrow I am coming with a full statement including your notings ...

SHRI RAJIV GANDHI: I would also request the Prime Minister to lay on the Table of this House all the documents of the Prime Minister's office on Bofors ... [Interruptions] ... Are you ready to place all the Prime Minister's office files on the Table of the House, Sir? [Interruptions]

SHRI VISHWANATH PRATAP SINGH: Yes, I am ready to place the document on the Table of the House. As regards what the Opposition Leader said, all the notings of the Prime Minister ... (Interruptions)

SHRI RAJIV GANDHI: All the PM's office files, not just the notings.

SHRI VISHWANATH PRATAP SINGH: All right.

SHRI RAJIV GANDHI: Is there not a separate noting where I have

---

[48] As the entire exchange is fascinating and not much known, I urge the reader to see the full exchange in the proceedings of the Lok Sabha, columns 408–15, 28 December 1989, reproduced *in extenso* at the end of the chapter by accessing the QR code.

categorically asked what the cost of cancellation will be, cost in terms of security, keeping in mind the security environment at that time, cost in terms of money loss which has already been paid, cost in terms of a new weapons that had to be bought? And if you look at that note, you will find that the cost was much more than the Rs 64 crores that you were getting back. [Interruptions] I am requesting you to lay all the files on the Table of the House.

SHRI VISHWANATH PRATAP SINGH: I will bring it tomorrow. I will lay it tomorrow on the Table of the House. Tomorrow itself, not much delay.

I was stunned. If Rajiv himself, or someone on his behalf, had taken the money for the personal use of the Gandhi family or even the party, why would the former PM (and now leader of the Opposition) wish to have all the information in this regard placed in the public domain? Which criminal has ever sought to lay out all the evidence that incriminates him? Did this indicate Rajiv's culpability or his innocence?

V.P. Singh never did fulfil his pledge to 'lay all the files on the Table of the House . . . tomorrow itself'. Instead, a selection of papers was made public, chosen by the government. Ironically, the process of Rajiv Gandhi's exculpation begins with the documentation V.P. Singh brought into the public realm to blacken his predecessor's reputation.

The Swedish Investigation Report and the PM's Reaction to It

Let me now return to the beginnings of the story two and a half years earlier. The SNAB reported its findings in early June 1987, two months after the Swedish radio broadcast, confirming that Bofors had indeed made payments into Swiss bank accounts, but, under Swedish commercial confidentiality laws, did not reveal the names of the beneficiaries nor Bofors' reasons for making the payments. I wish to particularly emphasize that RG could not refer to these matters in public as he was bound by his oaths of office to keep whatever was secret highly secret and covered by the oath of secrecy till V.P. Singh made the papers public in early 1990. That is why he could not refer to them in Parliament interventions, public speeches or media interviews till V.P. Singh placed the papers in the public domain.

My perusal of the papers placed on the Table of the House in early 1990 revealed that the minute he was informed of the SNAB report, on 4 June 1987, while touring Gujarat, Rajiv Gandhi recorded in my presence (without my seeing it) his critical set of questions to his deputy at the defence ministry, Arun Singh, in his own hand. I reproduce the questions as posed by the PM in full and in bold type, and explain their import in my words in normal type below each question:

(a) **'What will be our defence strength without the Bofors?'**
For at least five years, our defence forces had been stressing our need for a reliable 155 mm howitzer. The PM had gone along with the CoAS's preference for the Bofors gun and taken the decisive step to acquire it. Could we now afford, from a national security perspective, to let go the very 155 mm howitzer we had just secured after such a long search and at such heavy expense?

(b) **'What are the possibilities of an alternative purchase?'**
This required careful evaluation. Even if we found an alternative supplier after cancelling the Bofors contract, might not the new supplier be wary and considerably hike the price?

(c) **'Cost?'**
Clearly, this would have to be evaluated after detailed consultations with the finance and commerce ministries and legal authorities before a political decision could be taken. It could not be done by the army chief or the defence ministry on their own.

(d) 'Can we acquire the same capacity?'
It was at the instance of CoAS Sundarji that the military evaluation was made that the Bofors gun was the best of the shortlisted guns on offer. How could any alternative have the *'same* capacity' when only a year earlier the CoAS had concluded that the Bofors gun had superior capacity? Either we did indeed have the best available 155 mm howitzer – or the army had been fooling the nation into its biggest and most expensive defence acquisition.

(e) 'What is the institutional arrangement for arbitration in Paris? Can we expect support?'
International arbitration of commercial disputes is undertaken by an international institute established in Paris and is the internationally accepted tribunal for the resolution of international commercial disputes. If the tribunal's verdict is not acceptable to either parry, they can even move the International Court at The Hague. In the event of a unilateral cancellation by us of the Bofors contract, Bofors was bound to approach the Paris Tribunal. The outcome in that international forum could not be predicted. Obviously it did not fall within the competence of our defence authorities to answer this question. It required wide consultation with other ministries, including law and commerce and external affairs. And that advice had to be factored into whatever recommendation the CoAS and the Raksha Mantralaya (defence ministry) would make. They did not do so; indeed, it never occurred to either of them that such a consequence would have to be considered. The CoAS was to tell a journalist later that if Bofors were threatened with a cancellation of the contract, they would divulge the names of the recipients of their largesse *'phataphat'*[49] (immediately). Even as I write, we have experienced two international arbitration awards (Videocon and Cairn) that have seen billions awarded against our government. That explains RG's insistence

---

[49] Raminder Singh, *India Today*, 15 September 1989.

on military advice from the Chief of Army Staff, not uniformed political advice.

(f) 'How will this affect our international standing and credibility?'
A most relevant question, especially when the CoAS and RRM seemed more concerned with their own domestic standing and credibility than with delving into the truth of the charges being flung here and there and carefully evaluating the consequences of cancelling the contract. If it turned out in the Paris Tribunal or in subsequent court proceedings that our allegations of bribery were without foundation (as the Delhi High Court determined in 2004),[50] India's reputation would have taken a most serious knock (such as Canadian PM, Justin Trudeau, is suffering on account of his failure to substantiate his claim that an Indian agent was behind the assassination of a Canadian Sikh citizen.)[51]

---

[50] See p. 139 and p. 142 below where Justice Kapoor and Justice Sodhi of the Delhi High Court respectively in their separate Bofors judgments of 2004 and 2005 witheringly remark:
Justice Kapoor, p. 139:
> This case is a nefarious example which manifestly demonstrates how the trial and justice by media can cause irreparable, irreversible and incalculable harm to the reputation of a person. He adds: This is one of such cases where public servants who are no more have met somewhat similar fate being victim of trial by media. They have already been condemned and convicted in the eyes of the public.

Justice Sodhi, p. 142:
> During the investigation a huge bubble was created *with the aid of the media* which, however, when tested by court, burst leaving behind a disastrous trail of suffering… Careers – both political and professional – were ruined… Many an accused lived and died with a stigma [emphasis added].

[51] By an interesting coincidence, today's newspapers *(The Indian Express,* 5 November 2023) report that a Dutch court has confirmed the award against the Government of India of $111 million compensation by the United Nations Commission of International Trade Law (UNCITRAL) in a 2005 case involving the lease of two communication satellites by the Mauritius-based Devas group of companies to Antrix Corp, a company set up by the Indian Space Research Organisation (ISRO). A US federal court had raised the compensation payable to $1.2 billion but a US Court of Appeal reversed that to the original $111 million. The Supreme Court of India, however, had held that fraud had been committed. So, the Government of India went to the Court of Appeal in the

The PM's note of 4 June 1987 received no substantial, well-considered reply from Arun Singh. Instead of faithfully and fully responding to the queries, General Sundarji brusquely sent a one-page note, forwarded to the PM by RRM Arun Singh without further comment, recommending the cancellation of the contract – which was not military advice but strayed beyond the bounds of propriety into politics. The PM was furious at this clear breach of discipline aided and abetted by the minister of state and defence for amounting to a kind of Bonapartism that the Indian government since Jawaharlal Nehru's time had sought to keep at bay ever since the time of Ayub Khan's coup d'etat in Pakistan in October 1958.

On finding that the RRM and CoAS were focusing on how to save their personal reputations rather than working on answers to the questions he had raised, the prime minister penned another note to RRM Arun Singh dated 15 June 1987 that elaborated on some of the questions raised eleven days earlier on 4 June, and added other points. It opens with a salvo: 'It is unfortunate that MOS/AS [Arun Singh] has put his personal prestige above the security of the nation before even evaluating all aspects.'

The PM concluded the opening paragraph of his note of 15 June with the following sentence: 'I appreciate his [Arun Singh's] feelings as he has been dealing with defence almost completely on his own with my support but that is not adequate reason to be ready to compromise the security of the nation.' He then meticulously repeated and elaborated his previous query of 4 June: 'has he evaluated the actual position vis-à-vis security?'

Netherlands to dismiss the compensation claim. The Court of Appeal rejected the Indian claim based on the Indian Supreme Court's decision. So, it was decided to approach the district court in The Hague. The district court has now ruled that there are 'no grounds for setting aside the Final Arbitral Award'. This illustrates RG's apprehension that the outcome of international commercial cases is inherently uncertain. RG knew this; Arun Singh and General Sundarji did not.

These remarks were clearly a reference to Arun Singh's pride at his stout defence in Parliament of the RG–Olof Palme accord, which was now putting Arun Singh's good name and reputation in jeopardy. It also referred to his evident failure to get the ministry and the CoAS to respond cogently and in detail to the queries put to him eleven days earlier.

Arun Singh had endorsed Sundarji's brusque view that Bofors would cough up the names if cancellation of contract was threatened. But this was obviously a gut reaction for Sundarji had not applied his mind to 'all aspects' of the issue. How could he know this without any experience of international diplomacy, commercial practice, or commercial law? His expertise lay in his technical grasp of military equipment, which had led to his recommendation of the Bofors gun and, indeed, to the cabinet's acceptance of the gun. It did not lie in answering the PM's questions on his own – except the ones on 'defence capability' that he just brushed over without any evaluation of the high risks to national security that any precipitate cancellation of the contract would involve.

It had been decided by the cabinet a little over a year earlier that acquisition of the howitzers, even with the unprecedented financial outlay they required, was in the interests of national security, as determined by our armed forces and the ministry concerned. How, without evaluating, in consultation with the relevant ministries concerned, any of the germane considerations set out by the PM, and just based on the gut feeling of one gung-ho general, could so consequential a decision as threatening cancellation of a signed contract be taken? Would not national security be compromised for the same reasons as trotted out fourteen months earlier at the highest military level to justify the single-largest purchase of defence equipment the government had ever made?

This was the crux of the matter. The CoAS was casually dismissing this possibility on the quite unfounded expectation that Bofors would take such a threat lying down. What if they challenged the cancellation by resorting to international arbitration in the tribunal located in Paris?

How long would proceedings drag on? Could we afford, from the point of view of national security, to wait perhaps decades for arbitration?

Sundarji had estimated that it would take but eighteen to twenty-four months to find an alternative gun from either the British or the French, and that we could play the one off against the other to secure a better price. But this conclusion came by guesswork and gut feeling. In hindsight, we know that in every matter with which Sundarji was involved – Operation Blue Star, Operation Brasstacks, Operation Pawan in Sri Lanka – his gut betrayed him. His instincts proved wrong at terrible cost to the country.[52]

In keeping with the format I have adopted for setting out the PM's queries in his earlier note of 4 June, the same procedure has been adopted for the queries he posed in his second note of 15 June after rejecting General Sundarji's brusque reply to his first note:

(g) 'Has he evaluated the financial loss of a cancellation?'
Obviously, this point had not been addressed. Did not our larger national interest demand that this prospective financial loss be factored into our calculations?

(h) 'Has he evaluated the degree of breach of contract by Bofors, if any?'
Were the payments made by Bofors cognizable offences? Would the cancellation of the contract make the punishment fit the crime? Would our position stand up in an international arbitration tribunal or UNCITRAL?[53] Had the law ministry or the MEA's Legal and Treaties Division or the commerce ministry been sounded? Had any international lawyers of repute been consulted? Obviously not. The RRM was standing on his 'personal prestige' and the general on his gut feeling!

---

[52] I jokingly remarked to RG that, given Sundarji's reputation for brains, we should henceforth ask candidates for the CoAS to take an IQ test – and pass them over if they passed!
[53] See footnote 50.

Moreover, the attorney general arrived at a precipitate conclusion: that the contract was being executed under Indian law and as the Bofors' payments were in clear breach of contract considerations, we could go ahead with threatening or actually cancelling the contract. On more mature consideration, however, he was to later tell the Joint Parliamentary Committee (JPC) on Bofors that caution should be exercised because the outcome of international arbitrations could not be predicted.

(i) 'Has he evaluated the consequences for all future defence purchases if we cancel a contract unilaterally?'
Again, obviously not. For neither Arun Singh nor Sundarji had any personal knowledge of these possible consequences. By cancelling one contract to appease uninformed (and possibly motivated) domestic outrage, might we not be jeopardizing future national security?

(j) 'Has he evaluated how rival manufacturers will behave in future?'
Would rival manufacturers not put the squeeze on us because we would no longer be negotiating from a position of strength? Would they not pitch their prices higher as a kind of insurance premium in case of another cancellation?

(k) 'Has he evaluated how GOI [Government of India] prestige will plummet if we unilaterally cancel a contract that has not been violated?'
India had built an excellent reputation for faithfully adhering to international contracts and obligations. Could we put that reputation at risk without carefully assessing whether there was definitive proof that would stand up in a court of law, including an international court or tribunal, of whether Bofors was in fact in breach of its legal commitments, as also considering the wide international ramifications of unilaterally cancelling the contract on what might be held to be flimsy grounds?

The PM then moved inexorably in his 15 June note to his conclusion:

> To the best of my belief, the Swedish Audit report *upholds the GOI position and does not contradict it*. What we need to do is to *get to the root and find out what precisely has been happening* and who all are involved. Knee-jerk reactions and stomach cramps will not serve any purpose. RRM has run the ministry fairly well but there is *no need to panic, especially if one's conscience is clear* [emphasis added].

Gopi Arora Withholds PM's Note of 15 June

Extraordinarily, Additional Secretary Gopi Arora withheld the file without telling the PM and did not send the PM's note of 15 June on to RRM Arun Singh. When V.P. Singh laid this note on the Table of the House in January 1990 at RG's bidding, I looked at the noting in the file carefully and discovered to my horror that while the note was signed by the PM on 15 June, it was not in fact received in the RRM's office till late in July after Arun Singh had resigned in a huff. I wrote about my discovery in my *Sunday* magazine column. Gopi read it in Washington, DC, and on one of his frequent visits to Delhi from the International Monetary Fund (IMF), asked me if I was blaming him for the Bofors fiasco. I replied that it was not a question of pinning blame but discovering why he had held up this key noting when his only duty was to immediately rush it to the RRM. Gopi replied that he deliberately decided to hold up the file in his office so as to not further aggravate the differences between the PM and the RRM. This was a gross breach of propriety which had the most deleterious consequences because the PM thought his queries had reached the RRM while the RRM and CoAS were kept in the dark about the information, evaluation, and analysis the PM was seeking. That Arora had exceeded his remit resulted later in his being denied the post on which he had set his heart: that of secretary to the PM on the superannuation of Sarla Grewal. But that was his personal misfortune; the national tragedy was that the rest of the story played out with neither the PM knowing his note of 15 June had been held up nor the defence ministry knowing that one PMO officer's dereliction had left them in total ignorance of this key minute by the prime minister.[54]

So, when the PM demanded a revised note, General Sundarji, not knowing that the PM had revised and updated on 15 June his list of queries, the CoAS cheekily just changed the date on which his earlier note had been written and returned it to the PMO through the ministers in the raksha mantralaya, who too had been kept by Arora in complete ignorance of the PM's 15 June note. Rajiv Gandhi was understandably furious at this gumption and relations between the western corner of South Block where the PMO is located and the eastern corner that houses the raksha mantralaya virtually broke down, principally owing to the games Arora was playing in violation of all known procedure without informing anyone else – a weird, unprecedented, and unforgivable breakdown of all known bureaucratic norms. He had just grown too big for his boots.

Astonishingly too no one in our thoroughly biased media took up this question despite my rubbing their noses in the mess through my columns in *Sunday* magazine in the first half of 1990. They just shut their eyes to the truth because they thought they had a 'story' on their hands. Justice J.D. Kapoor of the Delhi High Court was to pull up the media for relentlessly conducting this kangaroo court in his judgment of February 2004.

Bofors Offers to Confidentially Disclose the Names of Recipients

In the face of the threat of the cancellation of their hard-won contract, Bofors, in late June 1987, offered to send a delegation to make full

---

[54] Unfortunately, Gopi Arora, who remained a close friend till his passing away on 5 November 2009, could not be shown this paragraph written in 2022. If he had, I would certainly have included his reaction.

disclosure. They, however, laid down the strict prior condition that the Indian government would never reveal in public information divulged to the government in the strictest confidence as divulging such commercial information in public would violate Swedish commercial secrecy laws. Arun Singh and Sundarji were desperate to clutch at this straw. They felt that once we had this information, we could then make the information public, whatever our prior commitment to Bofors.

It was left to Rajiv Gandhi to stress that if he were to stoop to this, the word of the prime minister of India would never more be treated as trustworthy. And, once he had the information, if he did not act on it, he would in effect, become an accessory after the fact to the crime. Either Bofors would have to unconditionally disclose what they knew, or the government would find its own way to the truth – wherever the search might lead.

This was not well understood and even wilfully ignored by not only RG's critics but even by his distanced school friend, Arun Singh, who suddenly resigned without explanation in mid-July and disappeared to Binsar in the high ranges of the Uttarakhand Himalaya. He has since refused to talk about these events to anyone, including me. A pity, as I would have loved to include his perspective of these dramatic developments.

Unfortunately, all these exchanges were hidden from public view owing to the oath of secrecy they were all obliged to take before assuming office. Meanwhile the press was free to publish any allegation, however wild, and any document, however clandestinely or unauthorizedly procured. That is the nature of democracy.

JPC

Parliamentary procedure provides a way out: a JPC where both accusers and defenders can freely state their case and bring on the record their speculations, conclusions, and any document that endorses their view.

This had been demanded by the Opposition in April 1987, when the scandal broke. The PM conceded the demand just four months later in August 1987. The Bofors JPC was constituted under the charipersonship of B. Shankaranand, a senior minister with legal training who resigned his ministry to take up the JPC chair.

The Opposition then raised absurd conditions to stall the proceedings of the JPC. These included the demand that the chairpersonship be handed over to a member of the Opposition, although they well knew that by established custom and usage, the chairpersonship of parliamentary committees, other than the Public Accounts Committee (PAC), had always been for the treasury benches to decide. And that if they were not content with the final JPC report, the Opposition members were free to submit dissenting notes which would be annexed to the report, unedited and unexpurgated.

Instead, as their misrepresentations were stripped bare during the proceedings of the JPC, the major Opposition MPs resorted to a cowardly walk-out in early 1988. In consequence, they could not participate in the drafting exercise or give dissenting notes. Only one of the non-Congress members, Aladi Aruna, furnished a long and detailed dissenting note that, after some procedural wrangling, the Lok Sabha speaker ordered be annexed to the report. This gave propaganda advantage to the Opposition but did not lead to their constructively leveraging the parliamentary devices available to flush out evidence.

The JPC's key conclusions were as follows:
- Every care had been taken, including adequate testing in field trials, to identify the best weapon.
- A superior gun system had been purchased from Bofors at less than the floor price offered by Sofma for a relatively inferior system.
- There was no evidence to show that any middleman was involved in the process of the acquisition of the Bofors gun.
- There was also no evidence to substantiate the allegation of commissions or bribes having been paid to any public official.

- Therefore, the question of payments to any Indian or Indian company, whether resident in India or not, did not arise.[55]

The JPC report was laid on the Table of the House on 26 April 1988 and debated in Parliament. After that the public discourse quietened for a year until T.N. Chaturvedi, the comptroller and auditor general (CAG), dropped a bombshell with his April 1989 report on Bofors.

Bofors and the Comptroller and Auditor General

In April 1989, about a year to the day after the JPC report had relatively stilled the controversy, extracts from the CAG report were leaked to the press damning the government for its handling of the Bofors matter.[56]

The main adverse findings of the CAG were:
- No field trials were conducted after 1982.
- While the French Sofma had been in the lead until February 1986 in terms of technical military evaluation, it was by 'adding some new characteristics and sub-characteristics' that, at the last moment, preference was accorded by the army chief for the Bofors gun.
- Moreover, 'none of these newly added characteristics hinged on the burst fire capability considered an essential feature of shoot and scoot tactics'.
- Minimum acceptable parameters were lowered by the army to prefer Bofors ammunition. The CAG estimated loss on this account to be Rs 329 crore.
- If the French offer of credit in German marks had been accepted,

---

[55] The JPC report has been admirably summarized in a book by one of the chief propagators of the allegations against Rajiv Gandhi, Prashant Bhushan, *Bofors: The Selling of a Nation*, Vision Books, New Delhi, 1990, pp. 76–84.

[56] Leaked allegations of the report were published in several newspapers in the summer of 1989 (April–July), and then in detail in an article by Raminder Singh and Paranjoy Guha Thakurta in *India Today*, 15 August 1989.

Sofma's offer would have been approximately Rs 70 crore lower than Bofors'.
- Bofors had resiled on its delivery schedule. This had been accepted by the defence ministry without demanding liquidation damages. These were sought (and secured) only after the CAG had raised the issue.

The JPC had already dealt with most of these points. Nevertheless, the CAG had the right to his views.

The CAG report was submitted *confidentially* to the PAC on 25 April 1989. In the normal course, as per established practice, it should have been referred to the PAC (invariably chaired by a leader of the Opposition) and then brought back to both Houses for a full debate. The government has the right and duty to assist the PAC. Thus, in the PAC, all shades of opinion are required to be taken into account to facilitate dispassionate consideration of the findings and recommendations of the CAG for the consideration of the Houses of Parliament. A report with recommendations is then prepared by the PAC and laid before Parliament for an open debate on its findings. This procedure has been devised to not let speculative, ill-informed public debate in the media pre-empt duly considered parliamentary examination.

All this was bypassed as the bulk of the Opposition tendered their resignations from the Lok Sabha on 24 June 1989 (but 'clung like limpets'[57]–

---

[57] The 'limpets' remark was made by RG in the context of the boycott of the House when it opened on 18 July 1989 by the Opposition members, where they were in small numbers, but clung 'like limpets' to their seats in the Rajya Sabha where they had a larger presence. RG on the floor of the House in the Lok Sabha on 7 August 1989, remarked 'in glaring contrast to their behaviour here, they cling like limpets to their seats' in the Rajya Sabha (*Selected Speeches and Writings*, Vol. V, 1991, p. 202).

Mentioned in *Outlook* of 5 February 2020 in an amusing article titled 'Not a Funny Bone under That Thin Skin': 'Rajiv Gandhi used this word (limpets) to indict his opponents for sticking to their chairs and being power-hungry. Critics were furious at being branded sub-human clingy invertebrates.' In fact, I had suggested this simile 'like limpets' as it is an expression often used by that brilliant humorist, P.G. Wodehouse, from whom I had picked it up.

in RG's telling phrase – to their relatively larger number of seats in the Rajya Sabha). This boycott by the Opposition of the PAC and Lok Sabha rendered the CAG report null and void in Parliament but remained of great propaganda value in the media. Clearly, the Opposition had decided to sit it out until the forthcoming Lok Sabha elections put them in a position to pursue their version of *l'affaire* Bofors from the treasury benches.

We now know from bitter experience that when the CAG wanders off its auditing track to attempt to make government policy without adequate inputs from experts, it can lose its way. For example, in the 2009 CAG report on 2G, absurd figures of 'notional' losses like Rs 12 lakh crore were trotted out, leading to detention in Tihar jail on judicial remand for more than a year of two MPs, A. Raja and Kanimozhi of the Dravida Munnetra Kazhagam (DMK). They were both later found by the courts to be innocent. We have also seen the direct outcome of the CAG's recommendations on competitiveness in the telecom sector in respect of resorting to the auction of spectrum. This has led to the emergence of an oligopoly verging on monopoly in telecom.

It is precisely to preserve the separation of powers that the PAC route for the initial examination of CAG recommendations is critical. It gives the government the opportunity of clearing its name and the Opposition the opening to press its accusations. In both the Bofors case and the 2G matter, the routine procedure was aborted. This led to the virtual lynching of those who were not given a fair opportunity of answering doubts raised by the audit authority (which anyway did not have the right to come to final judgement without further legislative examination and judicial adjudication on the substance of government policy).

The CAG, T.N. Chaturvedi, was well rewarded by the National Front and the BJP. He was conferred the Padma Vibhushan by a grateful V.P. Singh government in 1990, then elevated by the BJP to a seat in the Rajya Sabha for two successive terms (1992–98 and 1998–2002) before being further elevated to a five-year term as governor of Karnataka (2002–07). On retirement from that post, he was conferred the chairmanship for the rest of his life of the prestigious Indian Institute of Public Administration. But all these honours were stained by being so obviously connected with the service he rendered, as CAG, to the partisan politics over their Bofors allegations of the National Front and the BJP.

The Bases of the Bofors Allegations

The crusade against Rajiv Gandhi rested essentially on three points:
i. The quality of the Bofors gun vis-à-vis the Sofma howitzer.
ii. The estimation of rival prices, especially between Bofors and the French Sofma howitzer.
iii. The role of AE Services that had suddenly been brought into the picture with an agreement being signed between them and Bofors on 15 November 1985 and valid only until the end of March 1986.

We shall examine each of these points in succession.

Quality of the Bofors Gun

First, as regards the CoAS changing Army HQ's preference from the French to the Swedish gun, Sundarji laid out his reasons in detail before the JPC. I hand over the narrative to Prashant Bhushan, the most vocal of those intent on getting at Rajiv Gandhi:

> Sundarji was examined by the JPC on 12 January [1988]. Strongly defending the choice of the Bofors gun, he justified the change on his own relative ratings of the guns on the basis that between October 1985 and February 1986 he learned that Pakistan was acquiring a sophisticated fire finding radar from the U.S. The radar could determine the position of the gun within 45 seconds of the firing of a salvo. Since counter-

bombardment could be expected immediately thereafter, the ability of the gun to 'Shoot and Scoot' became important. [Also] since the Bofors gun has a better burst firing ability as it could fire a burst of three shells in 13 seconds as opposed to 15 seconds of Sofma, he changed the preference.[58]

Let us now bring in the authentic voice of General Sundarji from the 12 January records of the JPC:[59]

Admitting that in December 1982, he had rated Sofma as superior, he explained, 'At that point in time, we were evaluating not only the towed gun but also the self-propelled gun as one package. The only weapon which figured in both lists was the French gun. Therefore, it was only the French gun which fulfilled all the requirements. This aspect weighed with me considerably'.

Sundarji then explained what made him change his preference by February 1986 when, as CoAS, he plumped for the Bofors gun:

When I took over as Chief of Army Staff, two major events had occurred. First of all, the US army had successfully developed the fire finding radar, the ANTPS-37, and had also included this radar in the package which they were giving to Pakistan ... Now what I had hoped as a threat which would not materialise till 1997 or so, unfortunately materialised much more rapidly ... This ability of the fire finding radar, the only such radar which exists today, is that when the first round is fired it is capable of tracking the shell in flight early enough and after taking a few successive readings in space, computerised calculations ... give a highly accurate

---

[58] Prashant Bushan, *Bofors: The Selling of a Nation*, Vision Books, New Delhi, 1990, p. 54.
[59] 'Report: Joint Committee to Enquire Into Bofors Contract', para 5.53 and 5.54, pp. 65–68, Lok Sabha Secretariat, New Delhi, April 1988, https://eparlib.nic.in/bitstream/123456789/783416/1/Investigative_JPC_Bofors_2008.pdf.

location of the gun . . . in a matter of about 45 to 50 seconds from the time it was . . . fired.

The 'shoot and scoot' ability of Bofors, which no other gun had, was crucial to the choice made, especially in the light of the US supplying the Pakistanis with 'heat-finding radar'.

He continued, explaining how the burst fire capacity of Bofors – even in 1982 superior to Sofma by two seconds in a burst of three rounds, which was relatively unimportant then – had acquired greater criticality: 'Hence, shoot and scoot assumed greater importance in 1986 and it could not be wished away . . . In the light of these changed circumstances, I re-evaluated the inter-se placement and decided that the Bofors gun . . . had an edge over the French gun though fundamentally both guns were acceptable.'

Sundarji added that another difficulty with Sofma was that their turret could not be mounted on our Vijayanta tanks. The director general of artillery had testified before the JPC that there were three specific advantages that the Bofors gun enjoyed: 'higher angles' and therefore 'the ability to fire in different projections' (irrefutably proved in the Kargil war); 'bursts fire'; and, third, 'the most important thing, its own auxiliary power unit'[60] to 'shoot and scoot'. Further, the JPC had before it a note prepared by Army HQ saying that in mountain trials, four Bofors guns had been able to maintain the same 'rate of fire' as six guns without Bofors' level of automation.

All these considerations were amply borne out when the Bofors guns were used in actual combat in the Kargil war (1999). It was the Bofors gun that proved decisive in turning the tide of war, so much so that, speaking in the Rajya Sabha, even Jaswant Singh, a principal baiter of Rajiv Gandhi, conceded that he was impressed, as was General Jagjit Singh Aurora, the hero of the Bangladesh liberation struggle.

---

[60] *Ibid.*

High praise was also bestowed on the Bofors howitzer by Major Mohinder Singh Puri, commander of 8 Mountain Division in the Kargil war. As cited by Rajiv Gandhi's aide, Wajahat Habibullah, 'Bofors had proven crucial in decimating Pakistani positions in Tololing, Tiger Hill and Pt. 4875. This opened the way for India's infantry to overrun Pakistani fortifications within weeks.'[61]

Air Vice Marshall (AVM) (retd) Arjun Subramanian, apart from himself evaluating Bofors' performance at Kargil, cites a number of other officers involved in the operation, including Captain (later Lieutenant General) Anil Ahuja, Colonel (later Major General) Alok Deb and Major V.K. Ahluwalia.[62] I excerpt AVM Subramanian's own encomium:

> The acquisition of the ... versatile 155mm F1-1-77B Bofors artillery gun added significant punch to India's strike corps for offensive operations in conventional conflict scenarios ... the gun has performed brilliantly under varied conditions ...

He then explains:

> ... the FI-1-77B 155mm field howitzer – as the Bofors gun is technically called – was inducted into the Indian Army between 1986 and 1989 to complement the Soviet 130mm guns ... In a bold and unprecedented decision, the Indian Army chose the path of acquiring a complete 'gun system' from AR Bofors [today BAE Systems Bofors]. It acted not only as manufacturer of the guns [410 were purchased by India in total], but also as the major single-point supply contractor for globally sourced items. These comprised equipment such as the Saab-Scania gun-towing and ammunition-hauling trucks [approximately 600 trucks in different

---

[61] Habibullah, *op. cit.*, pp. 132–33.
[62] *Full Spectrum*, HarperCollins, Noida, 2020 pp. 23, 34–36.

variants], Barracuda camouflage nets, Marconi systems, Quickfire, fire-control systems, Fairey Australia muzzle-velocity radars, BEAB sighting equipment from Wild of Switzerland and navigation equipment from Ferranti UK.

He goes on:

A highly mobile platform despite its weight of 12 tons, the Bofors gun can be driven at speeds upto 70 kmph on paved roads – with excellent off-road mobility too. The gun's USP is its high rate of sustained fire of six rounds per minute – it is said to have sustained a short rapid rate of fire of fifteen rounds per minute during the Kargil conflict. Capable of achieving ranges of slightly over 30 kms, it has been known to hit targets at 35 kms in the rarefied atmosphere of Siachen and Kargil.

I would much rather believe in the field experience of senior, objective, and well-informed army officers than the CAG who either could not or did not call in the military experts and was in no way qualified to weigh the relative qualitative merits of the howitzers on offer. Yet the CAG gave his opinion. The JPC, on the other hand, had the benefit of detailed expert military advice.

The JPC concluded: 'It is most unfortunate that uninformed criticism has been levelled to insinuate that Bofors was picked up on extraneous considerations. The Committee find there is no force in such allegations and that the best gun has been selected for the Indian Army.'

What is underplayed, even perhaps deliberately overlooked, is CoAS Sundarji's clarification of his preference for the Bofors gun over the Sofma that he spelled out in an interview to Raminder Singh of *India Today*, published in its issue of the fortnight beginning 15 September 1989.

Sundarji said in the interview that it was '*after* the announcement that I was to be the next Chief' (emphasis added) that Arun Singh 'asked me, officially but orally, about my views on the relative merits of the two systems'.

He candidly admits that when he was serving as vice chief of army staff four years earlier, he found both the French and Swedish guns 'were good guns, close to each other and I did not give any special weightage to the Swedish gun at that point (December 1982)'. Operation Blue Star (which made or unmade Sundarji's reputation) was yet to happen, Indira Gandhi seemed set to be PM for another decade and her government was cautiously treading towards a decision after years of deliberation. He was not again involved with the choice of guns till the announcement of his appointment as CoAS in the autumn of 1985.

In response to a request from Arun Singh, Sundarji says, he 'requested Major General Ajay Singh and then Brigadier T.P. Singh, both from the Directorate of Weapons and Equipment (DWE), to do a thorough, objective analysis in the light of the two factors which had undergone a change in 1985'. They plumped for Bofors.

CAG Chaturvedi just did not bother to make such a detailed comparison. As an IAS officer, not a weapons expert, he probably could not have done so on his own and had no one on his staff to undertake such a technical exercise. Had the CAG report gone to the PAC, the committee would have doubtless asked the defence experts to clarify matters. That is what happens when procedures are short-circuited and the media sets up kangaroo courts.

Prices

The second point of the Opposition/CAG/media crusade related to the relative prices of the Bofors and Sofma guns.

It is beyond contest that the French Sofma gun was rated cheaper than Bofors until 21 March 1986. The decision to award the contract to Bofors was then taken on the basis of the final recommendation of the negotiating committee. The valuation of comparative price offers was then examined by the ministry of finance. And the file on which the Bofors 155 mm howitzer was recommended was signed off by none other than then finance minister, V.P. Singh!

The JPC dealt with the financial aspects at length. Their basic finding was that while on 10 February 1986 the Bofors offer of Rs 1,619 crore stood well over the Sofma offer of Rs 1,509 crore, by 21 March both parties had revised their offer downwards, Sofma slipping to their 'rock bottom' final offer of Rs 1,427 crore, and Bofors reducing its offer further to Rs 1,436 crore, Rs 9 crore more than their French rival. Bofors then slipped in the sweetener of ten free guns. It was also pointed out by the additional financial adviser that whereas the Sofma gun needed a crew of seven, the Bofors gun needed a crew of only six. If, therefore, the Bofors gun was chosen, our savings would be in the region of Rs 125 crore over twenty years. The JPC concluded that 'a superior gun system had been purchased from Bofors at less than the floor price offered by Sofma for a relatively inferior system'.

In the Lok Sabha debate on 4–5 May 1988, the Opposition stuck to its unproven allegations while the new Raksha Mantri, K.C. Pant, congratulated the negotiations committee, which had successfully negotiated the reduction of the prices by Rs 200 crore.

In the Rajya Sabha debate on 11–12 May 1988,[63] P. Chidambaram stressed that the final Sofma offer was a 'rock bottom affair'. Bofors had beaten that 'rock bottom'. To drive home his point, he argued that it would have been impossible for Bofors to have been able to cushion bribes of Rs 64 crore into their highly reduced price. He rammed home his argument: 'If it is the best gun that is available to you, and it is the best price which the nation could have paid – where is the question of bribe?'

There is a final nugget of information about the so-called 'Bofors

---

[63] 'Short Duration Discussion [RAJYA. SABHA] Parliament Committee on report of the Joint on Bofors Contract', column 198, https://rsdebate.nic.in/bitstream/123456789/293096/1/PD_146_12051988_14_p191_p243_11.pdf.

scandal' that needs to be highlighted. In his interview to Raminder Singh,[64] Sundarji is quoted as having been told by Arun Singh, 'Do you know something, till the actual day on which [defence secretary] S.K. Bhatnagar signed the contract, Rajiv Gandhi didn't know which gun we were choosing?' So, if the PM got to know Bofors was the chosen gun only on 24 March 1985, how could he or someone on his behalf (the never-named 'Gandhi Trustee' lawyer, 'Q' or 'N' or whoever) have informed Ardbo nearly six months *earlier* that Bofors was the preferred howitzer and that if Ardbo wanted the contract he had better pay up through AE Services' account? The fact is Rajiv Gandhi had nothing to do with these shenanigans. Any payment to AE was not a 'commission' but payment for services rendered, however dubious those services may have been. Yet Rajiv Gandhi was pilloried for telling Vir Sanghvi of *Sunday* magazine that AE was an outfit for 'industrial espionage'.[65] As per Bhushan,[66] responding to the interviewer's remark, 'there could be no genuine work they were paid for', RG replied, 'gathering information about the French weapon, for example. That is industrial espionage, you cannot grudge them for that.' The words 'industrial espionage' were torn out of context and the media went to town baiting him for that.

AE Services, the Ardbo Diaries and 'N'

In June 1985, Rajiv Gandhi, accompanied by his parliamentary secretary, Arun Singh, had visited Paris for the Festival of India. There, Rajiv Gandhi informed President Mitterand that the Government of India would not acquiesce in there being any intermediaries in the 155 mm howitzer deal, then in the offing, with the French firm, Sofma, being among the most favoured. Arun Singh also stressed this to his counterpart, the secretary general to President Mitterand. This was in line with the much-applauded

---

[64] *India Today*, 15 September 1989.
[65] *Sunday* magazine, 13–19 November 1988.
[66] *Ibid.*, p. 101.

policy announcement made almost immediately after RG became an elected prime minister that intermediaries and middlemen were no longer acceptable in defence deals with India. Hence his being lauded with the appellation 'Mr Clean'.

A few months later, in October 1985, RG attended the session of the UN General Assembly in New York. On the sidelines of that session, he met Olof Palme, the prime minister of Sweden, with whom he enjoyed a close relationship. They both agreed that no intermediary would be used by the Swedish armaments manufacturer, Bofors, the other strong contender for the India contract. Indeed, Palme went further and instructed his foreign office to formally inform Bofors of the decision taken by the two PMs and issue a statement to this effect.

Yet, on 15 November 1985, just a fortnight after the two prime ministers had formally announced in New York their mutual agreement to do away with all middlemen in this defence deal, Martin Ardbo, head honcho of Bofors, actually appointed a new agent, AE Services of Guildford, Surrey, UK, through his old partner of many previous dubious deals, 'Bob' Wilson who headed AE Services.[67]

The AE deal is of the highest relevance to the Bofors controversy for a number of reasons. First, it was stipulated that AE would get paid only if the Indian government awarded the contract to Bofors by 31 March 1986. This condition was fulfilled: the contract was actually signed a week earlier, on 24 March 1986. For Indians, at least, this stipulation need have caused no surprise as our financial year ends on 31 March and the howitzer deal involved such unprecedented expenditure that it would have to be factored into the budget for the next financial year, 1986–87. It did not need an 'insider' to know this.

Second, the payment of $35 million was to be made in five equal instalments to coincide with the instalments in which Bofors would

---

[67] A facsimile of the Bofors–AE agreement has been reproduced in Bhushan, *op. cit.*, at pp. 266–69.

receive payments from the Indian authorities. Eventually, only one tranche, valued at a little over $7 million, was ever paid. This was in September 1986, but no further instalments were paid, or even sought, although some $27.5 million was outstanding in dues to AE Services. Was it only coincidence that payments to AE stopped once Arun Nehru's falling out with his cousin, the Indian PM, was made public, and he was sacked from the Council of Ministers on 22 October 1986?

If, on the other hand, Rajiv Gandhi was involved with the AE deal, as was being alleged, why should an incumbent PM suddenly terminate a contract he himself had illegitimately fostered after securing only a fifth of the take and that too *a full year before* anyone knew anything about what was going on? The obvious answer: Rajiv Gandhi was not involved in the AE Services shenanigans.

Third, what was the nature of services to be provided by AE? This was not specified in the leaked documents but when Rajiv Gandhi suggested 'industrial espionage' in an interview to Vir Sanghvi of *Sunday*, an argument he must have made to his ministerial colleagues, his political opponents and the bulk of the media scorned the suggestion. Yet, according to an article by a Swedish journalist, Bo G. Andersson,[68] that could be the most plausible reason for Bofors to employ AE who had done yeoman clandestine work for Bofors, including 'Bofors' export of arms to the Middle East via Singapore [to sidestep Swedish law that prohibited arms exports to regions at war] which first blew up into a major scandal and Ardbo lost his job'.[69] After all, it was known by 15 November 1985 that Sofma of France was neck and neck with Bofors, with the Sofma gun, at that time, preferred by the then vice CoAS, Sundarji. This was further confirmed when Carl Aaberg, the undersecretary of state for trade in the Swedish foreign office, visited India on 25 November 1985 and,

---

[68] Translation of extracts published in *The Illustrated Weekly of India*, 28 October 1990.
[69] Andersson, cited by Coomi Kapoor in *The Illustrated Weekly of India*, 28 October 1990.

according to Andersson, was sternly told by Arun Singh (who had, in the meantime, become the RRM) that 'the price of the [Bofors] gun was wrong'; India 'would choose an alternative which was not only technically sound but where the price was right'; and that India was interested not only in a 'one-time contract' but in 'long-term cooperation'. This made it even more important for Bofors to spy on Sofma in France, especially as Bofors' long-time agent in India, Win Chadha, had been rendered out of play by the RG government's policy of 'no middlemen'. 'Bob' Wilson of AE was Ardbo's first preference.

Moreover, as revealed in the trove of secret documents leaked to Chitra Subramaniam (more on this later) and published in facsimile by the *Indian Express* on 13 October 1989, in the 'Agreed Summary of Discussions between the Government of India and the Bofors Delegation' in early 1987, Bofors had informed the Indian side that AE Services 'has represented Bofors in India and some other countries' and that AE was paid for providing 'information about competitors'. PM Rajiv Gandhi was aware of this, which is why he designated the Bofors–AE contract as payment for 'industrial espionage'.

There was also something strange about the consideration of $35 million due to AE Services for keeping an eye on Sofma. Indeed, Lindstrom told Subramaniam that he thought the AE contract was 'known only to Ardbo'. Why then did the Swedish Investigative Agency not explore the possibility of Ardbo having been taken for a ride by 'N' and Bob Wilson, perhaps with the collusion of 'Q', taking advantage of Ardbo's ignorance of India, his obvious gullibility and, perhaps also, his cupidity?

Fourth, among the documents published by the *Indian Express* on 13 October 1989 was a sentence by Bofors' chief financial officer (CFO) on his interrogation by the Swedish National Bureau of Investigation: '*On AE Services, I was not pressed*' (emphasis added).

Why was he 'not pressed' if the AE Services agreement was the smoking gun, as believed and relentlessly propagated by RG's critics? Why was the CFO 'not pressed', especially considering that Sten Lindstrom, heading the investigation by the Swedish police, had told Chitra Subramaniam that 'during the interrogation [in 1987] it became clear that to us that the AE Services payoffs were in some way linked to "Q"'? This shows the Swedish authorities were aware of the industrial espionage in which Bob Wilson's AE Services specialized. While this was clear to the PM, it was apparently (or deliberately) not clear to the PM's critics in politics and the media.

Much was also made by the *Indian Express* of AE being located in obscure premises above what looked like a grocery store in the small town of Guilford away from London, but a moment's reflection will show that a shadowy entity engaged in secret business is hardly likely to advertise its work with posh offices on Oxford Street.

What really called for investigation was the manner in which AE's activities in India seemed to have coincided with shifts in Arun Nehru's political fortunes. After the story broke on Swedish Radio in 1987, revelations began getting published from early 1988, somewhat piecemeal, arising out of leaks from documents submitted to the Swedish parliamentary committee investigating Bofors' misdeeds in the Middle East. These leaks covered dispatches from the Swedish embassy in New Delhi to Stockholm and revelations of others involved in the investigation, above all, the head of the investigation in the Swedish police (Sten Lindstrom, possibly 'Sting', the code name used by Chitra Subramaniam). A book by a Swedish author, Henrik Westander, titled *Hemligstamplat* (Classified) is also cited. These findings were summed up by Bo Andersson in an article for the widely circulated Swedish newspaper *Dagens Nyheter*, and succinctly reported to readers of the *Illustrated Weekly of India* (28 October 1990) by Coomi Kapoor.

The story revealed that Arun Nehru (who, as MoS for power at the time had no official connection with defence deals) called in Rolf Gauffin, acting ambassador of Sweden, on 21 June 1985, and ordered Gauffin to ensure that Bofors' 'number one' man reach Delhi in the 'first week of July' with 'total authority to negotiate all conditions'. Further, Arun Nehru 'stipulated firmly' that 'no experts were required at that stage'. (Curious, as how could 'all conditions' be discussed without experts?) Accordingly, Martin Ardbo, managing director of Bofors, arrived on his maiden visit to India all alone on 3 July 1985 and held a 'secret meeting' with Arun Nehru 'which', according to Bo Andersson, 'seems to have been of the greatest importance in the continuation of the deal'. Ardbo appears not to have met anyone else, not even Arun Singh, and the entire mission was clouded in a cloak of confidentiality.

Then, in a surprise development, Gauffin was again called in by Arun Nehru on 11 July and told, 'I am not in [the] picture and have done my part of the job.' Reporting this, Andersson asks, 'Which part of the job had [Arun] Nehru completed?' and himself provides the answer: 'Nehru and Ardbo might have discussed the 'dubious side of the affair'. Andersson adds that 'it was Arun Nehru who played a key role in the affair'. 'N' anyone?

Much later, on 18 March 1990, after Rajiv Gandhi's government had fallen, Arun Nehru, as a minister in V.P. Singh's government, claimed before the Indian Central Bureau of Investigation (CBI) that he had indeed met the Swedish envoy but 'on the instructions of then Prime Minister Rajiv Gandhi'.[70] He produced no corroborative evidence and, since, 'within months of Nehru taking over as MoS Internal Security reports of a rift between [Arun] Nehru and Rajiv [Gandhi] began making the rounds',[71] clearly the CBI should have asked what caused the rift. The CBI didn't. It was a token interrogation that did nothing to answer the question: had Nehru been authorized by the PM to speak to the Swedes

---

[70] United News of India (UNI), 18 March 1997, carried on Rediff on Net, 19 March 1997.
[71] *India Today*, 30 September 1990, report by Tarun J. Tejpal and Prabhu Chawla.

to fix a deal? And, if so, why just three weeks later, on 11 July 1985, did Arun Nehru tell the Swedish Ambassador Axel Edelstram that he had 'done his job' and henceforth Bofors 'should be dealing directly with the Defence Ministry'? We shall never know, although, as pointed out by *India Today* (30 September 1990), 'If Nehru does speak out, the lid will be taken off the Bofors case.'

On 15 November 1985, around the time AE Services entered the picture, Arun Nehru was at the height of his powers as the just appointed MoS for internal security. In an article by Prabhu Chawla of *India Today* (cited earlier), he was anointed by the magazine as second only to the PM in terms of the political clout he wielded. But within days of the signing of the Bofors contract on 24 March 1986, Nehru fell from grace. This was partly to do with his role in the opening of the Babri Masjid locks and perhaps because the PM may have obtained information about Nehru's extracurricular dealings with Bofors. When Arun Nehru had a heart attack in Dachigam near Srinagar in April 1986, about three weeks after the Bofors contract was signed, everyone was astonished that, instead of rushing to the side of his influential cousin, Rajiv Gandhi contented himself with sending his personal physician.[72]

That may or may not have had anything to do with information that came RG's way of games being played with the Bofors contract. The moot point we need to come back to is that AE Services eventually received only the first of the five instalments to which it was contractually entitled, as I have previously noted. After the first payment in August–September 1986, while Nehru was still in office, Bofors cancelled its contract with AE and abruptly stopped all payments immediately after Nehru was kicked out of the Council of Ministers in October 1986. Why should the

---

[72] My own acquaintance with the falling out was the consequence of the PM having asked me to check proposed domestic tour programmes with the two Aruns. When one of my proposals in April received no reply for several weeks, I asked V. George if he knew why. He guffawed and replied, 'Don't you know that Arun Nehru is out?'

payments have ended? If RG was involved in contracting AE Services on the terms set out, he, unlike Arun Nehru, remained very much in office for the next thousand days. Yet AE received only $7.5 million and had to forgo $27.5 million, to which it was contractually entitled, after Arun Nehru was removed from office.

As Goldfinger might have asked, 'Happenstance? Coincidence? Or enemy action?' Take your pick and weigh it against Arun Nehru being the principal cause, according to both Chitra Subramaniam and Prashant Bhushan, of the V.P. Singh government holding back on rapidly pushing the pace of investigations. How much of Arun Nehru's own role might not have been uncovered if the Indian investigations, *sarkari* or *patrakari*, had gone into mysterious corners relating to Nehru's role in the AE–Bofors contract?

On my reading of the Ardbo diaries, Arun Nehru seems to have been involved with Ardbo in bringing AE into the picture. The Ardbo diaries used initials – 'H', 'Q', 'R' and 'N' in connection with the AE Services deal – to refer to its key players. While media investigators played up their speculation that 'H' stood for Hinduja, 'Q' for Quattrocchi, and 'R' for Rajiv, the hostile sections of the media, in particular the *Indian Express*, took so little interest in ascertaining who 'N' was that more than a decade later, the subeditors of *Outlook* magazine headlined an interview with me '"B" for Bofors. "N" for Nobody?'[73] There were other howlers in the diaries such as Ardbo misspelling the most famous name in India, Nehru, as 'Nero' and well-known UK-based Indian businessman Swraj Paul as 'Serge Paul'. Also, who was the mysterious 'Gandhi Trustee lawyer' mentioned in the diaries? No evidence has been adduced as to his identity and the media let that trail run cold although the so-called 'lawyer' had obviously been brought in by the conspirators to lend 'verisimilitude

---

[73] Reproduced in *Outlook* magazine, 5 February 2022.

to their otherwise bald and uninteresting tale'.[74] This intrigued me but apparently not the investigators bent on pinning infamy on Rajiv Gandhi.

So, it is just as well that the Rajiv Gandhi government had not given in to the motion moved by Major Jaswant Singh (retd), MP, on 10 August 1987 to cancel the Bofors contract if the company did not reveal the details of all the payments made. In fact, all these details were eventually revealed but there was nothing pointing to bribes having been routed either to the prime minister or any public servant, as detailed by Justice Kapoor in the Delhi High Court judgment of 4 February 2004, to which we will be coming shortly.

Bofors after JPC/CAG

In the year that elapsed between the presentation of the JPC report in the spring of 1988 and the CAG leak of April 1989, the Opposition and the government inveighed against each other (the Opposition more successfully), but no one got anywhere near the smoking gun.

This interregnum was used by the media, in particular the *Indian Express* and the *Hindu*, to throw at the public a huge number of mysterious initials, foreign names and foreign banks, obtained largely by Chitra Subramaniam of the *Hindu* through clandestine channels (as is the right and duty of the media). These included:

(a) Lotus, Tulip and Mont Blanc – purportedly names of accounts in Swiss banks that had received payments from Bofors.
(b) Other bank accounts held with companies, or dummy companies, going by the names of Svenska, Anatronics, Ciaou Anstalt and its managing agent, Sedes Anstalt, besides PITCO (Parmanand International Trading Co., named after the father of the Hinduja brothers), Moresco and Moineau (French for 'sparrow'), Alcari, Interseco of Panama, Cambria Ltd, Jubilee Finance and others.

---

[74] Disraeli's famous retort to Gladstone in the House of Commons.

(c) Swiss and Swedish banks receiving payments from Bofors, including Riksbanken, Skandiniska Enskilda Banken, Société Générale, Nordfinanz, Manufacturers Hannover Trust Bank, Crédit Suisse and an investment company called Colbar.

(d) Dozens of individuals that would require an index for instant recall. Some grew relatively familiar through repetition: Martin Ardbo, Anita Gradin, Hans Ekblom, Peter Ove Morberg, Per Mossberg, Pierre Schmid, Myles Stott, Lars Ringberg, Bo. G. Anderssen, Marc Bonnant, 'Bob' Wilson, Rolf Gauffin, Lars Gothlin and a mysterious Jordanian, Mubar Melikia.

(e) Others less frequently mentioned whom even the most avid Bofors aficionado would be hard-pressed to remember (I'm sure I've left out a few): Anders G. Carlberg, Thorsten Cars, Thomas Fischer, Jan Mosander, Carl Fredrick Algernon, Eva Arnvig, Anders Bjork, Rainer Burkhardt, Steven Samos, Paolo Bernasconi, Dieter Jan-Corrodi, Ursula Eid, Norbert Gansel, Borje Remdahl, Rony Halberg, Lars Jederlund, Jorg Kistler, Reinhart Kramer, Maria Leissner, Lars Erik Thunholm, Emile Marshi.

(f) Then there are the Indians, including the alleged recipients: Win Chadha, the Hindujas, 'N' and 'R' and one Italian long resident in India, 'Q'. The initials are easily identified as Q: Quattrocchi; R: Rajiv; and N: Arun Nehru? There is also a passing reference in the Ardbo diaries to 'Serge' Paul, clearly Swedish argot for the well-known British industrialist of Indian origin, Lord Swraj Paul.

(g) Towering over this mine of information are three unidentified sources pseudonymously named 'Kaa', 'Snowman' and 'Sting'.

Impressive work as far as 'investigative journalism' is concerned, but did this mosaic of letters and this telephone directory of names lead anywhere? Yes, of course, said the journalists and their editors – if only the Rajiv government would follow the leads that their investigations were revealing day after relentless day. While journalists may be proud of their clandestine efforts in turning up confidential documents, Rajiv Gandhi actually went one step further by requesting the Swedish authorities to pursue the investigation – with the conviction that as he had nothing to do with any bribes paid, an independent investigation would only exonerate him and his government.

Bofors after V.P. Singh's Electoral Triumph

The opportunity the Opposition was so anxiously awaiting was given to them by the outcome of the November 1989 election. The incoming prime minister, V.P. Singh, had on several occasions during the election campaign pulled out of his pocket a piece of paper and, waving it dramatically before his audience, proclaimed that written on it was the number of the Swiss bank account that would nail Rajiv Gandhi. V.P. Singh repeatedly claimed that within a fortnight – sometimes amended to thirty days – of his becoming PM, Rajiv Gandhi would be sent to jail and made to pay for his sins. The electorate was persuaded that Rajiv Gandhi would, indeed, be imprisoned in the immediate aftermath of the election.

So, the public waited with bated breath for V.P. Singh to act. It took a fortnight from his swearing-in for V.P. Singh to secure a vote of confidence in his government from Parliament. And then a month from that date to table a select few of the Bofors papers in the House. It then took him yet another month to put together his Bofors team. When the team finally emerged from the woodwork it turned out to be akin to Inspector Clouseau leading a posse of Keystone Cops. They totally bungled the first requirement of Swiss law: the presentation of a letter rogatory in a Swiss court.

A month after they had taken office, the new government had not even filed an FIR with the police. Without this, they could not approach even any Indian court for a letter rogatory, let alone turn up in Switzerland.

Having barred Bofors from doing any business in India, the V.P. Singh government was patiently waiting for Bofors to reveal the names. What is more, it became obvious to the lead newshound, Chitra Subramaniam, that it was 'pretty clear from day one that a lot of people at all levels had no interest in Bofors proceeding as a straightforward investigation. Some of these were powerful ministers in V.P. Singh's government and ran independent and conflicting power centres around the prime minister.'[75] Was she referring to N? It does not require a Hercules Poirot to identify who she was pointing to.

We thus see that at the end of the period of thirty days, the actual progress made by the new government had been limited to reviving the predecessor government's request to the Swiss for assistance! When at long last an FIR was registered on 22 January, only three persons were named: Martin Ardbo, managing director of Bofors; Win Chadha of Svenska/Anatronics; and G.P. Hinduja. No senior Indian politician was named. Rajiv Gandhi certainly wasn't.

Although Chitra Subramaniam, the Geneva-based journalist for the *Hindu*, was not involved in any way with the government, she was detailed by V.P. Singh to accompany the first of several investigative delegations to Switzerland. That was when she made her acquaintance with Arun Jaitley 'who talked non-stop, had a theory a minute about the payoffs and looked over his shoulder constantly to see if we were being followed. He gave the distinct impression that for him the whole investigation was something like a "catch-the-thief" exercise.' In Geneva, Jaitley 'mistook static electricity in his room door-handle for electricity, and concluded their rooms were wired'![76]

On 9 February 1990, the letter rogatory was delivered in Berne. In the normal course, it should have taken a few days, or at most weeks, for this

---

[75] Chitra Subramaniam, *Bofors: The Story Behind the News*, Penguin/Viking, 1993, p. 220.
[76] *Ibid.*, p. 223.

to be acted upon by the Swiss authorities. In this case, the response did not come until months later. On 4 July 1990, Subramaniam, responding to a message received from one of her contacts, reached Berne to meet Dr Pierre Schmid, in charge of international assistance in legal and political matters, Federal Office of Police, Berne. Schmid said he 'didn't know which leg to dance on ... We have received an urgent message from India asking us to revive the old tax fraud request ... if we reply to this, you know we will have to turn down the request.'[77]

He then told her the letter rogatory had been rejected on 'technical grounds'. What technical grounds? Schmid left the talking to his colleague. I turn the narrative over to Chitra Subramaniam:

> Incompetence, he kept repeating, as he read out from some documents and his notes ... The Indian request was thrown out because many documents presented to the (French-speaking) court were in English, the rubber stamp on some documents was so large it covered the matter rendering it illegible, there were hand-written notes on some pages, ball-point pens had been used to make certain annotations, translations were neither signed nor dated, pages had been numbered haphazardly and some photocopies had matter cut off, missing lines completed by hand and some faxed messages were included as part of the documentation, even though it is common knowledge that faxes have no legal tender ... There were so many mistakes in the documents presented by the Indian side to the court, and such basic ones, that it seemed almost deliberate.[78]

This was Additional Solicitor General Arun Jaitley's singular achievement. He had turned the whole letter rogatory story into a laughable farce. Do you see why I talked of Inspector Clouseau and the

---

[77] *Ibid.*, p. 220.
[78] *Ibid.*, p. 234.

Keystone Cops? Is it any wonder that notwithstanding all of V.P. Singh's tall talk, no real progress was ever made by Jaitley in uncovering anything of note in Switzerland?

Virtually no progress on this matter had been made when V.P. Singh started what was to be the downfall of his government by tabling, in August 1990, his acceptance of the Mandal Commission recommendations. Immediately thereafter his government started coming apart, caught in the battle between, as Vajpayee remarked, 'Mandal and *kamandal*' (the holy vessels sadhus carry). Within some sixty days, his government lost its majority and it limped along until it lost the vote of confidence on 7 November 1990, within eleven months of being sworn in (validating my predictions in *Sunday* magazine). V.P. Singh and his band had thus gone the way of the Jaitley-drafted letter rogatory.

Meanwhile, the media continued to flog the dead horse. Although Rajiv Gandhi's questions were out in the open, and ought to have occurred to commentators on their own, there was no consideration of the issues raised. It was pretty obvious that the V.P. Singh government was deliberately not cancelling the contract, which had been the principal Arun Singh–Sundarji recommendation, probably for the same reasons RG had raised: we needed the gun and Bofors was the best 155 mm howitzer for our needs and the outcome of any international arbitration or court ruling if the contract were cancelled was uncertain.

There was not even any attempt at asking Bofors to disgorge full information about payments and beneficiaries after extending assurances of non-disclosure of such information. The only tepid step V.P. Singh had taken was to order no further commercial dealings with Bofors, with the result that while we got the guns (and V.P. Singh and his successors paid for them), we lost out on supplies of shells and ammunition and transfer of technology. So, we never got around to manufacturing the guns ourselves; three decades later, we have a pale indigenous version!

Apparently, it was more important to somehow get the goods on one man than ensure our national security. The prospect of seeing Rajiv Gandhi 'twisting slowly, slowly in the wind'[79] was the imperative for the V.P. Singh government and his avid supporters in the media; they were incapable of understanding the former PM's motivations: he had served the national interest by refusing grand, knee-jerk gestures even if it meant losing elections – that is true patriotism.

Fortunately for India's prospects in the Kargil war, the Bofors gun was acquired on technical military grounds and ignoring the advice of the favourite duo of V.P. Singh and his cohort, Sundarji–Arun Singh, that the Bofors contract be cancelled to save the 'honour' of the country. The V.P. Singh government had, however, stopped the import of shells and ammunition from Bofors. The howitzer operated in Kargil on supplies hastily imported from South Africa.

Bofors and the Bachchans

On 30 January 1990, just as Arun Jaitley was gearing up to ready his letter rogatory to the Swiss authorities, the Swedish newpaper *Dagens Nyheter* ran a sensational story under a titillating banner headline proclaiming 'Breakthrough for Indian Bofors investigators, Gandhi friend received the money'. The 'friend' was named as Ajitabh Bachchan, brother of the film superstar Amitabh, Rajiv's childhood friend. Even Bollywood could not have ground out more masala. According to the Swedish newspaper, the mysterious 'sixth account' that investigative reporters had turned up in Switzerland was none other than RG's *benami* account held by his long-standing 'best friend', screen star Amitabh, the idol of millions of

---

[79] This expression became widely known after John Erlichman, White House chief of staff to President Nixon, used it in arguing that Patrick Gray III, former chief of CIA, should not be considered for a seat in the Senate since he had not performed well in his interrogation by the Senate Watergate inquiry committee. The phrase came into the public domain when the White House tapes, which Nixon had installed to bug himself, were summoned by the inquiry committee.

fans. The Indian press swallowed the story hook, line, and sinker. The Bachchans accepted the advice of their solicitor, Sarosh Zaiwalla, that they pursue their case in London, 'the libel capital of the world', instead of suing in Sweden. The case for *locus* (jurisdiction) came up on 25 March 1990 and, after a copy of the newspaper had been obtained from a London newsagent and displayed in court, Mr Justice Davies held that 'the English court had jurisdiction'.[80]

On 12 July 1990, hearings started at the London High Court in the case of *Bachchans vs Dagens Nyheter*. Chitra Subramaniam was expected to be fielded as a key witness as it was she who had unauthorizedly been supplied some 350 documents by Sten Lindstrom, the head of the Swedish police's investigation of Bofors. (Curiously but tellingly, his name does not figure in Chitra's book but figured pseudonymously.) However, as 'Lindstrom had not revealed that he was the source ... *Dagens Nyheter* could not call him as a witness'.

Zaiwalla claims, 'We had acquired information ... about one of the witnesses who was to give evidence for the Swedish newspaper. This was so damaging it effectively made it impossible for Carter-Ruck [the libel litigation specialists hired by *Dagens Nyheter*] to prove justification, which was their defence. They decided they had no choice but to settle.' In consequence, a Carter-Ruck solicitor approached Zaiwalla just as the doors to the courtroom were opening and Zaiwalla realized 'that the settlement was on'.

Thereafter, a joint statement by the complainant and the defendant was read out in court which included the sentence, 'A remarkable feature of this case is that the defendants received the information on which they based their story from sources close to the present Government of India [that is, V.P. Singh's government].' The defence lawyers subsequently confirmed in open court that 'they were misled earlier this year in trusting

---

[80] All quotes in this segment are from Sarosh Zaiwalla's *Honour Bound*, HarperCollins, Noida, 2020, pp. 82–91.

information from persons directly involved in investigations into the Bofors transactions on behalf of the Indian [V.P. Singh] government', adding that the allegations had 'also caused embarrassment to Rajiv Gandhi'. And thus was it established that Arun Jaitley and his merry band were involved in maliciously spreading lies while wrecking India's reputation by filing a comical letter rogatory.

In court, one of the defence lawyers read out an apology from *Dagens Nyheter* to Ajitabh for libelling him. The judge ruled that damages be paid to Ajitabh. Ajitabh's counsel had 'submitted a report by a leading British investigative agency, that the entire story about the sixth account was *fabricated*' (emphasis added).[81] For his part, Zaiwalla says, 'client privilege means I can never disclose the events that forced *Dagens Nyheter* to settle'.

What of Chitra Subramaniam, who won her spurs purveying to the gullible public stories sourced in large measure from anonymous/pseudonymous sources under cover of names like 'Kaa', 'Snowman' and 'Sting'? In a single sentence she dismisses the proceedings of the UK High Court: 'The Bachchans won their case, but did not go the whole way.'[82] Neither, indeed, does she 'go the whole way'!

Chitra Subramaniam refused the *Dagens Nyheter* newspaper's request to testify. She also has nothing to say about Sten Lindstrom ('Sting'?) being the source of the leak of some 300 or more documents. However, in 2015, a decade after the Delhi High Court judgments that exonerated RG, and after Lindstrom's retirement when he no longer needed to hide his identity, Lindstrom granted an interview to Chitra Subramaniam published on the website The Hoot, in which he admitted that there was 'no evidence that he [Rajiv Gandhi] had received a bribe'.[83] *Der aayaa lekin durust aayaa*, as we say in Hindustani (late in coming but right in

---

[81] *India Today*, 15 August 1990.
[82] Subramaniam, *op. cit.*, p. 231.
[83] Chitra Subramaniam, 'The Bofors Story, 25 Years After', The Hoot, 24 April 2012, http://asu.thehoot.org/media-watch/media-practice/the-bofors-story-25-years-after-5884.

coming). Lindstrom adds that Rajiv Gandhi might have been masking someone else who received illegal payments but gives no evidence for this allegation. The point was pursued in Indian courts all the way to 2018, but no evidence emerged of Rajiv Gandhi having protected anyone.

Thus, the quest for the truth of Bofors was sacrificed to partisan political interests. That is why Rajiv Gandhi, in addition to what he said in Parliament within a month of his defeat, later told Pritish Nandy in an interview:[84]

> **Are you worried about what the Bofors investigation might reveal?**
> Not at all. On the contrary, I welcome any effort to get at the truth ... I am, of course, very concerned that just at the time when tensions with Pakistan are increasing, this government's policies have resulted in silencing our 155 mm howitzers. Our defences have been seriously jeopardized.
>
> It is now clear that the National Front's claim of revealing the names of the recipients within 30 days was a hollow lie.
>
> It is also shocking that the Prime Minister has gone back on his word to lay all the files on Bofors on the Table of the House.
>
> Let the investigations be pursued vigorously. Its results will only confirm what we have been saying all along.

That is exactly what happened as shown in the next section, 'Bofors in the Courts'. Prashant Bhushan and Chitra Subramaniam (and, of course, the *Hindu*, the *Indian Express*, the *Statesman* and the *Illustrated Weekly of India, India Today*, et al.) are entitled to their self-righteous views. But the judicial system is the final authority. This narrative now turns to the long saga (1990–2018) of the pursuit of Rajiv Gandhi, alive or dead, through the judicial process.

---

[84] *The Illustrated Weekly of India*, 1 March 1990.

Bofors in the Courts

A kerfuffle arose in the first quarter of 1990 when one H.S. Chowdhury, an advocate claiming to be the general secretary of an organization called the Rashtriya Jan Parishad filed a Public Interest Litigation (PIL) against the grant of letters rogatory by the designated court (the CBI trial court) to allow the CBI to pursue matters in Switzerland. Chowdhury's petition went before Justice M.K. Chawla of the Delhi High Court. Justice Chawla delivered his two-fold findings in August 1990:[85]

i. He ruled that Chowdhry had no *locus standi* to file the petition, and the initiation of the proceedings under Article 51-A could not come within the true meaning and scope of PIL.
ii. Taking suo moto cognizance under Sections 397 and 401 read with Section 482 of the Criminal Procedure Code, Justice Chawla directed the registrar 'to register the case under the title, *Court on its own motion vs. State and CBI*'.

The aggrieved parties went before the Supreme Court who decided on 20 December 1990 to grant an interim stay on Justice Chawla's order. Substantively taking up the case, the division bench of the Supreme Court, comprising Justice S.R. Pandian and Justice K.J. Reddy, decided on 28 August 1992 to endorse the Delhi High Court's first finding that Chowdhry had no *locus standi*, but quashed Justice Chawla's decision to pursue matters under *Court on its own motion vs State and CBI*.

The way was thus cleared for the CBI to pursue its investigations in Switzerland, Sweden, and elsewhere. The CBI sought and received hundreds of documents, the last instalment being delivered to the CBI in Berne, the capital of Switzerland, by the Indian ambassador, K.P. Balakrishnan (my batchmate) amidst much fanfare and publicity in

---

[85] https://delhidistrictcourts.nic.in/feb/3938.htm.

1997. In 1990, with the installation of the VP government, the CBI had already initiated the laborious business of understanding, absorbing, and synthesizing the vast number of documents leaked to Chitra Subramaniam and other Indian reporters and published with enthusiasm by their editors. After 1992, and particularly after 1997, an even larger number of documents were added to this trove and CBI officials staggered back from Switzerland with these in hand. The CBI was then engaged in joining the dots to its principal target, a dead man, the former prime minister, the late Rajiv Gandhi.

When the BJP returned to power for the third time in October 1999, its first action was to lean on an as yet unprepared CBI to file a chargesheet in the CBI-designated court. The chargesheet carried Rajiv Gandhi's name in the list of accused in column 2 but in the last column it was helpfully clarified that he was not being sent up for trial since he was no more.

The Congress was infuriated. In my first speech following my return to the Lok Sabha after a gap of three years on 26 October 1999, I said:

> We demand of the Government the deletion from column 2 of the name of Shri Rajiv Gandhi... This has been done with malice aforethought; this has been done with a vicious intent; this has been done with a political purpose; and this has not been done to further the cause of discovering what happened...
>
> There is no link that has been established which would indicate any justification for it to be there. It is furthermore extremely malicious to include his name... because not even... will he be given the opportunity to clear his name...
>
> We repeat what Shri Rajiv Gandhi stated in this House twice over. Once, on the 28th of December 1989, he said, 'We would like you to find the people who have taken the money because we know when you find the people all the accusations that you have made all these years will

turn out to be false.' There is nothing in the recitation of the chargesheet which establishes anything other than that Rajiv Gandhi was in no way a beneficiary in any manner to whatever payments that have been made.

The treasury bench's only response, which came from the law minister Arun Jaitley, was that without RG's name, no purpose would be served by the prosecution, thereby reinforcing my charge of malicious political motivation.

On 14 November 2002, the special judge in the CBI trial court wrote an editorial rather than a judgment. After quoting Rajiv Gandhi telling the Opposition in Parliament, 'You show us any evidence that there has been any involvement of middlemen, of payoffs or commissions, we will take action and we will see that nobody however high up is allowed to go free', the special judge, without adducing any evidence said,

> How encouraging and bold! As if there is a ring of sincerity and the Prime Minister is out to find the truth. Rajiv Gandhi was not naive and impetuous. He pretended to be a maverick. All this was, however, a deliberate posturing and part of a well-conceived plan to apparently show the non-involvement of middlemen/agents in the deal and to achieve the oblique purpose by direct negotiations on the one hand and to have secret middlemen on the other hand.

The learned judge did not provide any evidence to validate any of these imputations. He then confessed it 'has not been possible for CBI to unearth' any proof of this but he is nevertheless persuaded that 'the moneys paid or a least a substantial part of the same paid to these so-called agents/middlemen was not meant for them but was obtained at the behest of Sh. Rajiv Gandhi to be passed on further'. Is this idle speculation or based on conclusive evidence?

The special judge then speculated: 'Clandestine manner of payment was adopted in this defence deal by the high and mighty involved in this case to ward off obvious dangers of ruining political and public life ... Layers of secrecy and privacy are thus laid to achieve the desired end.' Again, where is the proof as required under the Evidence Act, 1872?

Little wonder then that Bofors, in its new avatar as Kartongen Kemi och Forvaltning AB, and the other private parties indicted went in appeal to the Delhi High Court where their petition was heard by Justice J.D. Kapoor who pronounced his judgment on 4 February 2004.[86]

The conclusions of the high court were summarized under the five laws invoked. Extracts from the order:

Indian Penal Code, 1860 (Sections 120B, 161 and 420/465)
- Nowhere [is it] alleged by the prosecution even remotely, that payment made by AB Bofors by way of commission constituted a bribe to the public servants.
- Public servants are completely absolved of all allegations leading to the offences punishable under section 120B read with section 420 of the Indian Penal Code – Prevention of Corruption Act, 1947, Section 5(2), 5(1)(d).

Evidence Act, 1872 (Sections 63 and 78(6))
- No evidence collected that the photocopies were taken out from the original documents. Documents are waste paper ... Certified copy cannot be taken to have been proved by way of secondary evidence.

Prevention of Corruption Act, 1947 (Sections 5(2) and 5 (1)(d))
- There is no evidence on record to suggest that either Rajiv Gandhi or Bhatnagar [defence secretary] used any direct or indirect influence on anybody.
- ... the element of dishonest intention is utterly wanting.

---

[86] The full text of the judgment may be read as reported by the Delhi High Court as 2004 (72) DRJ 693 and may be accessed at http://indiankanoon.org.

- Charges for the offences of having entered into a criminal conspiracy with the public servants ... and taken illegal gratification ... are quashed.

Before coming to this conclusion, Justice Kapoor pointed out:

Interestingly the CBI did not file the charge sheet for the offences punishable under section 161 and 165A [relating to bribes to public servants] ... The prosecution even did not seek sanction for prosecution of the public servants ...

Justice Kapoor then went on to put the CBI in its place:

Result of thirteen long years of investigation by the CBI ... during which period a large number of officers of CBI hopped to foreign countries to collect evidence against public servants but returned empty-handed as till date there is no evidence to show that public servants had taken bribe in awarding the contract of guns to M/s. AB Bofors & Co.

Justice Kapoor then trained his guns on the investigative journals and journalists:

This case is a nefarious example which manifestly demonstrates how the trial and justice by media can cause irreparable, irreversible and incalculable harm to the reputation of a person.'
He adds: 'This is one of such cases where public servants who are no more have met somewhat similar fate being victim of trial by media. They have already been condemned and convicted in the eyes of the public.

The judgment scrupulously sums up the arguments on behalf of the CBI made by the additional solicitor general; the arguments and subsidiary or complementary points put out by Kapil Sibal on behalf of the accused public servants; the arguments and subsidiary/complementary points of Ram Jethmalani appearing for the Hindujas; and, the 'two fold arguments' of Alok Sen Gupta representing Bofors plus his subsidiary/complementary points.

Justice Kapoor then drew his conclusions:

77. . . . (after) sixteen long years of investigation by a premier agency of the country, viz. CBI could *not unearth a scintilla of evidence* against them [Rajiv Gandhi and S.K. Bhatnagar] for having accepted bribe/illegal gratification in awarding the contract in favour of Bofors. All efforts of CBI *ended in fiasco*. . . (emphasis added as this became the most famous sentence of the judgment)

78. Again not an iota of evidence has surfaced that may even remotely suggest or suspect that the money received as 'commission' by them [Win Chadha, Quattrocchi, the Hindujas] was held by them as money for the public servants for such a long period.

80. Similarly, Quattrocchi also held the money on his own account and had been transferring part of monies in different accounts opened by him. To allow the imagination to fly that AB Bofors paid bribe to public servants through Hindujas, Chadha and Quattrocchi to get the contract and in return they held the amount of alleged 'commission' paid by AB Bofors for more than a year or so is nothing but to deceive oneself. This itself rends the CBI's case from foundation to cornice.

87. . . . offence of 'illegal gratification' has to be proved by way of evidence . . . not even a trace of evidence has surfaced inspite of stupendous efforts made by CBI . . .

89. Charges . . . have been framed purely on the basis of irrelevant inferences, presumptions, surmises, conjectures and through rioting

imagination ... criminal trials cannot proceed or even succeed on such premises without there being any material or evidence corroborating those inferences.

90. Learned Special Judge has by framing charges for these offences fallen into a grave erroneous concept of criminal trial by traversing beyond realm of offences committed by public servants and the petitioners.

96. ... if the army changed its mind in favour of Bofors, it did not do so because of intervention of public servants or Bofors or present petitioners or Quattrocchi or Win Chadha. It was purely an opinion of a body of experts.

97. ... there is no evidence that the official report of the Army in favour of Bofors was managed, manipulated, or procured (by) corrupt or illegal means. Since the best judge of the weapons to be used by the Government was the Army or its Committee of Technical Experts the Government had no business or role to overturn that decision.

101. ... no evidence was there to show that Indian politicians and defence personnel ... actually received pay-offs ... How can a judge create evidence of his own when there exists none?

107. ... the element of dishonest intention is utterly wanting.

117. Even on legal premise trial qua public servants cannot proceed as both the public servants viz Mr. S.K. Bhatnagar and Mr. Rajiv Gandhi are dead ... That is basic criminal jurisprudence that court cannot give findings against a person who is not in a position to defend himself.[87]

Perhaps the phrase used by the learned justice that reverberated the

---

[87] Paras 77–144, pp. 729–46 of Justice Kapoor's judgment which may be accessed at the website provided in footnote 70. The link to the judgment can easily be accessed at http://indiankanoon.org.

most in the public mind was his finding that not a 'scintilla of evidence' had been produced regarding the alleged 'bribing' of public officials, including Rajiv Gandhi.[88] So what was all the fuss about? A good man, a decent man, an innocent man was calumnized in life, and even after his brutal assassination, by an incompetent media, deeply prejudiced commentators, and a motivated Opposition.

However, while exonerating public servants Rajiv Gandhi and S.K. Bhatnagar, Justice Kapoor ordered further proceedings against 'Srichand Hinduja and Others' (that is, Bofors). They in turn went in appeal against the order before Justice R.S. Sodhi of the Delhi High Court.

Justice Sodhi, in his judgment of 31 May 2005,[89] damned the CBI for 'launching a persecution based on a political agenda'. He went on to hold that the 'remuneration payable to the Hindujas was for market expenses ... [and] has obviously nothing to do with securing the Bofors contract' – the precise point that Rajiv Gandhi, as PM, had been making. Before 'quashing all proceedings against the Hinduja brothers', the justice expressed his 'disapproval at the investigation that went on for 14 years' and 'cost the Exchequer nearly Rs 250 crores'. He added: 'During the investigation a huge bubble was created *with the aid of the media* which, however, when tested by court, burst leaving behind a disastrous trail of suffering ... Careers – both political and professional – were ruined ... Many an accused lived and died with a stigma' (emphasis added).

After the Modi government entered office, the CBI filed an appeal in the Supreme Court in the form of a Special Leave Petition. The Supreme Court in its order dated 2 November 2018, signed by the chief justice, Ranjan Gogoi, and fellow justices, K.M. Joseph and Hemant Gupta,

---

[88] Yet, without any evidence to back the charge, vicious critics like Tavleen Singh maintain (as recently as *Sunday Express*, 20 August 2023) that Quattrocchi was acting on Rajiv's behalf.

[89] The full text is reported as 2005 SSC online DEI 676 and may be accessed at http://indiankanoon.org.

held: 'We are not convinced with the grounds furnished by the petitioner for the inordinate delay of 4522 days in filing the present Special Leave Petitions . . . We, therefore, are not inclined to entertain the present Special Leave Petitions.'[90]

And that is where the matter finds its last resting place. The media continue to fester in their compost heap.

Bofors: A Final Assessment

Now that all doubts have been set at rest by final judicial pronouncement at the highest level, it is clear that Rajiv Gandhi insisted that all the Bofors files be laid on the Table of the House because he was innocent. He also insisted that the Swedish and CBI investigations be carried out in full until the whole truth was unearthed, for he knew it would end in acquittal for him and his family. He had asserted as prime minister, on the floor of the House on 6 August 1987: 'I categorically declare in this, the highest forum of democracy, that neither I nor any member of my family have received any consideration in these transactions.'[91]

This affirmation was received with howls of scepticism by the Opposition and those sections of the media that had become so-called crusaders in this matter. So, after he ceased being PM, Rajiv Gandhi reiterated on the floor of the House on 28 December 1989:[92] 'We would like you to find the people who have taken the money because we know that when you find the people, all the accusations you have made all these years will turn out to be false.'

---

[90] Unabridged text of the order is reported as 'CBI VS. Srichand Hinduja & etc.' at diary no. 4176 of 2018 as decided on 2 November 2018. Also see http://indiankanoon.org.

[91] Simran Bhargava, 'Bofors Debate in Parliament Brings Out Star Performers', *India Today*, 31 August 1987, https://www.indiatoday.in/magazine/special-report/story/19870831-bofors-debate-in-parliament-brings-out-star-performers-799246-1987-08-30.

[92] 'Lok Sabha Debates (English Version), columns 408–09, Lok Sabha Secretariat, New Delhi, 29 December 1989, https://eparlib.nic.in/bitstream/123456789/410/1/lsd_9_I_28_12_1989.pdf.

After decades of investigation, all 'the people who have taken the money' were identified and hauled before the courts; the final judicial finding was that the moneys paid were by way of 'winding-up charges' not 'bribes'; and that there was not an iota of evidence against Rajiv Gandhi 'nor any member of [his] family'.

RG's intention in seeking to end middlemen in defence deals was honest and genuine. And if he had not warned his close friend Arun Singh and Singh's selection for the CoAS against 'knee-jerk' reactions and had gone along with their 'panic-stricken' public relations advice to cancel the Bofors contract, the Kargil war may have been prolonged, leading to further needless deaths and injuries for our jawans – or even ended differently. Fortunately, all 410 guns arrived by the end of the eighties and proved their worth and more in every theatre of war they were deployed. Bofors is one of the many instances where RG put the national interest above his own. He was a brave man who took on his chin the consequences of his principled decisions. True, he lost the 1989 Lok Sabha election, but on Bofors he won the moral war. His 'conscience was clear'.[93]

---

[93] Before I conclude, I think I should refer to our then ambassador in Stockholm, B.M. Oza, who published a book titled *Bofors: The Ambassador's Evidence* (Konark, 1997) which made minor waves at the time. It largely centred on his resentment at him, as the ambassador, being bypassed in direct telephone conversations between Indian officials and political leaders with Swedish authorities. It reflected his rather antediluvian view of diplomacy in an age when technology had made possible channels of international communication that did not exist in the heyday of ambassadorial diplomacy. (According to Ronen Sen in a recent conversation with me, he also resented the ministry summoning him back from London where he was on holiday meeting friends and family and then dragging their feet on reimbursing his travel expenses.) The germane point is that *The Ambassador's Evidence* was brought on record when he spoke to the Indian investigating agencies ten years after all Bofors documents relating to the Indian howitzer deal had been secured by the CBI from the Swedish and Swiss authorities. When the Indian investigative agency went before our judicial authorities, Justice Kapoor of the Delhi High Court dismissed in 2004 the rubbish as not containing a 'scintilla of evidence' against Rajiv Gandhi. Later, the Supreme Court in 2018 finally ended the farce.

Yet, nothing so damaged Rajiv Gandhi as Bofors. I was never in the inner circle and, therefore hardly had any opportunity to share my views. I merely watched aghast from the sidelines. At the time, I reckoned RG was relying on the advice of a whole series of political and civil service heavyweights, advice that was pushing him into a corner. On reflection, I have come to the conclusion that he was not being 'advised' by anybody. I believe while RG was listening to what he was hearing, in the end he was acting on his own, especially at crucial turning points, confident about his own clean hands.

Early on, a colleague, Ronen Sen, who was dealing with the external aspects of the Bofors affair told me he had discreetly enquired whether he should hold his hand back in any manner, only to be sharply reprimanded by the PM that the officer's one and only duty was to get out all the facts.

To another colleague, rather more in the know of things, I bluntly put the question – not once but every time another mound of documents was unloaded – whether he knew whose hand was in the till. Each time I received the reply that he really did not know, and no one else seemed to know either. There was nothing to support the view that RG was involved.

Then there was the man himself. A more unlikely-looking crook is difficult to imagine. In every encounter with him, over a long spell of six years, dealing with hundreds of matters ranging from the really trivial to the really revolutionary, I found him consistently honest, straightforward, upright. Between the Rajiv I knew and the image painted of him in the media was a yawning gulf that grew wider by the day.

I was content, therefore, to leave those who dealt with Bofors to mind their business, assisted by the thought that, happily, it did not fall to my lot to unravel Arun Shourie's never-ending sentences.

Conclusion: 'Not a Scam but a Sting'

I saw him on most days throughout this trying period of nearly four years. He never looked stressed. He was never fazed. His dazzling smile never left him. (I recall asking him once on a flight back to Delhi as to when he thought the crisis with President Zail Singh would peak. At just that moment, a steward entered the cabin to say the home minister was waiting for him on the tarmac. Rajiv beamed at me and said, 'Now!') That others who did not share his values took advantage of his good intentions is evident. Bofors was not a scam, but a sting operation mounted by this cohort on the inside track and their allies in the media and the Opposition. The inner party conspirators, already restive over what they saw as Rajiv Gandhi handing over Congress-run states to Opposition parties (never mind the national interest), rallied around V.P. Singh and Arun Nehru as they saw the prospects of huge funds from defence deals slipping out of their hands. It was they who went on to form the National Front that toppled the Rajiv government – albeit for no more than a few months before they were consigned to the dustbin of history.

While his enemies and detractors went all out in their scandalmongering, the PM maintained his concentration on issues that mattered more to him than rebutting false charges on Bofors. These included the crusade for secularism; peace overtures to China and Pakistan; interventions in the Maldives and Sri Lanka; the universal nuclear disarmament initiative; the campaign to end apartheid in South Africa; the Technology Missions, ranging from high-tech telecom and supercomputers for better weather forecasting to the humble oilseed; drought-proofing and rural development; efforts to bring the geographical and social peripheries of our country into the national mainstream; cultural outreach through the Zonal Cultural Centres and the Apna Utsavs; and RG's determination to strengthen the grassroots of our democracy through Panchayat Raj (I was deeply involved with the latter two).

It is to these constructive issues that we will turn in the next chapter.

See detailed footnotes and endnotes by scanning the QR code above.

3

Foreign Policy Initiatives

Nuclear Disarmament, China, Pakistan, AFRICA Fund, Maldives

Nuclear Disarmament

In January 1987, the Indian journalist Kuldip Nayar, probably at the instance of the Pakistan government, was specially invited to meet A.Q. Khan, the 'father of Pakistan's bomb' at his hideaway in Kahuta, Pakistan, where Pakistan's atomic weapon facilities were housed. There, in an on-the-record interview, Khan revealed to India and the world that Pakistan had the bomb. Nayar visited the Indian high commissioner, S.K. Singh, in Islamabad to inform him of this startling revelation from the horse's mouth, as it were, and later published the interview in the London *Observer*. This revelation was probably a deliberate move on the part of the Pakistan establishment to warn India at the height of the tension over Operation Brasstacks. Reportedly, the Indian chief of army staff dismissed Khan's claim as stuff and nonsense. The experts at the Bhabha Atomic Centre were also sceptical. Nevertheless, the news was a political time bomb.[1]

---

[1] P.R. Chari, 'Nuclear Signaling in South Asia: Revisiting A.Q. Khan's 1987 Threat',

Rajiv Gandhi's immediate reaction was to prepare the Action Plan for a Nuclear-Weapons-Free and Non-violent World Order to be presented to the Third United Nations Conference on Disarmament, scheduled at New York in June 1988. Preparing the plan was largely the handiwork of our leading foreign service expert on disarmament issues, Additional Secretary Muchkund Dubey, under the intense and detailed supervision of the PM who was keen on getting right the technical minutiae of what he was proposing. As I was kept out of the process until it came to drafting the speech, I don't know the details of the fashioning of the action plan, but given the passion with which Dubey went about the task, I would call the initial draft of the plan principally his handiwork.

The single most important concept at the heart of the action plan was to wean the world away from the 1968 Non-Proliferation Treaty's (NPT) binary perception of the world as divided between the Nuclear Weapon Powers (NWPs) and Non-Nuclear Weapon Powers (NNWPs). Rajiv Gandhi alerted the international community to the emergence of a clutch of countries, including, above all, India, that had acquired the capacity to make nuclear weapons but were restraining themselves, or being restrained by the NPT, from demonstrating their capacity to test-explode the bomb. These were the Threshold Nuclear Weapon Powers (TNWPs). He called this an 'even worse' danger: 'Left to ourselves, we do not want to touch nuclear weapons. But when tactical considerations, in the passing play of great power rivalries, are allowed to take precedence over the imperatives of nuclear non-proliferation, with what leeway are we left?'[2] He went on to stress that it was only if the international

---

Carnegie Endowment for National Peace, 14 November 2013, https://carnegieendowment.org/2013/11/14/nuclear-signaling-in-south-asia-revisiting-a.-q.-khan-s-1987-threat-pub-53328.

[2] This and other quotations from his UN address of 9 June 1998 are extracted from the full text which may be perused at pp. 335–44 of *Rajiv Gandhi: Selected Speeches and Writings, 1988*, Vol. IV, Publications Division, New Delhi, 1989. Given its importance to understanding Rajiv Gandhi's values and *weltanschauung* (world view), I have reproduced

community replaced the highly discriminatory NPT with an international convention which outlawed 'the use or threat of use of nuclear weapons', could these nations that 'are capable of crossing the nuclear threshold solemnly undertake to restrain themselves'.

RG proposed a detailed, *time-bound*, *phased*, *verifiable* action plan for *universal* nuclear disarmament founded in a *non-violent* world order within twenty-two years, that is, by 2010. Each one of the words in italics in the previous sentence was accorded a special significance, with meticulous provision for their interpretation and implementation. It is particularly important to note that each stage of the staggered process was regarded as a link in a chain that would, in twenty-two years, lead to a world without nuclear weapons; in other words, there could be no cherry-picking of individual elements and expecting them to be endorsed by India unless the link were part of a chain leading inexorably to time-bound and complete nuclear disarmament. That is why the Comprehensive Test Ban Treaty (CTBT) passed by the UN in 1996 did not find endorsement by India. It had been cherry-picked from the action plan and was considered in isolation from the ultimate goal of definitively ending the era of weapons of mass destruction in *anyone's* hands, whether NWPs, TNWPs or NNWPs.

Rajiv Gandhi summed up his action plan's chief characteristics as, first, 'a binding commitment by all nations to eliminating nuclear weapons, in stages, by the year 2010 at the latest'; second, 'all nuclear weapon states must participate in the process of nuclear disarmament' and 'all other countries must equally be part of the process'; third, at each stage, 'there must be tangible progress towards the common goal'; and, fourth, to put in place doctrines, policies and institutions 'to sustain a world free of nuclear weapons'.

The new treaty – proposed to replace the NPT, which at the time was

---

it on the website of this book at http://rajivmisunderstood.com which may be accessed by scanning the QR code at the end of the chapter.

scheduled to expire in 1995 – 'should give legal effect to the binding commitment of Nuclear Weapon States to eliminate all nuclear weapons by the year 2010' matched by an equal and reciprocal commitment on the part of NNWPs/TNWPs to 'not cross the threshold'. The implication was clear: if the NWPs did not immediately commit themselves to fulfilling their NPT commitment to cap, reverse, and eliminate their arsenals of nuclear weapons, there would be no alternative to TNWPs like India (and Pakistan) going over the threshold to testing, possessing, and deploying nuclear weapons. (TNWP is my invention; RG actually described them as 'non-nuclear states on the threshold'.)

The NWPs did not heed the alert. The action plan was never adopted or acted upon. The world, therefore, has the five de jure NWPs of NPT days and at least five TNWPs that have de facto crossed, or are on the verge of crossing, the threshold: India, Pakistan, Israel, the Democratic People's Republic of Korea (North Korea), Iran. A possible sixth is Japan. This exponentially aggravates the danger to which Rajiv Gandhi drew attention in 1988 that nuclear war will mean 'the extinction of four [now seven] thousand million people'[3] and the 'end of life as we know it on Planet Earth'. In my view, the fact that we in India have acquired nuclear weapons does not obliterate the horrid consequences of nuclear conflict that RG so dramatically placed before the international community in 1988:

> The balance of nuclear terror rests on the retention and augmentation of nuclear armouries. There can be no ironclad guarantees against the use of weapons of mass destruction. They have been used in the past. They could be used in the future. And in this nuclear age, the insane logic of mutually assured destruction means nothing survives, that none lives to tell the tale, that there is no one left to understand what went wrong and why.

---

[3] Subhas Chakravarty of the *Times of India* enjoyed pointing out to me orally that despite the draft having undergone seventeen revisions, the population of the world in 1988 had been underestimated by an entire billion!

Rajiv Gandhi became the only head of government ever to present a detailed and practical road map, verifiable at all stages, to the elimination of nuclear and other weapons of mass destruction. His presentation was accompanied by a carefully thought-out and well-argued introductory speech on the imperatives of a nuclear-weapons-free planet (which went through seventeen drafts before it was readied!) It was the last throw of the dice.

The speech was well received by UN standards, but I was left a little bewildered when I ran into the PM in the UN Delegates Lounge a few minutes after he had finished speaking. 'The British ambassador,' he said, 'was saying your speech was very good.' Flattering, but why '*your* speech'? Was it a case of giving credit where credit was due – or was he distancing himself from what he had just read out?

On reliable reports being received of Pakistan's advances towards acquiring nuclear weapons, the PM, I have since learned, passed secret orders to the Atomic Energy Commission to start preparing for a test explosion. But he did not give orders for actually testing the bomb, possibly because we were not quite at that stage in his remaining year in office. The test was eventually undertaken a whole decade later on 11 May 1998 during the thirteen-day interim rule of Atal Bihari Vajpayee. I was in a TV studio when I heard about it. I was horrified at the news, so much so that when I returned home, my mother-in-law anxiously enquired of my wife whether someone in my family had died.

After the nuclear bomb tests of May 1998, I had a sense of the ambivalence with which Rajiv Gandhi saw the issue of India going nuclear. There were three occasions on which he shared with me his private concerns. He once told me, to my disquiet, 'You know, Mani, if Pakistan really does have the bomb, even I cannot stop India from going down the road to nuclear weapons.' In the second instance, he remarked, 'Well, you see, India and Pakistan both already have the bomb.' I looked at him quizzically. He explained, 'The Canadians have gifted them to us. We have the Bhabha Atomic Centre reactor in Bombay and the Pakistanis have the Candu reactor in Karachi. All that it would take for devastating nuclear explosions that would destroy both our commercial capitals would be for kamikaze pilots from either country to fly an aircraft straight into the reactor of the other.'

The third and last: 'You know, Mani, why our nuclear energy programme is such a flop and our space programme such a success? It's because Dr Ramanna is an obsessive bombwalla, while Dr Satish Dhawan never lets his focus wander to the military uses of outer space.'

These were passing thoughts – even 'idle' thoughts. I believe, however, these were also serious concerns that the PM was bouncing off me although I was in no way privy to the discussions between him and his inner circle of senior advisers, including Gopi Arora (an avid advocate of a muscular foreign policy), Chinmay Gharekhan (a sceptical realist), Dr A.K. Kakodkar (a leading nuclear scientist with a firm understanding of nuclear policy), perhaps K. Natwar Singh, MoS for external affairs (also a pragmatist), and maybe someone hawkish (there is no lack of them) from the armed forces or the defence ministry. Of course, the group most privy to the prime minister's innermost views and concerns included his principal foreign policy aide, Joint Secretary Ronen Sen, with whom I had the following recorded exchange several years later. Sen told me, 'The world has lots of weapons and needs a little hope.' To which my reply was: 'You are saying the world has lots of weapons and needs a little hope, and I am saying the world needs lots of hope and only some weapons.'

I was involved only in the public relations exercise of drafting what I understood to be the PM's public expression of his thoughts. I stress all this only because two decades later, long after Rajiv Gandhi was no more, I was entrusted by Dr Manmohan Singh in 2010 with the chairmanship of an expert group to review and update RG's Action Plan for a Nuclear-Weapons-Free and Non-violent World Order. It was then that I discovered there were wide differences of perception from even within Rajiv Gandhi's PMO as to what his real objectives were in drawing up the action plan: a feint to distract the world's attention from India's plans of going nuclear; or a last desperate attempt to stop India from going nuclear if the phased implementation of his action plan was not seriously considered by the international community.

I sincerely believe it was the latter, but in full recognition of the alternative of India going nuclear (and Pakistan doing the same) if, as dolefully expected, universal nuclear disarmament was not accepted by the international community (and the two superpowers of the day, in particular) as an immediate goal to be attained with all deliberate speed. Having skimmed through his subsequent speeches, including the Jawaharlal Nehru birth centenary speech on 13 November 1989 which was his last as PM, I find that whatever his orders about readying for the bomb, he was consistent in arguing for and explaining the imperative for a world without nuclear weapons. Therefore, I believe he was entirely sincere in presenting his action plan to the international community at the UN on 9 June 1988, a date we should seek to make the International Day for a Nuclear-Weapons-Free and Non-violent World Order, especially as it coincides with the date in 1950 when Niels Bohr, the Danish scientist most responsible for discovering the scientific and technological route to making the bomb, passionately pleaded at the UN for an end to the era of nuclear war. I hope the Congress will act on this suggestion if Narendra Modi, the current PM, is defeated in 2024.

Two last incidental memories. While going through one of these seventeen revisions, the PM picked on my expression: 'the system, like a whirlpool, sucks us into its vortex'. His point was that a whirlpool is a vortex; so how could anything be sucked into a whirlpool's vortex? When I contested his remark, he asked Vincent George to bring in a dictionary. The PM took a while to reach W for 'whirlpool' and then, his face wreathed in his famous smile, read out from the dictionary that a 'whirlpool' is a 'vortex'! I had to admit defeat and offered to withdraw the scientifically incorrect phrase, but he graciously asked me to leave it in as it 'sounds nice'.

Another related memory: Jawaharlal Nehru's year-long birth centenary celebrations were to commence on 14 November 1988. It had been decided to invite a large number of NGOs from all around the world to a conference on nuclear disarmament to kick off the celebrations. The conference was to be inaugurated by the PM. I was tasked with drafting his address. I decided to use this opportunity to test a hypothesis of mine. So, I filled the draft with quotations from Jawaharlal Nehru on the subject of nuclear weapons, adding little of Rajiv's own thoughts.

The draft was, as usual, circulated in advance and I spotted Muchkund Dubey fuming as I walked into the meeting, the PM presiding. I began by asking for permission to read my draft without interruption, promising in advance to thereafter tear my draft to shreds and rewrite it. RG was intrigued but agreed. As I read through all the quotes, I saw the PM's eyes widening. So, I was not surprised when he asked me out to the garden as soon as the session ended. I joined him on the lawn outside and he said, 'This guy talks just like me.' I coughed and replied, 'No, sir, you talk just like this guy!'

I went on to ask whether he had picked up his ideas on nuclear disarmament from his grandfather. He said, 'No,' adding that his grandfather was always preoccupied and there was no opportunity to really sit down and talk to him, except at breakfast where there was a family rule that all conversation had to be in Hindi. Or on holidays. 'But where,' added RG, 'was there the opportunity to discuss nuclear disarmament when we were diving off the houseboat into the Dal Lake!' I remarked I had suspected as much, which is why I had included the quotes. These ideas had seeped into RG's mind from his grandfather by some process of psychic osmosis. The speech to kick off Nehru's centenary was redrafted and finalized to the satisfaction of Muchkund Dubey and all concerned!

Endnote

While Rajiv Gandhi's action plan has mouldered in the cupboards of foreign offices around the world, the current international position has undergone a sea change. This flows from Rajiv Gandhi's reasoning of forty-four years ago:

> It is already widely accepted that a nuclear war cannot be won and must not be fought. Yet, the right is reserved to resort to nuclear weapons. Therefore, we propose that all nuclear weapons be leached of their legitimacy by negotiating an international convention which outlaws the threat or use of such weapons.

Such a convention has now – four decades after RG spoke – come into effect. This is the story:

In 2017, the UN General Assembly through resolution A/Res/71/258 of December 2016 adopted on 7 July 2017, set up a UN Conference to negotiate a legally binding instrument to prohibit nuclear weapons. This is standard UN procedure to create a new treaty. Accordingly, a Treaty on the Prohibition of Nuclear Weapons was adopted by a majority of 122 member states (with just one abstaining and one voting against). In its essentials, the treaty is clearly premised on much the same arguments as presented to the UN by Rajiv Gandhi in 1988, nearly three decades earlier. The treaty was then opened for signature and came into force on 22 January 2022 after 50 countries had signed it. As of the date of writing (21 October 2023) 93 memberstates have signed the treaty and the number of state parties which have declared their adherence to the treaty by intimating the Depository, namely, the UN secretary-general, now stands at 69.[4] The numbers may increase in view of the abject failure of the latest NPT review conference, the tenth, in August 2022. On the other hand, because of Putin's nuclear threats in the context of the Ukraine war, the numbers might diminish. But the treaty has entered into force and is now part of established international law. And the rationale of the treaty reflects the substance of RG's arguments in favour of his 1988 action plan.

So, Rajiv Gandhi was not wrong; he was just way ahead of his time.

I, personally, remain in favour of universal nuclear disarmament and, failing that, for India to become the only NWP to take the lead in signing, ratifying and bringing into universal effect the Treaty on the Prohibition of Nuclear Weapons. This is not the popular view in twenty-first-century India, which revels in being a member-elect to the evil club of recognized de jure NWPs, but that remains my strong maverick conviction if we are to remain true to Mahatma Gandhi's teachings.

China

On the evening before we flew out to Aizawl in February 1987 to inaugurate the new full-fledged state of Mizoram, V. George rang me to say that the PM wanted me to also include a quick visit to Itanagar, the capital of Arunachal Pradesh, before returning to Delhi the same evening. I protested that the sun set so early in the north-east that the logistics were impossible. George replied that organizing the visit was my business; his job was to convey the PM's instructions to me!

Fortunately, I had Air Commodore Trevor Keeler, a brilliant officer, as liaison at the Airforce Headquarters. We worked out a complex schedule that would get the PM by helicopter from Aizawl to Silchar, then by aircraft to Dimapur, from where he would take a helicopter to

---

[4] See the website https://disarmament.unoda.org/.

Naharlagun in Arunachal, followed by a quick motor ride to Itanagar. Meanwhile, the aircraft would be repositioned at Dibrugarh to get RG back to Delhi by dinner time.

At the Itanagar rally, I stood at the edge of the stairs leading up to the platform, my usual vantage point, to listen to the PM. I was perturbed to hear him announcing full statehood for Arunachal Pradesh, just as he had done for Mizoram earlier in the day. I feared he was jeopardizing with this move the anticipated huge diplomatic triumph for him in China. So, I went into his cabin as we took off from Dibrugarh to express my concerns. He listened to me carefully and then gave me one of my most telling lessons in diplomacy: 'But, Mani, if we do not know where our frontiers lie, how can we expect the Chinese to know?'

My very marginal involvement with RG's China policy began with my delight on learning in March 1985, when I joined the PMO, that Rajiv Gandhi had charged Additional Secretary Gopi Arora and Arun Singh, then his parliamentary secretary, with taking a fresh look at India–China relations. I later found this had been in the works since Indira Gandhi returned to office in 1980. In 1983, she had received an invitation from Deng Xiaoping to visit China. The preparations for this were reset at the start of RG's premiership.

But this was made known only on a 'need-to-know' basis – and I had no need to know! It was proving almost impossible to reach Gopi Arora's desk as the floor of his office was strewn with MEA files on China. My IFS colleagues dealing with China were extremely hush-hush. But I did gather trouble was brewing in the valley of the Sumdorong Chu (river). This caused concern as it was believed that Tawang could be protected only if the Hathung La pass was in our control, and this required continuous surveillance of the Sumdorong valley.

In the summer of 1984 we had established an 'observation post' at Wangdung on a bank of the Sumdorong Chu. Arunachal Governor R.D. Pradhan describes this as 'India's clumsy attempt to set up a border patrol station *in an area that even by the Indian survey maps was in Tibet*' (emphasis added).[5] For a while, the Chinese chose to ignore the post, but in the summer of 1986, an Indian patrol came upon a team of Chinese putting up 'permanent structures' on the banks of the river. We lodged a formal protest with the Chinese against these 'intrusions' and the Chinese responded by building a helipad at the site in August.

In September, we proposed to the Chinese that if they dismantled their facilities when they withdrew from the winter snows, we would not move back in the summer. The Chinese appear not to have been impressed with this bravado. Deng Xiaoping retaliated with the threat that he would teach the Indians a lesson.

India answered the threat by Parliament passing a Bill on 8–9 December 1986 conferring full statehood on the union territory of Arunachal Pradesh. As recounted above, the state was formally inaugurated by the PM in Itanagar on 20 February 1987. Meanwhile, a heavy build-up of troops on both sides of the border took place as the snows thawed. India–China relations also thawed with the raksha mantri and external affairs minister visiting Beijing in quick succession in April– May 1987[6] while both armies started withdrawing from the Sumdorong Chu area. By mid-1987, preparations for the prime ministerial visit to China were back on track.

There are those who believe it was because we gave a strong military response to the Chinese in 1986–87 that they were ready to make political

---

[5] *Dragon's Shadow over Arunachal Pradesh*, Rupa, New Delhi, 2008, p. 138.

[6] It may be noted that in the current stand-off in Ladakh that started in April 2022, neither the defence minister nor the external affairs minister has visited Beijing although some unstructured conversations have been held with the Chinese foreign minister on the sidelines of different international fora. Also, at the level of local army commanders, there have been discussions and operational decisions to defuse tension at some points of potential confrontation in Ladakh. But none of this is the same thing as high-level ministers visiting Beijing or being invited to visit New Delhi. And Xi Jing Ping has brushed off PM Modi's somewhat pathetic attempts to engage him in Bali and Johannesburg.

progress in 1988. I am in the minority who do not accept this view. The Chinese leadership was quite as keen as RG was to put the relationship back on an even keel after a stand-off lasting over a quarter of a century. All the military alarums on the border were on account of our establishing an 'observation post' on the Tibetan side of the Line of Actual Control. It was the PM's firm commitment to responding positively to Chinese political signals that brought about the December 1988 breakthrough in Beijing. Military perceptions might have helped yet would have added up to nothing but for the firm political leadership on display on both sides. It is a useful lesson for us to remember in the first quarter of the twenty-first century as disengagement gathers pace in the areas of Ladakh occupied by the Chinese in April–May 2020.

A great deal of quibbling followed on whether we should proceed to 'a reasonable overall solution to the border problem' on the basis of 'Mutual Understanding and Mutual Accommodation' or 'Mutual Understanding and Mutual Adjustment' or 'Mutual Acceptability' rather than 'accommodation' or 'adjustment'. But it was generally agreed that some form of 'MU MA' held the key to a settlement.

Far more to the point than these word games was Deng's handshake with Rajiv Gandhi in the Great Hall of the People that, by some accounts, lasted for eight and a half minutes, giving ample time for the world's cameras to inform the world that a new chapter was opening. Of course, other steps were taken, such as the establishment of a Joint Working Group (JWG) on the boundary question at the level of the Indian foreign secretary and the Chinese vice minister of foreign affairs. The JWG had the twin mandates of ensuring peace and tranquillity along the Line of Actual Control and working towards a 'fair, reasonable and mutually satisfactory settlement' of the boundary question. In addition, there were agreements signed on science and technology; civil air transport; and the executive programme under the Agreement on Cultural Cooperation for three years, 1988–90. But these details paled in relation to the handshake.

The consequences of the handshake manifested themselves in a joint communique stating that 'the two sides agreed to restore, improve and develop good neighbourly relations based on the Five Principles of Peaceful Co-existence'. The communique also affirmed the joint will of the two sides 'to resolve the border dispute according to mutually acceptable solution'.[7]

Since April/May 2002, with the two armies glaring at each other across the Shyok river, in the Galwan valley, the Depsang plains, Hot Springs, and Pangong Tso, and at other points on the 4,000-kilometre-long border between India and China, it seems to be important to retrieve the Rajiv–Deng spirit of December 1988. We must return to the fundamentals of the political and defence parameters generated by RG's China visit that yielded rich dividends for three and a half decades until April 2020. With disengagement taking place at several points as a consequence of talks between local force commanders, there is now some easing of political tensions. In the winter of 2023 as we go to press, it appears feasible to consider this as such engagement on the Rajiv model seems to be back in the realm of possibility – provided we get over what sometimes seems to be a visceral national suspicion of China and moderate our dallying with our 'natural ally', the US in its anti-China crusade born of jealousy that China has emerged as the alternative superpower.

Of course, much has changed in the three decades that have passed since RG visited China. While a significant gap had already opened up between China and India in economic terms at the time of the visit to China in 1988 (for example, China's foreign exchange reserves were three times India's), the gap now is much larger (while we have at last exceeded the level of Chinese foreign exchange reserves three decades

---

[7] Joint communique released in Beijing on 23 December 1989. See the website of the *Indian Journal of Asian Affairs* at jstor.org/stable/41950350. See also the joint communique when Dr Manmohan Singh visited China dated 19 December 2010, which reiterates the 1988 position and moves matters further forward.

ago, even now China's reserves are five times India's) and will take ages to close, if ever.

What I am confused about is why do we begrudge the economic lead that China has taken over India? I can understand our wanting to catch up with China and overtaking them if we can in the economic realm, but I do not think it is necessary to consider the India–China economic gap a military threat, provided we persist in negotiating a reasonable settlement of the border with China. True, China's military strength has also increased exponentially, and we are putting in strenuous efforts to keep up with them at least on the northern border. We are clearly in an arms race at the border, but does the answer lie in intensifying that arms race or does it lie in earnestly searching through diplomatic channels and patient peaceful negotiations for solutions to the border question?[8] Experts will reply that we have put in our best effort, it is the Chinese who are dragging their feet. Accepted, but is there an alternative to persisting in peaceful coexistence and keeping the dialogue going? And is it in the potential military dimension of the Quad (the quadrilateral economic and security cooperation arrangement between the US, Japan, Australia, and India, which might yet acquire a military dimension) that we are going to seek the answer?

On the global stage, the same Washington, DC, that was benevolently viewing China's economic rise in 1988 and immensely benefiting from China's integration with the global economy, has now woken up to the Chinese economic 'threat'. That, to my way of thinking, is an exaggeration as China has a long, long way to go before catching up with US standards of living, and perhaps never will. But in terms of economic heft and

---

[8] See Nirupama Rao, *The Fractured Himalaya*, Penguin/Viking, Gurugram, 2021. A brilliant exposition and analysis of the pendulum swings in India–China relations. It was published too close to the finalization of my manuscript to be mentioned in the detail it deserves in this book. Perhaps I will return to it in my sequential volume, *A Half-Life in Politics*, likely to be published by Juggernaut towards the end of 2024 or early 2025.

military power, and, more importantly, increasing political influence in Asia and the world generally, China is certainly a significant world power. We would be as foolish as the USSR was under Gorbachev if we were to attempt to match Chinese military power at the cost of the welfare of our people. That is also perhaps the reason we are shying away from the military dimensions of the Quad. I for one applaud that. I do not think the border issue can be resolved by matching China gun for gun and soldier for soldier. The only way forward is to negotiate a settlement of the border in full recognition of the historical fact that Aksai Chin was never ours; that we inherited 'flexible frontiers'[9] on the north from the British; and that, indeed, India did not even claim all of Aksai Chin until Nehru, in 1954, ordered the Survey of India to stop showing Aksai Chin as undemarcated. Why, if we really believed Aksai Chin was ours, did we not then set up a district administration in Aksai Chin in the years following 1954 as we had done in Tawang in 1951?

I also recognize that the longer the border simmers, the more complex it becomes to extricate our country from border tensions carrying the risk of a wider war. I do not understand our stand that we will never give an inch of our territory to the Chinese without quite knowing where that inch lies, and what we would do with it if we ever got all that we covet.

I stress that India and China are neighbours and need to live in peaceful coexistence as good neighbours. I discount theories of China wanting to hold down India as a regional hegemon, for I can't understand why we should aspire to be a hegemon. Surely we should be prioritizing the settlement of our border disputes with China in full recognition of no settlement being possible without an element of give and take? That is the necessary prerequisite for the cultivation of friendly relations with China. This should be matched by the cultivation of friendly relations with Pakistan – for, among other reasons, we must recognize

---

[9] A term I owe to my IFS colleague and former vice-president of India, the Hon'ble Shri M. Hamid Ansari.

the weightiest reason of all that China is no longer on the other side of the Himalaya. It is positioned in today's Pakistan, at the very point where Alexander stood on the banks of the Indus when he was poised to invade India in 326 BCE!

There is no denying the need to define and limit the exact location of the Line of Actual Control to arrive at a settlement in a pragmatic, purposeful, and mutually acceptable manner. Most Indians (and perhaps most Chinese) are unwilling to give an inch. Fantastic dreams are entertained over 'retaking' Aksai Chin as if this can be done without a war that would extinguish much more than just an arid mountain desert where 'not a blade of grass grows'[10] in Nehru's famous phrase.

The Chinese have settled their borders with twelve of their fourteen neighbours (India and Bhutan being the exceptions, and Bhutan is struggling at the Indian leash) including surrendering to Russia tens of thousands of square kilometres earlier claimed as 'Chinese'. All these accords have come through patient and peaceful negotiations, while attempts to impose their will on Vietnam by force ended in failure for China. There is nothing China or India can gain from going to war.

Pragmatically, with give and take, we can come to rational, reasoned solutions provided we give a sustained impetus to the negotiating process instead of dragging our feet over technical details like their refusing to share their maps over their claim lines. We are informed on the authority of Ambassador and Foreign Secretary Nirupama Rao, one of the brightest envoys we ever sent to China, in her brilliant book, *The Fractured Himalaya*, that it has been the Chinese habit to not share maps, in advance, of what they claim. This makes it easier for them to 'sell' the necessary compromises that arise out of the negotiating process to their leadership and people. For decades, we have regarded this as proof of

---

[10] Quoted by Rakesh Sinha, a BJP MP and leading intellectual, in 'History Headline: Aksai Chin, from Nehru to Shah', *The Indian Express*, 18 August 2019, and frequently cited ever since Nehru said this in Parliament in 1959.

their malintent, but I cannot see why this point cannot be overcome by ever more persistent negotiation.

My final point is that if, since Simla 1972, we have wanted to change the Line of Control in J&K into an international border, why don't we do the same with the Line of Actual Control with China after firming it up to remove the haze of the 1962 and 2020 conflicts? Otherwise, it is virtually certain that we will align ourselves with the Americans, as some Indians yearn for, and others like me dread. Then, when the fighting breaks out, India will be the Belgium of the Third World War.[11] The conflict will occur in the triangle that marks the conjunction of India, Pakistan and China.

I also do not believe we are obliged in the name of 'nationalism' or 'patriotism' to retain or lay claim to 'every inch' of what Mother Victoria left us, which was not what was claimed in the name of Mother India. Mother India (Bharat Mata) is altogether different from Mother Victoria. Mythologically and ritually, in the *Sankalp* that marks the start of Hindu prayers, India's northernmost point is named as Mount Meru in Garhwal (which was not conquered until a half-century after Edmund Hillary and Tenzing Norgay reached the Everest summit!); there is no reference in the *Sankalp* to Aksai Chin.

I recognize that the stand I take is not that of the large body of China experts who have made it to foreign secretary and national security adviser, and even external affairs minister. But then I am no longer bound

---

[11] Belgium is where the Battle of Waterloo was fought in 1815 between France, on the one hand, and Britain and its ally, Prussia, on the other. Belgium was not a combatant, but Napoleon's dominance was fought on the broad plain of Waterloo, a few kilometres to the west of the capital, Brussels. It was then declared 'neutral' territory at the Congress of Vienna and remined so till Kaiser's Germany violated the treaty at the start of World War I, and through the war devastated and destroyed much of Belgium where the fighting was intense. This was repeated in World War II (see Hugo Claus, *The Sorrow of Belgium*, Pantheon Books, New York, 1990). God forbid Indian territory becomes the killing fields of World War III.

by the discipline of the IFS (if I ever was). Indeed, I was persuaded when I was the joint secretary (UN) at the age of forty-two that I would never make it to the upper echelons of the service because I was too much of a maverick in my thinking, and that if by some accident of fate I were to make the grade, I would soon be out on my ear for having expressed my own views instead of faithfully sticking to the government line, particularly on the highly sensitive issues of China and Pakistan.

This maverick approach was consistent with my reading of the national tragedy of 1962, that the disaster was brought on as much by Nehru's and Defence Minister Krishna Menon's political mistakes (which have been worked to death in the literature) as by military incompetence starting right at the top from the CoAS, General P.N. Thapar, down to the 4 Corps Commander, B.M. Kaul (which is why the military sections of the Henderson-Brooks–Bhagat report[12] are being suppressed from public reading for well over half a century while the political findings damning Nehru/Menon have been leaked and widely reported).

Nehru's Views on China: 1950

Indeed, as far as Nehru's views on China are concerned, while everyone who denigrates his handling of Tibet and China cites the letter that Sardar Patel wrote to the prime minister on 7 November 1950 (drafted apparently by Nehru's own secretary-general in the MEA, Girija Shankar Bajpai), what is almost never mentioned is the brilliant point-by-point reply that Nehru personally drafted as a Minister for cabinet a fortnight later, on 18 November 1950. After all these years and so many ups and

---

[12] For the benefit of generations that did not go through the trauma of the 1962 disaster, it might be clarified that the raksha mantri, Y.B. Chavan, announced in 1963 a two-man committee comprising senior army officers, Lieutenant General Thomas Bryan Henderson-Brooks, and Brigadier (later Lieutenant General) P.S. Bhagat, to enquire into the causes and consequences of the reverses India suffered in 1962. It is now some sixty years since their report was submitted but it has never been officially released although extracts have been leaked to the press and academia.

downs over the past seventy years, I think it is the fundamentals of Nehru's note[13] that need to be retrieved.

Nehru urged that 'we should be clear in our own mind as to what we are aiming at, not only in the immediate future but from a long-term view'. The first consideration he took into account was that 'present-day China [that is, Communist China] is going to be our close neighbour for a long time to come'. Secondly, he stressed, we have 'a tremendously long common frontier'.

From these basic considerations, he went on to underline that 'China will take possession, in a political sense at least, of the whole of Tibet'. He added that 'there is no likelihood whatever of Tibet being able to resist this or stop it'. Further, 'it is equally unlikely that any foreign power can prevent it'. He then added the crucial line: 'We cannot do so.' He bluntly asserted, 'We cannot save Tibet', adding that it is only by operating at the 'diplomatic level' and 'by avoidance of making the present tension between India and China worse', that 'we might be able to help Tibet retain a large measure of her autonomy'. There was no dreaminess, only hard-headed assessment, in the making of his Tibet/China policy.

He conceded that while China might formally grant Tibet 'autonomy', that autonomy 'can obviously not be anything like the autonomy verging on independence that Tibet has enjoyed during the last forty years or so'. Please note the period 'forty years or so' that Nehru underlined: that the history of Tibetan virtual 'independence' is no longer than four decades; also, that such autonomy merely 'verged on independence'. It was a plea for a realistic assessment of the situation and not entertaining fantasies about anyone being able to materially change that reality.

He went on to argue that while there was 'practically no chance of a major attack on India . . . there are certainly chances of a gradual infiltration across our border and the possibility of entering and taking

---

[13] Tripurdaman Singh and Adeel Hussain, *Nehru: The Debates that Defined India*, HarperCollins, 2021, pp. 171–78.

possession of *disputed* territory' (emphasis added). Many will point to 1962 as having refuted this relatively sanguine view of China's intentions vis-à-vis rival Indian and Chinese claims to 'disputed territory'. To them I would say, as I told the IFS interview board in London in 1963 when the humiliating military setback of the previous October–November was very much on our minds, that the Chinese thrust beyond Thagla ridge was a 'riposte' to Nehru's orders to the Indian army to 'throw the Chinese out'. If the Chinese had really wanted to seize and possess undisputed Indian territory, would they have withdrawn unilaterally from the very edge of the Brahmaputra valley when all of the north-east, with which they had racial similarity, lay before them? Did they not withdraw unilaterally from even Tawang? Nehru was as right in 1950 as he is in hindsight in 2023/2024: there would be 'infiltration' but mostly in 'disputed territory'.

Moreover, Nehru added that we must 'take all necessary precautions to prevent this' but bear in mind that 'to make full provision for a feared attack' would 'cast an intolerable burden on us, financial and otherwise', as also 'weaken our general defence position'. We needed to remember, he cautioned, that 'our major possible enemy is Pakistan'. He was proved right in 1965, 1971 and 1999, when not only was Pakistan the aggressor but China did not come to Pakistan's rescue. Presciently, Nehru added that 'if we fall out completely with China, Pakistan will undoubtedly take advantage of this'. This we must remember now more than ever before, as the Chinese presence in Pakistan just across the Indus on the vast Indo-Gangetic plain stretching into Bangladesh is the overwhelming 'fact' of the first quarter of the twenty-first century for India.

Nehru also considered the argument that was rampant then (and has been resurrected by many of our China experts now – especially after the Galwan incidents of 2020) that 'Chinese communism means inevitably an expansion towards India'. Describing this attitude as 'rather naïve', Nehru added, however, that 'it may mean that in certain circumstances'. Seven decades on, that point retains its validity: it is only if we allow 'circumstances' to drift towards irretrievable hostility that such a prediction, now being made in the context of China's rise to Great Power status, would arise. If such views are encouraged and constitute our fundamental appreciation of the Chinese, then, of course, we will bring upon our heads the very thing we wish to avoid: war between the two most populous nations of the world, both armed with nuclear weapons.

Hence Nehru's alternative path, as valid in 1950 as it is today, that 'if China and India are inveterately hostile to each other . . . there will be repeated wars bringing destruction to both'. But if 'India and China [are] at peace with each other, [it] would make a vast difference'. He concluded that although 'we should be prepared, to the best of our ability, for all contingencies, the real protection that we should seek is some kind of understanding with China'.

It was, alas, a route – 'understanding with China' – that Nehru himself tragically forsook after the Chinese became aggressively militant in 1959 and unhappily abandoned in 1960 when Zhou Enlai came to Delhi for a week in April with very reasonable proposals as a starting point for negotiations to settle the border. This was possibly because Nehru's cabinet colleagues sought confrontation not resolution, and the mood of the country was such. But in 1988, thirty-eight years after Nehru's note was written, and twenty-two after the brief Chinese incursion in October–November 1962, Rajiv Gandhi journeyed to China in search of precisely such an 'understanding'.

I had the good fortune to travel there with him. Of course, I was not involved in any of the highly confidential confabulations in preparation for the visit, nor in the secret talks at the summit, but I was involved deeply with the public projection of the prime minister's reasons for making the visit and its outcome. I draw on these speeches[14] to explain

---

[14] The full texts of Prime Minister Rajiv Gandhi's major speeches in China may be seen at pp. 404–20 in *Rajiv Gandhi: Selected Speeches and Writings, 1988*, Vol. V, Publications Division, New Delhi, 1989.

the significance of the historic breakthrough that gave us thirty-five years of peace and tranquillity at the border.

At the welcome banquet, he underlined that 'stable and friendly relations between India and China' are 'crucial to the future of humankind' as it is these relations that will 'determine the destiny of our region' and vitally 'influence the course of world history'. His peroration affirmed that this visit 'solemnizes' our 'pledge' to work for 'peace among peoples and co-operation among countries'.

In his definitive oration at Qing Hua University, he remarked that 'in contrast to the warmth of our friendship' in the early years, 'the last thirty years or so have been a period of estrangement'. Yet, it was over these very years that both China and India had advanced to the point where there is 'comparability and complementarity between what we have achieved'. So, 'I have come to office with the firm conviction that, between ourselves, we must make new beginnings. I am heartened that the Chinese leadership is more than prepared to put behind us past rancour and past prejudices' – proof of which was the political determination at the highest levels to find solutions 'within a realistic time-frame' and the practical measures taken to set up joint working groups to deal with issues of enhanced cooperation. The key decision was to institute high-level talks on the border between the Indian foreign secretary (later, national security adviser) and the vice minister concerned on the Chinese side.

This initiative fructified in the Treaty on Peace and Tranquillity on the border concluded in 1993. But the search for an 'acceptable solution to the boundary question within a realistic time-frame', as sought by Rajiv Gandhi, ran out of steam thereafter, and the eighteen rounds of talks on the border, plus several rounds recently at the military level, have not resulted in an acceptable solution based on 'mutual understanding and mutual confidence'.

While we are back to rancour and prejudice as these lines are typed, we must recall, as I noted earlier, that the accord reached in 1988 led to thirty-five years of peace and tranquillity on the border. Tragically, they did not lead to solutions to the border issues. That, I suspect, is because Rajiv Gandhi's determination to settle differences on the border was not matched by equal ardour on the part of his successors and perhaps not on the part of Deng's successors. But that is the only sensible path to pursue. Not the Narendra Modi path of being all things to all men. What is said to Xi must be consistent with what was or is whispered to Trump or Biden.

My claim to being a maverick explains why I hold a maverick view of China, begging the pardon of all our experts on China who know why we should be at odds with China but are unable to show us the way out of the maze.

Amid the solemnity of the Rajiv Gandhi China visit, there were moments of levity too. I recall three such interludes. At the banquet the first day, a Chinese lady, who knew nothing of India but had a smattering of English, was seated at my table. While making stilted conversation, she enquired whether we ate Chinese food in India. We nodded. She then remarked that there were so many different kinds of Chinese cuisine, which did we prefer? Before anyone else could answer, I butted in with 'Sino-Ludhiana'. The Indians all laughed but we left behind one thoroughly confused Chinese lady!

A second opportunity for a laugh arose when we were getting into the long car-cade that was to drive us to the Great Hall of the People. Invariably I had to share a car with my insufferably pompous IFS and PMO colleague, G. Parthasarathy (Partha). Before the car-cade started, a very ruffled-looking Ambassador C.V. Ranganathan (Rangi) ran up to my car calling out, 'Where's Partha?' I had seen Partha clambering in beside one of the senior ministers. So, I replied, 'Oh, up in front with the ministers, climbing, as usual, the greasy pole.' Next day, as we were leaving for Qing Hua University, the commerce minister Dinesh Singh asked me to get into his car. To my chagrin, Dinesh's car stopped at the university right next to Ambassador Ranganathan. 'Aha,' Rangi called out, 'and who's climbing the greasy pole now?' Pointing a thumb at the minister who was descending from the other door, I replied, 'Frankly, Rangi, I don't know whether it's him or me!'

The third laugh arose out of my personal involvement in the visit being limited to the drafting of speeches. An unexpected hurdle arose when Rajiv Gandhi's additional secretary for economic affairs, Montek Singh Ahluwalia, raised an absurd objection to the first draft including 'biotechnology' among possible areas of future India–China cooperation. I decided to ignore the petty objection and continued to include it in further revisions. But at each reading, Montek continued to object with a steadfastness better bestowed on a more substantive matter. The more he objected, the more stubborn I grew.

With my reference to 'biotechnology' still adamantly in the draft, we eventually went before the prime minister. Montek once again stuck to his stand, arguing that the Chinese were so far ahead of us in biotechnology that there was no scope for our working together. I, of course, held that this was the precise reason for flagging it as a potential sector for cooperation. The PM ended the dispute by winking at me to let the point go. But when we were together in the aircraft carrying us to Beijing putting final touches to RG's Qing Hua University address, he wickedly suggested that as Montek was not present, I smuggle the word back into the speech. I did – gleefully.

At Shanghai, we were hosted to lunch by the mayor. The menu included 'King Prawn's Balls' as the starter. I couldn't resist it. I marched across the banquet hall to where Montek was seated and, in everybody's hearing, proclaimed, 'Montek, I must apologize, you were right. These guys have grafted testicles on to their king prawns and all we've succeeded in is grafting a turban on to a Sardarji.' There was a loud roar of laughter. The PM summoned me to the high table to ask what all that was about. I solemnly replied, 'There are some things, sir, not fit for a prime minister's ears.'

Pakistan

Rajiv Gandhi came to office determined to put India–Pakistan relations on the right track. To this end, he met with the Pakistan president General Zia-ul-Haq no less than six times in his very first year in office. When Zia visited on 17 December 1985, this resulted in a signed 'time-bound, phased agreement to normalize relations'.[15] So close were the two leaders that, as Rajiv Gandhi told *Sunday* magazine after he demitted office, 'I could pick up the phone when we were on the brink of shooting each other ... We were able to defuse the situation and not go to war.'[16]

When Rajiv Gandhi viewed matters in retrospect, in his August 1990 interview to *Sunday* magazine, there were four significant strands that went into the constructive relationship he was trying to weave with our 'distant neighbour'.[17] First, that he always felt it was easier 'to deal with a hawk who had behind him a strong government'. Second, it was only with a dictator like Zia that 'a very hard deal could be struck on parts of the Kashmir border'. Indeed, Zia 'was willing to come and sign on the dotted line just a few days before the accident'. Third, 'we took a softer line with Benazir' because hers was a 'minority government' and she needed time to 'stabilize before we took a hard position'. Fourth, that the restoration of democracy made things easier provided she didn't 'forget that I am the Prime Minister of India, and I will not forget that you are the Prime Minister of Pakistan'.[18]

Thus, before going to Islamabad on 28 December 1988 for the SAARC summit, the prime minister sent a clear and public signal to Pakistan's new PM, Benazir Bhutto, from Qing Hua University in

---

[15] *Sunday* magazine, 12–18 August 1990.
[16] *Ibid.*
[17] The much-quoted title of the book by Kuldip Nayar on Nehru's visit to Pakistan in 1960.
[18] All quotes cited in this paragraph are from the same issue of *Sunday* referenced in footnotes 15 and 16.

Beijing earlier the same month that 'the emergence of a democratically elected government' had 'opened up encouraging prospects for enduring friendship and good will between our two countries, reflecting the natural affinities and affection which the people of India and Pakistan have for each other'. This was followed by a secret visit to Benazir Bhutto by Ronen Sen (of which I have only just learned) where plans were drawn up for how the visit was to be structured.[19]

As these breakthrough visits reflected my own views on how our relations with China and Pakistan should evolve, I regard December 1988 (and his second visit to Pakistan in July 1989) as the high point of my years in the PMO, confirming that I was on the same page as the prime minister about our relationships with our two most important neighbours.

At the SAARC summit in Islamabad towards the end of December 1988, RG delighted Benazir less by what he said than by what he did *not* say. All the other statesmen had begun their addresses praising the contribution that the late President Zia-ul-Haq had made to the progress of SAARC. The Indian PM, pointedly, made no mention of Zia. It was then put out that the new Pakistan PM was so thrilled that she begged Rajiv and Sonia Gandhi to stay on for an afternoon after the closing session to make this the first 'bilateral' visit by an Indian PM to Pakistan after Nehru had visited in 1960, twenty-eight years earlier. (It has been confirmed to me by Ronen Sen that this was not in fact spontaneous but planned in advance during his secret visit to Karachi.) Substantively,

---

[19] Since the lines were written, more details have been provided in Satinder Lambah's posthumous publication *In Pursuit of Peace: India–Pakistan Relations under Six Prime Ministers*, Penguin Random House/Viking, Gurugram, Haryana, 2023, pp. 80–81.

Alas, Ronen Sen refuses to put pen to paper about his many years in the PMO, working under four prime ministers from Rajiv Gandhi, through V.P. Singh and Chandra Shekhar to PVNR. I wish he would, but he loves hugging his secrets. That is the character of the man and probably contributed to his serving, after his long stint in the PMO, as our ambassador to Berlin, Moscow, London and Washington – arguably the most distinguished diplomatic career of any IFS officer ever.

during the course of that afternoon's talks, an agreement was reached on the two countries 'not attacking each other' and progress made towards resolving visa, trade, and other issues. Most importantly, a framework was agreed for the resolution of the Siachen dispute. It was also agreed that a more formal visit would be scheduled the following year.

The formal bilateral visit took place on 16 July 1989, which Lambah describes as 'a landmark visit'.[20] For me, it was the fulfilment of a dream I had nurtured since my spell in Karachi. Here I was travelling with the prime minister to Pakistan as his principal speechwriter. I threw all I could into drafting the banquet speech. Of course, the pernickety PM went through my draft with a toothcomb and would not let it pass until he had read and reread and subjected to the scrutiny of his advisers every word, indeed every comma of the draft, so that, by the end of this exhausting exercise he had absorbed the full import of the draft into his DNA and could own everything written in it. So, I would vouch for the sincerity of every sentence and every phrase in the oration.

RG began by pointing to the generational change that was signalled by both PMs being in the prime of their youth, which meant that 'when our two countries attained independence, I was a child, almost an infant and you, Madam, were yet to be born'. In this, he saw a great portent of what India and Pakistan could achieve by putting the past behind them and working together as 'friends and good neighbours'. Of course, there are 'real problems on the ground and real problems of perception', but he saw progress as possible on three key issues: an end to actions aimed at infringing our sovereignty; an end to clashes and conflicts in the 'forbidding, ice-bound terrain of the north'; and an end to 'disputation' in forums 'where other interests prevail'. He stressed, 'We are summoned to greater tasks than assiduously aggravating the scars of history. We must rise above the stoking of petty problems, unworthy of

---

[20] Satinder Lambah, *op. cit.*, p. 81.

our larger destiny ... it is a destiny we can achieve together, as friends and good neighbours.'

He then moved to his peroration:

> As anyone who has been to the Gulf or West Asia, Europe or North America will testify, when an Indian and a Pakistani meet, as human beings in a human encounter, there is an instant mutual recognition, an affection that swells from some inner core of our existence, an embrace that transcends the passing passions of politics. Why must we go abroad to meet each other? Why can we not meet in each other's hearths and homes? It is incumbent on us to give joyful expression to the natural affinities that bind our peoples.[21]

It was the distilled essence of all I had learned of Pakistan and Pakistanis in my three years in Karachi. And here it was pouring forth from the mouth of the prime minister!

Substantively, as I have noted, secret talks had been held in Karachi in mid-December 1988 on the eve of the SAARC summit between Ronen Sen, personally representing Rajiv Gandhi, and the new Pakistan PM, Benazir Bhutto, on the issues to be taken up and, if possible, settled on the sidelines of the SAARC summit. Besides the standard questions of trade, visas and people-to-people contacts, the focus was on Siachen and an agreement to not attack each other's nuclear installations. The latter led to a signed agreement between the two countries that the listed nuclear installations on either side would be immunized from attack by the other.

On Siachen, the discussions focused on a settlement based on 'mutual force withdrawal from recorded actual ground position locations and establishment of a jointly monitored demilitarized zone' – narrower in scope than earlier talks between the intelligence chiefs of the two

---

[21] The full text of his banquet speech may be seen at pp. 263–64 of the Publication Division's *Selected Speeches and Writings, 1989*, Vol. V.

countries in Amman and Geneva facilitated by the crown prince of Jordan who was married to a prominent Pakistani.[22]

Yet it came to nothing, for Prime Minister Rajiv Gandhi was out of office within four months. Benazir was first overwhelmed by her army, then removed from office within two years. And both were assassinated within a decade.

The issue, however, was almost resolved when P.V. Narasimha Rao became PM in 1991 following Rajiv Gandhi's assassination. Pakistan was invited to send a delegation to India for defence secretary-level talks on a possible settlement of the Siachen issue. A close friend of mine from my Karachi days, Salim Abbas Jilani, Pakistan's defence secretary, reached Delhi in October 1992 to negotiate a final accord on Siachen with our defence secretary, N.N. Vohra, building on the Rajiv–Benazir initiative of three years earlier. Hurdling impossible difficulties, an agreement was reached and a high-profile event was scheduled in front of the media for the formal signing of the accord the following morning at Hyderabad House. But the signing ceremony never took place.

For, at the same time, P.V. Narasimha Rao was deep into a doomed attempt to negotiate his way out of the Babri Masjid imbroglio with BJP president L.K. Advani. The BJP objected to a major breakthrough with Pakistan just as they were trying to bring their foot soldiers on board a settlement with Rao. So, literally at the last minute, late at night as the Indian and Pakistani negotiators were going to bed content that they had reached agreement, PM Rao called in Defence Secretary Vohra and ordered him to cancel the signing ceremony.[23]

The mutually agreed accord was thus aborted, illustrating the myriad thickets through which India–Pakistan issues have to be negotiated

---

[22] Satinder Lambah, *op. cit.*, p. 79.

[23] Based on personal telephone conversations with both defence secretaries, N.N. Vohra and Saleem Abbas Jilani.

if issues with Pakistan, a matter of external affairs, are mixed up with domestic issues. As Sati Lambah says, it is essential that 'the process of engagement is insulated from domestic and electoral compulsions'.[24] Jilani, who went on to become defence minister in an interim government, remains unfazed, still convinced that ways can be found to bring viability to the India–Pakistan relationship. Vohra shares this view. So, we must soldier on, as much on Siachen as on other divisive issues.

AFRICA Fund at the Non-Aligned Movement Summit, 1986, Harare

Prior to attending the Non-Aligned Movement (NAM) summit in September 1986 in Harare, Rajiv Gandhi undertook an extensive preliminary visit to several countries in southern Africa in May that year, including Tanzania, Malawi, Zimbabwe and Angola, for briefings by the heads of these states and freedom movements about their views on their principal problems and the role they envisaged for NAM in settling these grave issues. I was excited about the lead role RG played in building up a NAM-wide movement to fight the three great menaces of southern Africa: apartheid in South Africa; foreign invasion in Mozambique; and colonialism in south-west Africa (now Namibia) and Angola.

Rajiv took the initiative to gather together in Harare, on the sidelines of the main conference, the major African NAM leaders to set up a fund to combat these three menaces. As he left for the meeting, he asked me to think up a suitable name. I suddenly hit upon an acronym that might do the trick. When Rajiv emerged from the meeting, he asked me what I had thought up. 'AFRICA Fund, sir,' I replied and explained the acronym, 'Action For Resisting Invasion, Colonialism and Apartheid'. RG was delighted. And thus was born a self-help movement that within

---

[24] *Ibid.*, p. 326.

a decade achieved all three objectives: Mozambique was freed of invasion from without; Namibia (and Angola) ended colonialism and achieved independence; South Africa freed Nelson Mandela and put an end to the disgusting practice of apartheid. It was my quiet moment of triumph.

Intervention in the Maldives

In the early hours of 3 November 1988, information was received that the Maldives was under attack from a group of mercenaries recruited by disgruntled expatriate Maldivian citizens, who arrived by ship and quickly captured key government buildings and surrounded the presidential palace. Fortunately, President Gayoom managed to elude the attackers and sent the Government of India a formal appeal for urgent military assistance.

Prime Minister Rajiv Gandhi, in a statement to Parliament the following day, explained that he decided to 'respond positively and go to the aid of a friendly neighbour facing a threat to its sovereignty and its democratic order'. He arranged for the Indian Air Force to dispatch two aircraft with about 300 paratroopers on a reconnaissance mission. They successfully landed near Male and completed their mission around 2.30 a.m. on 4 November, without there being any Indian casualty. The PM then announced that 'we would like to withdraw our troops at the earliest'. He added that 'the country is proud of the speed and efficiency with which the operation was planned and executed'. He hailed the intervention as proof that 'countries in the region can resolve the problem ... free of outside influences'.[25]

While this was undoubtedly a high point in Rajiv Gandhi's premiership, it unfortunately encouraged establishment hawks to raise the decibels on India having become a 'blue water' power. It contributed to the gung-ho

---

[25] The full text of the PM's statement in Parliament may be seen at pp. 367–68 of the Publication Division's *Rajiv Gandhi: Selected Speeches and Writings, 1998*, Vol. IV.

spirit that animated the IPKF disaster in Sri Lanka. I was, of course, in favour of the quick and efficient action taken to forestall the coup and delighted that we had decided to 'withdraw our troops at the earliest', but, unlike most of my fellow bureaucrats in the PMO, I was deeply concerned at what appeared to be the beginnings of India becoming the 'regional policeman' and flexing military muscles. The temptation to do so had been exponentially increased by the Maldives intervention and colleagues like Gopi Arora were thrilled at the prospect of making this the exemplar of future Indian military action in the region – our very own Monroe Doctrine.[26] I was not. The IPKF experience sobered down these ambitions.

Having reviewed Rajiv Gandhi's major foreign policy initiatives, we now turn to his major domestic policy initiatives, including a special chapter on his major constitutional initiative, Panchayati Raj, with which I was deeply involved.

See detailed footnotes and endnotes by
scanning the QR code above.

---

[26] As stated in Wikipedia, 'The Monroe doctrine (pronounced in 1812 by President James Monroe, 5th President of the US) is a United States foreign policy position that opposes European colonialism in the Western hemisphere. It holds that any intervention in the Americas by foreign powers is a potentially hostile act against the United States. The doctrine was central to American grand strategy in the 20th century' and was reiterated as central to US policy after the 9/11 terrorist attack on the Twin Towers in New York.

4

Innovative Domestic Initiatives

Technology Missions, Zonal Cultural Centres and Apna Utsavs, Island Development Authority, Drought-Proofing, the Economy

Technology Missions

Many would rate Rajiv Gandhi's Technology Missions as his most important contribution to taking India into the twenty-first century by linking science and technology to the basic requirements of the people. Perhaps it is because I was not involved in these missions that I rate them below Panchayati Raj! But I am tempted to modify my ranking after rereading RG's last address to the Science Congress in Madurai on 7 January 1989.[1] I also draw extensively on the February 1989 issue of *Seminar* monthly magazine, exclusively devoted to the Technology Missions, sent to me by Sam Pitroda, the leader of the Technology Missions. Pitroda is described by his deputy Jairam Ramesh in his

---

[1] Given the importance of the address, extracts may be seen on my website at https://rajivmisunderstood.com or by scanning the QR code at the end of the chapter. The address may also be seen at pp. 127–35 of the Publications Division's *Rajiv Gandhi: Selected Speeches and Writings, 1989*, Vol. V.

article as 'a catalyst, an idea-broker, a trouble-shooter, and a problem-solver'.[2]

PM Rajiv Gandhi underlined in his speech to the Science Congress that these Technology Missions were not designed for the exotic realms of 'hi-tech' but directly related to 'our highest priority, the war on poverty'. He sought to make 'the application of S&T [science and technology] to development a people's movement'. He wanted to marry 'technological and technical ability with district and village-level administration'. Specifically highlighted was 'immunization' as a particular concern to reduce morbidity and mortality among pregnant women and infants by a massive programme of mass vaccination, cold chains to store vaccines, and self-sufficiency in the production of vaccines.

His speech placed a strong emphasis on the 'drinking water' mission which would link the remote sensing of aquifers to the plumber, the mason, and the electrician installing hand pumps in villages. A major mission was to exponentially increase the output of oilseeds, mostly grown in rainfed areas that are mostly bypassed by the monsoon rains, as edible oil constituted our second largest import after crude oil. This mission succeeded in doubling oilseed production over the 1980s, a feat not emulated since. The missions, moreover, were tasked with considering questions of indigenously produced cold chain equipment for deployment in rural India; solar-powered pumps oriented towards our rural needs; and improved designs for oil presses. The PM also prioritized the promotion of adult illiteracy by supplementing administrative methods with such technological measures as plastic blackboards and dust-free chalk.

RG went on to highlight embryo transfer technology for dairying that has resulted in India becoming the world's biggest producer of milk. He emphasized 'the pressing need for indigenous solutions tailored to our particular requirements in infrastructure areas like energy, transportation,

---

[2] *Seminar*, Vol. 354. Ramesh's article is at pp. 18–25 and is titled 'Charkha, Chip and Community'. Ramesh's fulsome tribute to Pitroda is at p. 21.

and communications, including telecommunications'. This led to astonishing strides in rural telephony, preparing the country to become the biggest user of cell phones. He also pledged massive financial resources for research and development.

The missions were supplemented by S&T projects in mission mode such as 'the control of iodine-deficiency disorders and integrated vector control for malaria eradication'. It amounted to the translation on the ground of RG's twin preoccupations with S&T (his favourite reading was *Scientific American*) and grassroots growth (as reflected in the time and energy he spent on promoting Panchayati Raj).

Jairam Ramesh explained in his *Seminar* magazine article that the Technology Missions were 'societal missions in which technological interventions form only a part'. In other words, the term 'Technology Mission' was something of a misnomer. The missions were aimed at generating 'useful and relevant technologies ... to translate knowledge from laboratories into actual use' in areas 'basic to development'. The aim was to bring together 'the vast and sprawling S&T infrastructure' in the country with 'the mainstream of development activity'. The final goal was described as 'self-reliance at the national level and self-help at the local level'.

Hence the choice of drinking water, immunization, edible oils, the telecom network, and dairy development for the missions, and specific S&T projects (also in mission mode[3]) for adult literacy; 'integrated vector control of vector borne diseases'; goitre control; cattle herd development; median range weather forecasting; development of amorphous silicon solar cell technology; and rehabilitation of the handicapped (especially victims of polio for whom universal vaccination was the key, since achieved).

---

[3] 'Mission mode' meant putting together in the same group representatives of different departments and ministries, including technical experts, so as to reconcile differences within the group instead of calling them for meetings, which has been Indian government practice since at least colonial times.

Unfortunately, hardly had the Technology Missions and S&T projects taken off than the Rajiv Gandhi period ended. A vicious V.P. Singh government just closed down the initiative; it briefly spluttered to life under P.V. Narasimha Rao before fading out again. Rahul Gandhi has been attempting to highlight it but has not been in office since entering politics.

Zonal Cultural Centres and Apna Utsavs

My first substantive assignment in the PMO arose out of my accompanying H.Y. Sharada Prasad to a meeting of the prime minister with the MoS for culture, K.P. Singh Deo, to determine the five-year agenda of that ministry. I was mesmerized by the argument put forward by the PM. He said independent India had made remarkable strides in reviving and rejuvenating all forms of culture – literature, the fine arts, the plastic arts, folk and tribal art forms, classical music, song and dance – through the Sahitya Akademi, the Sangeet Natak Akademi and the Lalit Kala Akademi, and projected this abroad very successfully through the Indian Council for Cultural Relations (ICCR) and the Festivals of India that his predecessor, Indira Gandhi, had planned for key cities around the world. But what were we doing to bring this cultural efflorescence to the general public in the villages and mohallas where they lived, to those who could not afford expensive tickets unlike the elite? He stressed that culture, particularly the performing arts, could be made a key effective instrument for the emotional integration of different parts of the country, on the principle of 'unity in diversity', the overwhelming requirement of nation-building.

RG suggested that we could build on the diversity of cultures, including folk and street culture, by setting up seven Zonal Cultural Centres (ZCCs) that would take the performing arts to the people at large by organizing intra-zonal cultural interaction in public spaces that could be easily accessed for free by the general public in rural villages and mofussil towns of the zone. This might be interspersed with interzonal interactions that could travel through different parts of the host zone. Also, to avoid rigidity in cultural demarcation, each state might be allowed, even encouraged, to join more than one zone. This would facilitate the holding of periodic national festivals of India in open spaces for the general public involving all seven zones. This was the germ of the idea which later led to an Apna Utsav in Delhi (1986) and another in Mumbai (1989). It was also agreed to set up the headquarters of the ZCCs in renowned cultural locations of the zone rather than in state capitals. So, the ZCCs came to be headquartered in Patiala (North Zone); Thanjavur (South Zone); Santiniketan (East Zone); Udaipur (West Zone); Dimapur (North East Zone); Allahabad [now Prayagraj] (North Central Zone); and Nagpur (South Central Zone). (I was always sorry we did not think up more imaginative names for these zones; our designations of regional zones brought to mind fertilizer distribution centres more than cultural havens, as my most active director of the North Zone, Geetika Kalha, put it, wishing her centre to be named 'Dhruva' for the northern star!)

I was tremendously taken up by the idea and threw myself into the work. As it was at the fag end of that meeting that the PM told Sharada Prasad he was giving him an extension, Sharada Prasad was more invested in the prolongation of his professional career than the ZCCs. So, the ZCCs and their festivals became my exclusive concern, and I thoroughly enjoyed this additional responsibility. My colleagues in the PMO were more than a little surprised at the zest and enthusiasm I displayed for what they took to be a trivial and somewhat eccentric preoccupation of the prime minister (an attitude that persisted into Panchayati Raj). The PM, on the other hand, was delighted to find in me an enthusiastic collaborator in what he considered a national priority.

RG spelt out his reasons for regarding culture as a key instrument for national integration in the Zakir Husain Memorial Lecture he delivered in April 1987.[4] He opened by citing Dr Zakir Husain himself: 'There could be no better instrument than the medium of music, dance and drama to bring about national integration.' He went on to explain that 'the performing arts are the most visible, participative form of arts, since on all occasions of joy, whether it is at birth, a wedding, or a festival we burst into dance and music'.

Ruminating about millions of Indians leaving their traditional homes as economic development proceeds apace and migrants are required to accommodate themselves to new ways of life, he pointed out that this led to 'the breakdown of their links with their traditional cultures'. He went on to argue that the challenge to national integration lies in preventing this great movement of people from becoming a platform for 'individual rivalries, community rivalries, or linguistic rivalries'. To this end 'participating in the performing arts is an osmotic process of building values, awareness, familiarity, respect and even reverence' for 'the different strands of the tapestry of our civilization'. RG went on to argue that national integration could not take place by limiting cultural performances to a few moneyed people in elite venues. It was imperative to organize cultural programmes from different regions of the country for the 'average person' (the '*aam aadmi*', to use a contemporaneous term) to come into contact with the diverse facets of our many-hued cultures.

RG was so deeply involved in this initiative that he personally inaugurated all but one (Allahabad) of these ZCCs. When we had them all up by mid-1986, he decided to hold a massive festival at seven different public venues in the capital which would be visited by each zone in turn to present to the general public *gratis* the full range of India's performing

---

[4] *Rajiv Gandhi: Selected Speeches and Writings, 1987*, Vol. III, Publications Division, New Delhi, 1989, pp. 317–21, extracts reproduced at this book's website https://rajivmisunderstood.com/, which may be accessed by scanning the QR code at the end of the chapter.

arts from north to south and east/north-east to west. After holding a public contest for an appropriate name for this festival, the choice fell on Apna Utsav (Our Festival) to give everyone a sense of ownership in the event. The very imaginative culture maestro Rajiv Sethi was set to putting his genius at work in organizing the first Apna Utsav. The second Apna Utsav, in Mumbai in 1989, was handled by another cultural icon, the cineaste and theatre personality, and extraordinarily creative Amol Palekar.

However, the initiative met with instant disapproval from high-level artistes and media critics, led by the cultural doyenne Pupul Jayakar, who were peeved that their monopoly over culture was being snatched from them and handed over to 'nautankis' (street performers and folk artistes – *theru koothu* in Tamil). RG encouraged me to respond to them although some of them responded to my responses with outrage! Nevertheless, the first Apna Utsav was held in November 1986 in Delhi, spread over two weeks and seven different venues. The PM was mobbed when he went to one site after having inaugurated the event from the ramparts of the Red Fort where he tried to teach the invaluable lesson that speeches are inappropriate on cultural occasions. Our estimate was that some 6,000 persons were present at each of the seven venues each day for those two weeks of the festival.

The person who most appreciated the essential idea of Apna Utsav was Dileep Padgaonkar, editor of the *Times of India*, who wrote on 8 November 1986:

A Momentous Event

The cultural festival that the Prime Minister inaugurates in the Capital today is arguably one of the most significant events in the history of independent India. We do not agree with the view expressed by some opposition parties and critics drawn from the cultural field itself that the expenditure incurred on it is extravagant and unnecessary. That view is cynical for it reflects a singularly narrow idea of the role of culture in the process of development and nation-building. Culture, in our view, is not an expendable luxury. On the contrary, it is, or ought to be, the basis and the end of all national endeavour. A people perceives itself as a people, as a distinct collective entity, through its culture. Culture channels its time-tested values and decisively shapes its vision of the world. To regard culture merely as entertainment or as a pastime of the privileged is to deny its potential as a potent force for self-fulfillment of individuals and the nation alike.

It is entirely to the credit of Mr Rajiv Gandhi and his able band of advisers on cultural matters that the government has given culture the respect, and the resources, it needs to play its rightful role in public life.

On 21 December 1987, the PM met the directors of the ZCCs and told them:

> The work that we as a nation have assigned to the Zonal Cultural Centres is, I feel, of crucial national importance . . . you have to fight not only the distortions in the press and the media, but you have to fight the government itself at times to see that the task that you have been given is completed.[5]

Unfazed by critics of the 1986 Delhi Apna Utsav, the PM fell in with my suggestion of holding the second Apna Utsav in Bombay (Mumbai) two years later, in January 1989. Initial soundings indicated opposition from the minister of human resources development, P. Shiv Shankar, under whom the department of culture fell. The PM asked me to summon Shiv Shankar to a meeting at 7, Race Course Road with him. We waited

---

[5] Full text at pp. 329–33 of the Publication Division's *Rajiv Gandhi: Selected Speeches and Writings, 1987*, Vol. III.

in somewhat awkward silence for RG to arrive. He fetched up a few minutes late and explained that he had been caught up in reading a children's magazine to which Rahul and Priyanka had subscribed when they were much younger. He continued that he had read a letter to the editor from a young child who said an injured vulture had landed in their garden and they had looked after it, but even after the injury had healed, the vulture had refused to fly out. The children were therefore obliged to adopt the vulture and find a name for it. So, they had decided to call it 'Pupul'. Shiv Shankar got the message and instantly withdrew his objection!

There was a final memorable moment connected with the Bombay Apna Utsav. I was with Rajiv Gandhi working on his speech to the Madurai Science Congress on the intervening night of 6–7 January 1989 when the phone rang at 3 a.m. and the PM took the call from Buta Singh, home minister. Buta Singh said one of the conspirators in the Indira Gandhi conspiracy case was due to be hanged on the morning of 8 January, and he was worried about the PM being scheduled to inaugurate Apna Utsav in Bombay the same evening. I had rarely seen RG ruffled by anything said to him, however grave, but on this occasion he sounded troubled and rhetorically asked why he should mourn the hanging of his mother's assassin.

Next afternoon, that is, 8 January 1989, just as we were readying to depart for Bombay, news came in that Emperor Hirohito of Japan had died. National mourning had been declared in India. Rajiv looked relieved. This gave him the perfect excuse to opt out of the cultural event. He decided to drop me off in Bombay before flying on to Delhi and left it to me to read out his message to the participants. The chief minister of Maharashtra then inaugurated the event. For me, substituting for the PM was a unique privilege!

The ZCCs continued in existence after RG's defeat. In 2010, I was appointed chairman of a committee to review the working of the ZCCs on their twenty-fifth anniversary. I will allude to the report at the appropriate place in the chronological narrative (that is, in the sequel to these Memoirs of my first fifty years, *A Half-Life in Politics*, likely to come out end 2024/early 2025) but limit myself here to saying that we found some of the ZCCs flourishing and fulfilling their duties in the spirt of Rajiv Gandhi's conception, but others becoming playthings of state governors as sources of entertainment for their special guests. There was also little supervision by the department of culture. It was, therefore, proposed that an inter-zonal committee be established to generally supervise the working of the ZCCs to ensure conformity to the letter and spirit of the initiative. I was immensely surprised and honoured when Sonia Gandhi arranged for me to be appointed chairman of this committee as well, *with cabinet rank* (emphasis added). Unfortunately for me, this appointment came only six months before the Congress crashed to its worst ever defeat in the general elections of 2014.

Island Development Authority

It was on his tour of Lakshadweep and Minicoy in November 1985 that the PM started thinking seriously of the sustainable development of these long-neglected islands off our south-western coastline and the islands of the Andamans and Nicobar off the south-eastern shores of mainland India. Hitherto, the islands had been given attention by independent India only as settlements for expelled immigrants from East Pakistan and Burma, and migrants seeking economic opportunity from some Indian states like Orissa (now Odisha), Andhra Pradesh, Kerala, and Tamil Nadu, or from a national defence perspective. Little thought had been bestowed on economic development without damaging either the environment or the individual, differentiated lifestyles of the varied inhabitants of these islands.

The PM also found to his intense disappointment that although these islands were administered as union territories, they were rarely, if ever, visited by Union ministers or mainland departmental officials. He felt it necessary to bind these outposts of the nation closer to the mainstream by making them familiar to the mainland and vice versa. He was also particularly concerned about the life of the tribals occupying many of the islands in the Andamans and Car Nicobar being left undisturbed, and, in the Arabian Sea, sensitivity being displayed to the Muslim tribals who lived in Lakshadweep and the Divehi-speaking people who occupied the distant Minicoy islands.

Romesh (Romi) Khosla, a well-known environmentalist who had served in many assignments with the UN around the world, was commissioned to write a report on the prospects and problems of bringing these islands into the mainstream of the nation's progress, bearing in mind their frail ecology and the need to leave undisrupted the cultures and traditional customs and usages of the tribal population.

To give substance to his plans, RG set up the Island Development Authority (IDA) to hold annual meetings with all Union ministers concerned in each set of islands to the east and west of the peninsula alternately. The first meeting was held in Port Blair, Andamans, in December 1986 and the next in Kavaratti, Lakshadweep, in December 1987. These meetings dealt with the nuts and bolts of development and the environment.

The Andamans were in some sense easier to handle because thriving communities of mainland migrants had been established on many of the islands and tourism was beginning to blossom. Also, the defence establishments – air force and navy – had assisted in the development of the local economy. Efforts had been made to establish contact (without disturbing their ways of life) with the Jarawa tribals living in the North Andamans and even with the poisoned arrow-wielding Sentinelese, as well as with the gentle Onge tribals of Dugong creek. (When I visited Dugong creek in 2004 after the tsunami, I was impressed to learn that not a single Onge had been drowned because they had noticed early in the morning that the sea was behaving unusually and all 300 of them walked up the mountainside in anticipation of the disaster that caused so much damage elsewhere.) In Car Nicobar, great pride was taken by the tribals in a school football team becoming champions in an all-India inter-school tournament. Fascinatingly, there is a village named after Guru Gobind Singh, with Sikh settlers, in Great Nicobar, far closer to Sumatra in Indonesia than to the Indian mainland. Indeed, the southernmost point of Indian territory, on the southern tip of Greater Nicobar – earlier Pygmalion Point and renamed Indira Point after Indira Gandhi – is only 86 nautical miles from Sumatra but hundreds of kilometres from the mainland. My personal introduction to the archipelago was a book called *Islands of the Marigold Sun* by an IAS officer, Kaushal Kumar Mathur, who had been one of my gurus at St Stephen's.

Even though Lakshadweep was closer to Kerala than Andaman and Nicobar to either Kolkata or Chennai, the islands in the Arabian Sea appeared more distanced and neglected than in the Bay of Bengal. The IDA meeting in Kavaratti changed this, largely on the basis of the Romi Khosla report and the observations of the commissioner, Wajahat Habibullah, who had earlier served in the PMO, enthusiastically endorsed by the PM.

It was decided to set up a council in the islands to which the people could elect their representatives, as also commercial, financial, and promotional state corporations or cooperatives for traditional economic occupations that would extend assistance for economic development such as protecting traditional fishing, upgrading fishing equipment, opening new markets for fish, and supplying live bait that was disappearing owing to coral mining in the lagoons. The IDA also decided to furnish more high-speed boats for inter-island transport and to build an airport at Agatti. An integrated communications telecom plan was drawn up, including four additional satellite earth stations and five very high frequency stations. A new standard trunk dialling (STD) facility was inaugurated in Minicoy by the PM. Transmitters were installed to enable All India Radio broadcasts and Doordarshan television to be heard and seen on every island. Several industries – aerated water, fish pickling factories, rice and wheat grinding mills – were in the pipeline, and employment opportunities were being expanded for Lakshadweep/Minicoy residents in the merchant navy and the navy proper. The annual plan outlay for the archipelago was doubled. Freshwater sources were sought by satellite. A master plan was under preparation to see how the construction of fishing boats could be undertaken with locally available material. Navodaya Vidyalayas were opened and facilities for educational training explored. The Islamic heritage of the islands, 'which is part of the Indian heritage', would be preserved and protected 'with loving care'.

I have gone into this in such detail only to show how the PM was concerned not only with broad guidelines but went into the minutiae of the requirements of the mere 25,000 inhabitants of these islands. He was looking not for votes – a charge often laid maliciously against him – but the welfare of Indians living on the geographical periphery of the country.

Drought-Proofing

Whereas in 1985 RG's domestic tours were principally aimed at acquainting the social and geographic periphery of the country with the prime minister and vice versa, from mid-1986 that changed with the worst drought since independence overtaking the country. At first, the drought was heavily concentrated in western India – Rajasthan, Gujarat, and western Maharashtra – but later spread over much of the country, even as far as Nagaland. The earlier tours had resulted in at least two major initiatives of the Rajiv era – Panchayati Raj and the Technology Missions – but the tours in 1986 and 1987 were principally focused on the drought caused by the El Niño disturbances in the Pacific and the spread of drought from traditional low rainfall areas to even some of the more fertile parts of the country. Apart from providing immediate relief to the affected people, the tours also led to a special emphasis on what Rajiv Gandhi called 'drought-proofing'.

He had an Action Plan for Drought and Flood Relief prepared and submitted it at a meeting of all chief ministers for their comments and consent. RG regarded distinguishing between immediate needs and long-term issues as essential. On the immediate front, he ensured substantial additional financial resources to be made available for providing work and, therefore, income to tide over the current crisis, over and above the drought relief grant already provided for in the budget. This required slashing other less essential non-plan expenditure. In consequence, to give one example, Rajasthan received more funds for drought relief and drought-proofing in one year than in all the preceding forty years taken together. Grain was used from the Food Corporation of India stocks to ensure that no one starved, agricultural loans were rescheduled, provision was made for reaching drinking water to remote villages, orders were issued for the advance release of funds for rural employment works, and additional edible oil imports were sanctioned.

But more important for the drought-threatened economy than these immediate measures was the prime minister's emphasis on drought-proofing through the creation of permanent assets that would help conserve water and improve irrigation. RG made several tours of drought-hit areas of Rajasthan and Gujarat, in particular, to supervise the construction of these 'permanent assets' and enquire if basic facilities were, in fact, being provided; whether wages were being disbursed on time; and whether strict vigilance was being maintained against malpractice. It was a signal to chief ministers that this had to be their own priority. He also urged state governments to associate voluntary agencies with drought relief work. Taking an even longer-term view, he stressed the key need for improved irrigation and watershed management, and warned against the rapid degradation of the environment, emphasizing the imperative of halting deforestation.

This was, of course, in addition to his visiting drought- and flood-hit areas in every affected state, sometimes at extremely short notice. I particularly remember his visiting during his lunch break (!) flood-hit Rajahmundry, on the banks of the raging, rampaging Godavari. He also traversed by road the entire length of the flood-ravaged Brahmaputra valley from Dibrugarh to Guwahati.

The Economy

Was Rajiv Gandhi a hidebound socialist or an early pioneer in the liberalization of the economy? Almost immediately after I joined the PMO in March 1985, the *Economist* of London sent down two correspondents to interview him. I sat in on the interview and saw his astonished expression when asked whether he believed in 'supply-side economics'! A few weeks later, I accompanied him to a meeting of the Confederation of Indian Industry where the chairman (an old Doon School buddy of the prime minister's) talked at length of 'India Inc'. While returning to South Block in his car, Rajiv Gandhi turned to me and asked quizzically, 'Do they really believe I am abandoning everything we have based ourselves on from Panditji's time?'

The fact is that Reaganism and Thatcherism were in vogue in the West. There was hope, even expectation, that in the young, modern-minded, Western-educated new Indian prime minister, the West had found its dream leader who would drag India out of the socialist camp (and, incidentally, out of the Soviet embrace as well) and into the glorious world of free enterprise. In fact, Rajiv Gandhi had no such intention. He recognized that changing times demanded changing policies. At the same time, he also recognized that times had changed only because of, and not in spite of, previous policies. Therefore, instead of throwing out the baby with the bathwater, as he was being urged to do by many Indian and world economists, some of his own economic experts, large swathes of the corporate sector, and the West (entirely unsolicited advice!), he emphasized 'adjustment' to contemporary times and not the overthrow of the past.

His line, as I understood it (many contemporaries will discount this view as being prejudiced by my own unredeemed faith in socialism) was that ours had never been an 'imported socialism'. We are indebted to neither Karl Marx nor the Utopian socialists of the nineteenth century. We are not even indebted to the twentieth-century Fabians. We had taken account of what they had to say and woven it into the wholly Indian concept of a 'socialistic pattern of society'. This uniquely Indian expression evolved between the Karachi Congress in 1931 (when 'socialism' was first underlined as basic to Congress philosophy) and the Avadi Congress in 1955, which had given rise to the expression 'socialistic pattern of society', that is, a planned 'mixed economy' in which the private sector continued to flourish but, owing to its relatively smaller size, the industrial economy would be dominated by a new public sector at the 'commanding heights' of the economy.[6] Under Nehru, few Indian enterprises were nationalized, a major exception being airlines. Most nationalization was resorted to with respect to private industrial and commercial entities (managing agencies) left behind by the departing Brits for which there were no Indian takers. (I had great difficulty in Baghdad explaining to bewildered Ba'athist Iraqis that Andrew Yule, Jessops and Balmer Lawrie were Indian public sector companies!)

Moreover, the 'licence permit raj' was introduced not because of addiction to state avarice, as has been often mis portrayed, but on account

---

[6] I would regard RG's two most important speeches on his economic policy as those he delivered in the Rajya Sabha and the Lok Sabha respectively on 17 and 18 December 1985, which may be found at pp. 147–61 of his *Selected Speeches and Writings*, Vol. I, 1984–85, brought out by the Publications Division, New Delhi in August 1987. It was in the Lok Sabha that he declared: 'Our goal is to develop a socialist society' (p. 159) but explained at length that times and circumstances change and so policies have to be appropriately adapted.

of the severe resource shortage in both domestic and external terms with which the country was faced in the mid-fifties, partly because of the priority accorded to building 'basic industry' such as steel, heavy electricals, petroleum, and fertilizer. Most important of all, massive land reforms were undertaken but agriculture (and allied activities) were left entirely in private hands.

That was 'Indian socialism'. Adjusting the mix of the public and private sectors was not some heroic 1991 revolution but part and parcel of a process that had been carried on since Independence. While questions of distribution were always in India allied to the important consideration of accelerated economic growth, the key consideration was that we would stick, come what may, to the democratic and constitutional path. There was no question of establishing a 'dictatorship of the proletariat' or any fascist suppression of fundamental rights in the quest for progress. True, there were some distortions that Rajiv Gandhi's predecessor PM had introduced into the Nehru model, but she herself had started unravelling some of her more extreme economic measures in her second coming, as foreseen in a brilliant little book written during the Emergency, *Economic Strategy for the 80s* by her favourite economic adviser, L.K. Jha, which is a kind of Deng Xiaoping tract for the Indian economy.[7]

India was always adjusting its economic policies to changing circumstances while strictly observing democratic and constitutional norms. Rajiv Gandhi continued and started intensifying that standard practice. Isolated quotations from Rajiv Gandhi can be used to buttress both sides of the argument. The authoritative version is perhaps to be found in Montek Singh Ahluwalia's *Backstage*, although it concentrates more on the Manmohan Singh phase starting mid-1991 after RG's assassination.[8]

---

[7] *Economic Strategy for the 80s: Priorities for the Seventh Plan*, Allied Publishers, New Delhi/Paris, 1980.
[8] *Backstage: The Story Behind India's High Growth Years*, Rupa, 2020.

I myself had nothing to do with economic policy formulation. That was Montek's domain (shared with an ideological opposite, the very Marxist Gopi Arora who betrayed his leftist tendencies whenever he used the word 'masses'!). I came in only after November 1985 as the draftsman of the PM's speeches. However, as my drafts went through the most rigorous emendations by his team of expert advisers and by the PM himself, the spoken text was definitely his and his alone. I find in my research of his speeches that his approach to economic policy was most succinctly articulated in his inaugural address to the Indira Gandhi Institute of Development Research set up by the Reserve Bank of India in Bombay on 28 December 1987. Montek accompanied us to Bombay, and as the speech was finalized in his presence on our flight there, I think it would be right to regard that speech as an authentic record of the PM's approach to economic policy in the late eighties.

Arguing that 'we have now come to the point in our development when it is especially important to stimulate new thinking', the prime minister went on to assert that it was 'the essence of good planning to set difficult targets and find ways of realizing them'.[9] Since 'the economy has become much larger than it was 20 years ago', he believed 'the nature of government regulation of industry must reflect these changes'. To this end, he urged 'the need to rationalize and simplify our regulatory system'. In these words might be found the genesis of the process of economic liberalization that was to make a huge impact on the country – and the world – a few years later.

Rajiv Gandhi, however, saw no contradiction between advocating economic reform and 'our commitment to socialism' which 'is unshakeable. Our socialism is our own. It is not a foreign transplant. It is not cast in someone else's ideological mould. It is rooted in our own history, our culture, our realities.' Jawaharlal Nehru's vision had been to transform

---

[9] The full text of this vitally important address may be found in the Publication Division's *Rajiv Gandhi: Selected Speeches and Writings*, 1987, Vol. III, pp. 139–43.

India into 'a modern industrial state assuring social justice and equality for all its citizens. That is our concept of socialism.'[10]

After his defeat at the end of 1989, RG closeted himself with a cabal of advisers led by V. Krishnamurthy to devise new economic policies for his return as PM. I was not included in the group and was never made privy to its proceedings, but I have been assured by some of the members that many of the reforms undertaken by Dr Manmohan Singh had their roots in the deliberations of that cabal. I only know that after I heard of the economic crisis in March 1991 from Dr Deepak Nayyar, chief economist in the finance ministry, I immediately carried the message to RG and he, in turn, asked me to call on Dr Manmohan Singh and request him to meet the Congress president. We will have to await Dr Singh's memoirs (if they are ever written or published) to learn the full extent of Rajiv Gandhi's endorsement of the reforms that were to follow his passing away.

See detailed footnotes and endnotes by
scanning the QR code above.

---

[10] In the course of our discussion, Rajiv Gandhi remarked that 'we are wedded to socialism'. I whispered to Montek, 'That's why we are getting screwed!'

5

Panchayat(i) Raj: The Defining Initiative

'I shall *work* for an India in which *the poorest* shall feel it is *their country* in whose making *they have an effective voice.*'

– Mahatma Gandhi, *Young India*, 10 September 1931

I have always felt the origins and substance of Panchayati Raj are to be found in these succinct words.[1] Please read the sentence again carefully, emphasizing in your mind the expressions in italics to get a full grasp of the significance of what Gandhiji was saying. The 'poorest' will have to feel it is 'their country' as it is 'their voice' that will have an 'effective' role in building the nation after Independence. That is the final goal of Panchayati Raj.

It was one of Gandhiji's greatest disappointments that the draft Constitution of India circulated by Dr Ambedkar in December 1947 did not contain even a passing reference to Panchayati Raj.[2] Eventually, after

---

[1] As there is some dispute among Hindi experts as to whether the right term is Panchayati Raj or Panchayat Raj, I use both expressions interchangeably.

[2] For a comprehensive exposition of Gandhiji's ideas on Panchayati Raj as the very foundation of the new republic, please see Sriman Narayan Agarwal, *A Gandhian Constitution for Independent India*, Kitab Mahal, Allahabad, 1946. Gandhiji wrote the preface, regretting that he did not have the time to pen the book himself but believed Sriman Narayan had accurately reflected his views.

debate in the Constituent Assembly, it was brought into the State List in November 1948 and made part of the non-binding Directive Principles of State Policy. I would, therefore, describe the Constitution as having brought into being a 'bourgeois democracy' that privileges the upper and middle classes, but severely limits the participation of the people, and especially the 'poorest', in the 'making of the nation'.

Nehru at first took little interest in the subject but realized as he embarked on his five-year plans that without a democratic, people-oriented administration at the grassroots, development could not be delivered at the last mile to the people. He set up a study group chaired by Balvantray Mehta,[3] and on the basis of its recommendations made the first attempt to spread Panchayat institutions through a model law passed by state legislatures in 1959. Nehru's vision for Panchayat Raj is best expressed in this indirect rendering of his own words: 'Panchayat Raj was the most revolutionary development in India because behind it were all the forces which, when released, would change the structure of the country.'[4]

But this initiative faded with Nehru's death in 1964. In 1977, the short-lived Morarji Desai government set up a committee under Asoka Mehta to revive Panchayati Raj but by the time its report came, the Janata government had fallen.[5] In 1986, Rajiv Gandhi introduced the idea of constitutional Panchayati Raj through amendments to the Constitution. To my mind, it is his most lasting contribution to this nation. The credit for this constitutional initiative goes entirely to Rajiv Gandhi although

---

[3] The name is often misspelt Balwant Rai.

[4] S. Gopal, *Jawaharlal Nehru: A Biography*, Vol. II, Oxford University Press, Delhi, 1989, pp. 398–401. The speech was delivered on 9 December 1960 at a meeting of state ministers of community development.

[5] Please see my short history of Panchayat Raj, 'Inclusive Governance for Inclusive Development: The History, Politics and Economics of Panchayati Raj', in Jean-Paul Faguet and Caroline Poschl (eds), *Is Decentralization Good for Development?*, Oxford University Press, Oxford, 2015, pp. 80–108.

many distinguished luminaries before and after him, starting with Mahatma Gandhi and Jawaharlal Nehru, and including Balvantray Mehta, Asoka Mehta and L.M. Singhvi, have made their respective path-breaking contributions to bringing grassroots democracy and grassroots development to the doorstep of every Indian, rural or urban.

I am privileged to have been associated intimately with the evolution and implementation of Panchayati Raj from the time of Rajiv Gandhi to the present. Apart from my work as a civil servant in drafting the constitutional amendments that were eventually numbered 73rd and 74th and included in the Constitution as Parts IX ('The Panchayats') and IXA ('The Municipalities'[6]) (the longest and most detailed amendments made to the Constitution since its proclamation in 1950), I worked on the passage of the amendments through Parliament (1991–92) and for more than a decade (1993–2003) both on the floor of the Lok Sabha and in the Joint Select Committee (1991–92), in both the Parliament Standing Committee for Rural Development (which dealt with Panchayat Raj) as well as from the Rajiv Gandhi Foundation (1991–2003) which prioritized the subject under a committee chaired by D. Bandyopadhyaya, former rural development secretary and later member of the Rajya Sabha. On behalf of the Rajiv Gandhi Foundation, and in consultation with the Bandyopadhyaya committee, I prepared a draft Action Plan and then undertook a journey around the country addressing over forty Congress conventions seeking endorsement of the draft, which drew from Sonia Gandhi, the President of the Congress, the encomium that 'it is truly remarkable that you have personally attended all the 40 conventions' and that 'this reflects your genuine dedication to the cause of panchayats'. She added that the Action Plan reflects 'your deep study of the subject and the sustained determination you have displayed'.[7]

---

[6] PM Rajiv Gandhi preferred the Hindi word 'nagarpalika' for 'municipalities' but eventually the Joint Select Committee of Parliament opted in 1992 for the English word.

[7] Letter dated 21 August 2003.

This was to result in her pressing for my inclusion as India's first-ever Cabinet Minister for Panchayat Raj in Dr Manmohan Singh's first government (2004–09). She did so in the face of some opposition from party hacks who never appreciated the significance of Panchayat Raj.

Later, Sonia suggested, and Dr Manmohan Singh approved, that I be designated chairman (2011–13) of the Expert Committee on Leveraging Panchayati Raj for the More Effective Delivery of Public Goods and Services. This Expert Committee produced a five-volume report, tantamount to an Encyclopaedia Panchayatica, which, however, moulders in forgotten cupboards since the Modi government assumed office in 2014 and has deleted the report from the website of the Panchayat Raj ministry. I propose including it in my personal website and hope the Congress will restore it and, more important, act on it as and when (and if) it comes to office again. However, I confess I am disappointed that the role of Panchayat Raj in radically rehauling governance in favour of people's participation has virtually dropped out of the current Congress vocabulary. This is despite Rahul Gandhi having assured me in March 2013, weeks after becoming vice chairman of the party, that whereas he was only '75 percent in agreement' with me earlier, 'now I think you are 100 per cent right'. He followed this up by picking me out of the audience in the AICC convention on 17 January 2014 to announce that my championing of Panchayat Raj showed me as just the kind of Congressman who gave hope for the future of the party.

That proved my swan song as the party's Panchayat Raj icon because in August 2013, I was requested by the party president to resign my post as national convenor of the Congress's Rajiv Gandhi Panchayat Raj Sangathan (2007–13) and for the past decade my continuing Panchayat Raj work has been transformed into a personal crusade, particularly in Karnataka and Kerala.

The fact remains that it was my close involvement with the drafting of the Panchayati Raj legislation that sparked off my opting out of the IFS to take up an alternative career in politics. This has made Panchayati Raj the definitive drumbeat of my life. I don't think any other foreign service diplomat would have made such a maverick transformation of his career.

In view of this, I hope the reader will bear with me as I take him/her through the long labyrinth of thought and action that has made Panchayat Raj ineluctable, irreversible and irremovable by giving constitutional status, sanction and sanctity for local self-government in our country.

Spread of Panchayati Raj

We now have about 2,60,000 institutions of democratically elected units of local self-government spread across our country. To these, we have elected some 3.2 million (32 lakh) representatives. About 6.5 lakh of these representatives and office bearers, as sarpanch or up-sarpanch, are from the Scheduled Castes (SCs) or Scheduled Tribes (STs). Moreover, almost half the representatives in local bodies, rural and urban – that is, about 1.4 million (14 lakh) – are women, some 1,00,000 of whom hold the post of chairperson or vice chair and include over 20,000 SC/ST women. The number of women democratically elected to positions and posts of responsible governance in India *is larger than the total number of elected women members in the rest of the world*!

Yet this astonishing political, social, economic, cultural, civilizational, and administrative revolution – arguably the most significant since freedom came at midnight – is not widely applauded or even acknowledged within the country. I suspect this is because it has not been matched by women's representation in our state legislatures and Parliament.[8] Elite women are, therefore, not much enthused by what has been achieved for and by their humbler sisters. Most unfortunately, the United Nations

---

[8] Although Parliament has passed legislation at its special session convened on 18 September 2023 to reserve seats for women in Parliament, the state assemblies, legal, constitutional, and administrative issues will probably push implementation to 2029 or even later.

Development Programme (UNDP) in its annual Human Development Report only takes account of the share of women in Parliament and the state assemblies, overlooking the social and political empowerment of 1.4 million women through reservations in the democratically elected local bodies. India would register an exponential jump on the index if elected women at the grassroots were included as a criterion for determining the extent of women's participation in national life.

The performance of these humble and often poor women from every social segment of our highly segmented society has been so impressive that while the Constitution mandates a minimum of 33 per cent reservation of seats and posts for women (while allowing states to raise that quota, if they wish) as many as twenty-one states, beginning with Bihar, have equalized the representation of men and women in their local bodies. It is time to ensure through a constitutional amendment that 33 per cent is raised to 50 per cent and made mandatory across the board. Also overdue is increasing in practice women's representation mandatorily through appropriate constitutional and legal amendments to ensure gender justice in the state legislatures and Parliament. Not until women's representation reaches these levels of proportion in the upper tiers of our democracy might we expect India to be regarded as home to the most outstanding example in the world of gender equality in democratic institutions of governance and government, assured and guaranteed through constitutional provisions.

SC/ST Reservations in PRIs

Equally, at every level of Panchayat Raj in both rural and urban local bodies, it has been constitutionally ensured[9] that elected SC representatives, and their share of representation in the local bodies,

---

[9] See Article 243D at Part IX of the Constitution.

reflect their share of the population *at each tier of the system* and that their overall share of reserved posts reflects their share of the population at the national level. Thus is 'elite capture' – the single most stinging criticism of local self-government in caste and gender discrimination-ridden rural society in India – sought to be elided. This also reconciles Mahatma Gandhi's impassioned advocacy of Panchayati Raj as the foundation of our democracy and Dr Ambedkar's equally impassioned opposition to village-based institutions which he regarded as 'sinks of localism' and 'dens of ignorance' and as 'the ruination of India' for their perpetuation of caste discrimination. Ambedkar's view of the Indian village was dismal:

> The existing village system has the effect of making the Scheduled Castes in the villages slaves of the caste Hindus ... Under the village system the Scheduled Castes are not allowed to live inside the village. They have to live on the outskirts ... They have no independent means of livelihood. They own no land ... They have to do forced labour day in and day out on pain of being driven away from their quarters by the Hindu landlords ... They have to live a life of degradation, dishonour, and ignominy from generation to generation. It is a state of eternal perdition.[10]

Rajiv Gandhi's unprecedented move to base the share of seats reserved for SCs/STs in proportion to their concentration at each of the three tiers of local self-government ensured due representation for SCs/STs at each tier and in posts of chairperson/vice chairperson. It reconciled the apparently irreconcilable and diametrically opposed perspectives of Mahatma Gandhi and Dr Ambedkar on village India.

As for the STs, they fall in three different clusters. First, states such as those in the north-east hills and Ladakh (listed in the Sixth Schedule) where they constitute nearly the entire population. Sixth Schedule areas

---

[10] Cited in Sukhdeo Thorat and Narender Kumar, *B.R. Ambedkar: Perspectives on Social Exclusion and Inclusive Policies*, Oxford University Press, New Delhi, 2008, pp. 270–72.

are exempted from the 73rd Amendment to enable their own local tribal governance systems to prevail. Second, there are concentrations of tribal populations in nine composite states identified in the Fifth Schedule of the Constitution where PESA – 'The Provisions of the Panchayats (Extension to Scheduled Areas) Act, 1996' applies, which exempts these tribal habitats from the 73rd Amendment and makes special provisions for exclusively tribal panchayats to act autonomously. And third, states other than these nine states where scattered ST habitations form an integral part of non-ST panchayat areas. In this third category, the same reservation provisions apply as to the SC.

PESA and Local Self-Government for States in Which They Constitute the Bulk of the Population

It may be particularly noted that PESA came about in consequence of the recommendations of an expert committee under the chairmanship of Dilip Bhuria, a tribal parliamentarian of long and respected standing. This resulted in the passage in December 1996 of The Provisions of the Panchayats (Extension to Scheduled Areas) Act – generally known by its acronym, PESA.

I regard PESA as the best example of conformity legislation in the country to give effect to the aims and objectives of the constitutional amendments incorporated in Part IX ('The Panchayats') because it provides for really effective and meaningful participation by the community as a whole in the executive functions of the tribal panchayats. This has been achieved primarily by making all decisions of the panchayat subject to approval by the gram sabha (village assembly) and the submission of Utilization Certificates (UCs)[11] also subject to explicit gram

---

[11] The UC, sent by the government official concerned under his authority and signature, is a key auditing device to satisfy the audit authorities that the sums have been duly appropriated through the prescribed process and have been spent properly for this

sabha approval – features not found in most state conformity legislation. Regrettably, but hardly surprisingly, most of the nine states concerned have been dragging their feet over embracing PESA in letter and spirit for the best part of the quarter-century since the legislation was brought on the nation's statute books.[12]

I am strongly of the view – which I expressed in the Rajya Sabha, leading to people of my ilk being dubbed as 'half Maoist' by Arun Jaitley, then leader of the Opposition in the Upper House – that had the tribal communities been genuinely empowered in Fifth Schedule areas, as provided in PESA, the Naxalite problem might not have spiralled into the nation's 'most dangerous internal security issue', as described by former PM Manmohan Singh, nor brought under relative control with so much cruelty, bloodshed, and crass commercial exploitation. (My riposte to Jaitley was declared 'unparliamentary' by Vice President Hamid Ansari and, therefore, cannot be published in this book, more's the pity!)

As for the tribal populations living in Sixth Schedule areas where they comprise an overwhelming majority, such as in most of the hill states of the north-east and Ladakh, the question of Panchayati Raj was considered in light of the imperative of safeguarding tribal ways of life, tribal customs, usage, and culture, as well as the fact of hallowed tribal self-government institutions that stretch back into the mists of time. Prime Minister Rajiv Gandhi, therefore, decided to exempt Sixth

---

particular purpose. It is believed that there is widespread misuse of the UC by officials because there is no check on them by the beneficiaries at large except under PESA, which statutorily requires the prior acceptance and approval of UCs by the tribal gram sabhas as being accurate and truthful.

[12] A study in Hindi of '25 Years of PESA', undertaken by Jitendra Chahar and Richa Pandey, and published by the National Foundation of India, was recently released at Constitution Club, New Delhi, and constitutes a thorough survey of progress – and the lack of it – in the last quarter-century in implementing PESA. One hopes the recently established National Tribal Research Institute, under the directorship of Dr Nupur Tiwary, at the Indian Institute of Public Administration, New Delhi, will particularly concentrate on propagating PESA.

Schedule areas that comprise principally tribal populations from the constitutional amendments for Panchayati Raj (unless, as in the case of Arunachal Pradesh, the state voluntarily opts to come in). This wise and compassionate approach was in a sense validated when the United Nations in 2007 held the local system of self-government in Nagaland to be among the most commendable in the world.

The origins of the largely silent revolution brought in by constitutional Panchayat Raj lie in RG's preoccupation with, and privileging of, 'responsive administration' as a key element of his governance agenda. Devolving economic and social development to empower the people – particularly women of the lower economic and social strata and, indeed, SC/ST men and women – to take control of their own lives and their economic and social development was the leitmotif of his domestic programme. (To this was added the OBC – Other Backward Classes – category at the penultimate stage of drafting the 64th and 65th amendments, not as mandatory but at the will of the state legislature concerned.[13])

Tours and Reflections

When he started out, RG appears to have regarded administrative reform as largely a managerial matter. He had been much impressed, as a general secretary of the Congress, by what a young collector had done in Ahmednagar to impart a human face to administration: the collector had opened a 'single window' in the collectorate where petitions could be handed in and responses received. The bane of most administrative offices is that the bewildered petitioner, who is usually little educated and socially overawed by the bureaucracy, wanders from desk to desk and office to office not knowing who will give him or her a hearing.

---

[13] Artcle 4D(6).

Securing a response, especially a constructive response, is a matter of 'Ram *bharose*' (trust in God). RG believed that contact with the people through a single window was an effective way of providing a people-oriented administration. A second innovation was a kind of Darbar-e-Aam (a public hearing) where, once a week, the collector would seat himself/ herself under the shade of a tree in the open with all the key officers in attendance and anyone – literally anyone – could come in and secure instant grievance redressal, or at least the promise of the matter being looked into with all deliberate speed.

As PM, RG began intensively touring the countryside (with me in tow). He was indefatigable. He met the most marginalized sections of society – the SCs, the forest-dwelling tribes, the denizens of urban slums – and also went to the geographically most distant regions – Lakshadweep and Minicoy; the villages of the Thar desert; the jungles of central India; the far reaches of the north-east.

He entered tiny huts, eating with relish their humble offerings, rarely making speeches, just listening to them. (The *Hindustan Times* described him as a modern-day Haroun al-Rashid.[14]) In the evenings, there would follow prolonged introspective sessions with local bureaucrats and political leaders. These conversations made clear to him the vast chasm separating the people from an administrative system allegedly designed to serve them. Four decades into freedom, the steel frame was as much in place as when the British, who devised it, were ruling the country. Was this, perhaps, the reason that the people felt almost as distant, even alienated, from their own democratically elected government as in colonial times, be it at the Centre or in the states?

Rajiv Gandhi's experiences as a constituency MP were reinforced

---

[14] As I believe is widely known, Haroun al-Rashid, the eighth-century Abbasid Caliph (Khalifa) would disguise himself to wander among his people to learn what they thought of his regime. This, I am given to understand by my publishers, is apparently not taught to the younger generation of Indians! (I would be happy to be corrected.)

by what he saw as PM of the political culture spawned by the absence of representative government at the grassroots. This was the political culture famously decried by him at the centenary session of the Congress (December 1985) where he tore into the 'brokers of power' – those who made a profession of interceding with the authorities on behalf of those without access to authority and ostensibly bridged the vast chasm between the elected representatives and the people. They may have succeeded in making the administration responsive to some but only because the administration was so cut off from the many – and the payment they extracted from hard-pressed beneficiaries for their intercession was usually high.

After about a year and scores of these tours, Rajiv Gandhi seems to have come to the recognition that managerial changes were not the answer; a thoroughgoing systemic change was required. It would be too much to expect the bureaucracy or local politicians on their own to undertake an institutional revolution for the people's active participation in their own welfare and development. The initiative would have to come from the Centre.

I got an early hint of how his mind was working when he accepted an invitation from the All-India Panchayat Parishad to address their inaugural session on 22 September 1986. Almost everything he said came extempore from his own head and heart, and not from my pen. The official English translation of his opening remarks in Hindi contains most of the key points that were to be elaborated over the next three years:

> The community must decide ... what activity would be most beneficial to it; what are the things that the central government must do, what the state governments must do, what can be taken up at the district level, and most important, what are things that the people must themselves do through the panchayats ... This task is for you, for the panchayats

to undertake. Till there is this involvement, [the] full benefits of the development schemes will continue to elude us.[15]

To the best of my knowledge, this is the first invocation of his campaign for 'inclusive development through inclusive governance'.[16]

For my part, I had been much taken with the idea of local self-government as an undergraduate at St Stephen's, largely because I found a Panchayati Raj enthusiast in my teacher for Indian economics, the colourful Professor Balbir Singh. More significant, however, was my experience of perhaps the world's best example of democratic decentralization during my most impressionable years in Brussels (1964–68 and 1973–76).

That city had no more than a million inhabitants. But their everyday needs were catered to by no less than nineteen 'communes' or municipalities. The commune office was just around the corner for everyone. Even passports were issued by the commune. There was also considerable local patriotism built around the commune – including a Brussels commune, Anderlecht, having one of the best football clubs in Europe, so much so that on one trip back from Dover to Ostend, I heard a cheeky young Belgian boy proudly reply to the British immigration officer who had asked him his nationality, 'Anderlecht'!

When, in my second spell in Brussels, we lived in Boisfort, the local commune brought out an artistically produced and heavily illustrated monograph tracing the history of the locality back to the twelfth century when it was a village. Thus is the community involved in building its identity and ensuring its welfare through its own locally elected representatives.

---

[15] *Rajiv Gandhi: Selected Speeches and Writings, 1986*, Vol. II, *op. cit.*, pp. 45–54.

[16] The title of a major paper by me, frequently referred to in academic discussion of the subject and widely popularized by me in public discourses.

Although Belgium is riven by linguistic and cultural divisions between the Flemish-speaking Flamand and the French-speaking Walloon, the country remains united because the principal interaction that the Belgian citizens have with governmental authority is the friendly local commune, where they are received with courtesy, given the most personal attention, and offered, to the extent possible, instant redressal. In short, a 'responsive administration'. This is what Rajiv Gandhi's Panchayati Raj seemed to me to be about.

Workshops with District Magistrates[17]

The PM embarked next on a programme of face-to-face interaction with district magistrates, drawn from every district in the land. At the very first of these workshops, in Bhopal on 10 December 1987, he voiced his concern that 'no matter what earth-shattering decisions or directions we give from the top, the implementation and delivery is at the district level' yet 'the lower level, where the delivery takes place, has generally been neglected or ignored'.[18] It started to dawn on him that the best of our administrators felt handicapped by the absence at the grassroots of any machinery for determining the will of the people. Interestingly, the dullards among the DMs insisted they could work best patriarchally, without consulting the people; they believed the ordinary people were illiterate or semi-educated, riven by class, caste, and communal prejudices, and could not make an intelligent contribution to welfare or development. Administration in a democratic country was being carried on without

---

[17] Also designated in some states 'collectors' or 'deputy commissioners'.

[18] *Rajiv Gandhi: Selected Speeches and Writings, 1987,* Vol. III, Publications Division, p. 122. The full texts of these mind-forming addresses at this and the next four workshops are essential reading for scholars and others interested and may be perused at pp. 120–29 of Vol. III and pp. 134–72 of Vol. IV of his *Selected Speeches and Writings* published by the Publications Division.

effectively consulting the people, or their elected representatives, on issues that most immediately impacted them.

At the second workshop, held at Hyderabad's National Institute of Rural Development (now renamed the National Institute of Rural Development and Panchayati Raj), the proceedings were conducted by the director, a Panchayati Raj enthusiast called Dr M. Shivaiah. That is where the shift from 'managerial to systemic' solutions was mooted and approved. At the Hyderabad workshop (13 February 1988), RG underlined the point that 'Development is being hampered by the dependency syndrome. The people in general today are just waiting for the government to do something, even waiting for government to do the simplest things which they can do themselves.' So 'how do we enthuse the local community? How do we involve the local community?'[19] His mind was inching towards the conclusion that the problems of a non-responsive administration were intimately linked to directly empowering the people so as to marginalize and, hopefully, eliminate the power brokers. This systemic solution became his priority, and he started working out the parameters in his mind.

This understanding transformed the workshops and led to a truly seminal breakthrough. In focusing on Panchayati Raj as the systemic answer to deficiencies in our governance, Rajiv Gandhi did not lay any claim to originality. On the contrary, he was intrigued by the failure of Panchayati Raj to take root despite being the fundamental prescription of Mahatma Gandhi, and a priority for Jawaharlal Nehru. Why had the recommendations of Sriman Narayan Agarwal, Balvantray Mehta, Asoka Mehta and L.M. Singhvi not taken root? Why had democracy at the grassroots so palpably failed when, equally palpably, democracy at the Centre and in the states had taken such deep root? Was this because provisions for Panchayat Raj in the Constitution were so rudimentary,

---

[19] *op. cit.*, Vol. IV, pp. 135–36.

especially compared to the reams and reams to ensure democracy at higher levels?

At the third workshop, on 2 April 1988 in Imphal, Manipur, RG talked of 'one of the fears that keeps being thrown up . . . is that the stronger groups, whether they may be at the village or district level, tend to take over and the weaker sections are just bullied'. The answer, he felt, lay in elections for 'if you have regular elections, then elections at the local level really break across these barriers'.[20] Assured local elections, with reservations for the weaker sections (including reservations for women) would obviously require changes in the Constitution. I think it was then that he started coming to the conclusion that the answer lay in amendments to our Constitution to bring in Panchayati Raj on a durable basis. Democracy, he underlined in conversations with me, flourished at Delhi and in state capitals because the Constitution made detailed provisions for the institution and protection of democracy at these levels. But the same Constitution treated local government in a most perfunctory manner, confining all mention of the subject to a mere three lines – and that too only in the non-binding Directive Principles of State Policy.

Since the responsibility for Panchayati Raj was vested in the political will of the states, it was the tug and pull of political compulsions in state capitals that determined the fate of Panchayati Raj. Most states had played ducks and drakes with grassroots self-governance. A few – Gujarat and Maharashtra, for example – had not. West Bengal under Jyoti Basu, and Andhra Pradesh under NTR, had introduced many useful innovations in local self-government. So, above all, had Karnataka under Chief Minister Ramakrishna Hegde and the minister for rural development, Abdul Nazir Sahib. The solution lay in making Panchayati Raj as much a constitutional obligation as for democracy in Parliament or state assemblies.

---

[20] *Ibid.*, pp. 150–51.

At the fourth workshop, held in Jaipur on 30 April 1988, RG explained the way forward lay in giving 'meaningful content to our basic equation, namely, that Representativeness and Responsibility (to the electorate) equal Responsiveness'.[21] This was the 'Three R' formula that encapsulated his vision.

The fifth and last workshop was held in Coimbatore on 5 June 1988. RG arrived after midnight at the end of one of the most exhausting tours I had ever experienced. We had commenced at 7 a.m. driving from Erode through north-west Tamil Nadu. The concluding public rally ended late at night, just before the PM entered the workshop. The participants must have been surprised at the vigour and zeal he displayed. After finishing his inaugural remarks, in which he stressed 'the pace at which democratic decentralization must reach below the zila parishad level to the mandal panchayat and gram sabhas',[22] he returned to his metronomic invocation of the 'three R' formula by asking for 'proposals for making our district administration more representative, more responsible and, therefore, more responsive'.[23] He then joined each of the working groups in turn until 3 a.m. although departure next morning was scheduled at 6 a.m. Such was his dedication to the cause.

I can go into much more detail to explain the process to demonstrate that no Indian prime minister ever before or since has involved himself or herself in such detail in a major reform of governance at the grassroots,[24]

---

[21] *Ibid.*, p. 164.

[22] *Ibid.*, p. 168.

[23] *Ibid*, p. 170.

[24] Interested readers (especially research scholars) are invited to look up the texts of all his key Panchayati Raj addresses at workshops, seminars, and symposia, and Parliament (both Houses) in the five indexed volumes of his *Selected Speeches and Writings* brought out annually by the Government's Publication Division, particularly Volumes IV and V, or many of them on this book's website https://www.rajivmisunderstood.com, which may be accessed by scanning the QR code at the end of the chapter, or by perusing the 'Panchayat Raj' section of his *Selected Speeches and Writings, 1989*, pp. 131–72.

but as this is not a treatise but a book for general readers, I shall restrain myself. A pointer is that the Panchayati Raj amendment is the longest and most detailed constitutional amendment.

Bringing around Others

Rajiv Gandhi quickly discovered that his quest for such a systemic revolution was a rather lonely one. Few of the senior administrators he consulted shared his perception of the imperative need for root-and-branch reform of administration at the grassroots. Even principal officers in the PMO – bar me – were sceptical or uninterested. Few of his political colleagues shared his enthusiasm for radical change. In state capitals, there was positive hostility to what was correctly seen as a move that would rob state ministers and state legislators of many of their (arbitrary) powers.

And the Opposition, by and large, condemned the workshops as an unacceptable transgression of states' rights and described RG's Panchayati Raj plans as an insincere political gimmick designed to distract the attention from Bofors. He, therefore, mounted a major campaign to build a nationwide consensus on what he came to see as the single most important platform of his agenda for taking India into the twenty-first century.

Apart from regional conventions of general local bodies' representatives drawn from all over the country, and separate conventions for women, SCs and STs, the prime minister also set in place a subcommittee of the Consultative Committee attached to the ministry of personnel, under the chairmanship of P.K. Thungon, a long-standing MP from Arunachal Pradesh. The report of that subcommittee became the basis for the next stage of the campaign.

A working group of the Congress Parliamentary Party was constituted to elicit back-bench reaction. The theme was taken up in public speeches and party forums. Meanwhile, some of the more positively inclined members of the Planning Commission were informally drafted into fleshing out the concept. And the Council of Ministers was sensitized into an appreciation of the significance of the endeavour.

It was not until the last days of December 1988 that Rajiv Gandhi felt the coast to be sufficiently clear to ask the Department of Rural Development (then part of the Ministry of Agriculture) to begin the exercise of drafting what was then numbered the 64th constitutional amendment. He made sure the exercise was not reduced to bureaucratic or legal technicalities by putting the same officials who were doing the drafting in charge of organizing face-to-face interactions between the head of the Union government and the people's representatives; it was undoubtedly the most profound attempt ever made at understanding the perceptions of the people through such means. In all, it was estimated that the PM interacted with some 25,000 people over this amendment. Never before or since has there been such close interaction on a legislative matter between a prime minister and the generality of the population.

The guidelines given to the drafting group constituted under the chairmanship of the rural development secretary, Vinod Pande, were to prepare as detailed constitutional provisions as were required but not to alter the constitutional place of Panchayati Raj, namely, its position in the State List. In other words, the proposed amendment would ensure full constitutional sanction, sanctity, and safeguards to the institutions of local government in rural India but would leave it to the states to work out the modalities for decentralization and devolution through conformity legislation in the state assemblies.

Above all, it was the revolutionary proposal on reservations for SCs/STs that led to disquiet among several of his own most senior cabinet members, particularly my former boss, Dinesh Singh. The PM asked me to put together a motley group of ministers, including SC, ST and 'savarna' (higher-caste) ministers holding contradictory views for him to discuss his unconventional and unprecedented plans for SC/ST reservations. The meeting was to be followed by dinner.

I did as I was instructed. We gathered in 7, Race Course Road at the designated time and gave ourselves over to stilted small talk as we waited for RG to arrive. To my astonishment, a message came through asking me to start the meeting.

It was unprecedented for a mere joint secretary to chair a meeting of cabinet ministers, but orders were orders, so I cleared my throat and started. After we had discussed the issue for about an hour in the PM's absence, another message came that the PM would be unable to join the meeting but would join us for dinner on the lawns when we had concluded our deliberations. Dinesh Singh was the first to understand that this was RG's way of signalling that they should shape up or ship out. After the SC/ST ministers had had their say, all speaking in favour of the PM's position, Dinesh Singh wound up the meeting saying I should inform the PM that all ministers were agreed that his plans should be put through. Rajiv Gandhi then joined us for dinner!

'May' and 'Shall'

From then on, I became the PM's principal envoy on Panchayat Raj issues to senior Congress leaders (and some Opposition luminaries, especially non-Congress chief ministers). I informed them about what RG wanted and acted as the feedback channel for the expression of their doubts and dissent. I realized that I was crossing the thin line of propriety between a civil servant's role and that of a political appointee; yet I felt this was an opportunity to seize even if it meant burning my bridges to the IFS. Indeed, when a front-page photograph appeared of me addressing a meeting of the Congress Working Committee, my neighbour, Mahesh Prasad, a senior IAS officer, called me to warn that I was putting my career in jeopardy. I admitted that – but I was not unduly concerned.

The PM's principal guideline was, in Law Secretary P.C. Rao's words at the Golden Jubilee retrospective in 1994: 'Don't give an impression that we are taking over local government whereas the constitutional mandate is that it be left to the State governments. We should not give the impression to anybody that through this amendment, we are taking over the subject.'[25]

To me, the PM remarked that as the Sarkaria Commission had just given its report on Centre–State relations, he wanted to go ahead with implementing Justice Sarkaria's recommendations aimed at strengthening the federal features of the Constitution and was concerned that the wrong signal might go out to state capitals if we were to overstep the mark in drafting the constitutional amendments relating to Panchayati Raj. He also did not want attention to be diverted to jurisdictional disputes between the two upper tiers, the Union government, on the one hand, and the state governments, on the other. His focus was on setting up and empowering the third tier of government.

The law secretary tried to reconcile these contradictory pulls by using the word 'shall' when it was mandatory and 'may' for the recommendatory provisions. When, in our group, anyone suggested that 'may' be substituted by 'shall', Rao would smooth ruffled feathers by holding that in the Constitution 'may' equalled 'shall'. One jurist who was not mollified by this explanation was Madan Bhatia, who had been Indira Gandhi's lawyer in her post-Emergency trials and had been rewarded with three successive terms in the Rajya Sabha. One afternoon, Bhatia exited the PM's office, with a thunderous look, muttering imprecations. I went in and asked the PM what all that was about. RG replied that he had shared with Bhatia the law secretary's view that in the Constitution 'may' equalled 'shall'. Madan Bhatia was furious at what he regarded as a travesty of correct jurisprudence.

---

[25] *Rajiv Gandhi's India: A Golden Jubilee Retrospective*, UBSPD, Delhi, 1997, Vol.1, *op.cit.*, p. 18.

Three decades later, I must say I have to agree with Bhatia that our attempt to treat 'may' as 'shall', especially with regard to effective devolution as a constitutional obligation, never really took off and even attempts to hold states to their own conformity legislation have not met with success. Law Secretary Rao may have been correct in law, but political exigencies are almost impossible to counter with legal arguments alone. So, looking back, we have in place all the mandatory 'shall' provisions but the 'may' provisions are suspended in a kind of limbo between applicable law and implementation. Yet, had we persisted with 'shall', the worst might have happened: the issue would have been converted into a tussle over states' rights instead of attention being focused on creating and empowering a third tier of what Article 243G unambiguously describes as 'local self-government' (not 'governance').

Rajiv Gandhi was also in dialogue with his senior party and cabinet colleagues, as well as Congress CMs and Opposition CMs, especially Jyoti Basu of West Bengal and Ramakrishna Hegde of Karnataka, and, to some extent, N.T. Rama Rao of Andhra Pradesh, who all ran innovative and estimable schemes of Panchayati Raj in their respective states. Serving and retired civil servants who had distinguished themselves in rural development were brought within the net of consultations. The questions arising were then put to the drafting group through me or directly when the PM personally interacted with the drafting group.

Loopholes

Some key questions remained unasked and unanswered. What should be the ideal size of a village panchayat (it varies today from 2,000 in Punjab to 30,000 in Kerala)? And what should be the role and functions of the gram sabha comprising all adult voters of the village and to whom should the elected members be responsible? We also failed to ask the question that has come to haunt the whole process: how to prevent Panchayat

Raj from becoming Sarpanch Raj. Was the sarpanch (the president of the panchayat) to be an independent authority or was he/she required to carry other members of the panchayat with her/him? What, in other words, was to be the role of the panchs? Were they to function as a collective or as individual representatives trying to secure what they could for their wards?

We also failed to fully examine and appropriately incorporate the mechanism for effective devolution and meaningful planning for economic development and social justice, having decided that this might be best left to states to determine. When I became India's first Union minister for Panchayati Raj (2004–09), I tried to fill this lacuna by circulating, through the Planning Commission, guidelines for district planning, prepared by the brilliant V. Ramachandran, vice chair of the Kerala Planning Board. Apart from Kerala's remarkable initiative in 'People's Planning', no other state has made satisfactory arrangements for planning at the grassroots to meet local priorities for development and welfare and social justice. Is this the fault of federalism being limited to the relationship of the Centre to the states? Or should 'cooperative federalism' extend the relationship of the Union and states to the third tier of self-government, that is, the panchayats, under the 73rd Amendment and to urban local bodies (for which Rajiv Gandhi preferred the expression 'nagarpalikas') under the 74th? And to ensure a measure of equity in the evolution and progress of local self-government, should rural and urban self-government have been placed in the rubric of a single ministry of panchayats and nagarpalikas at the Union level and a common department of local government at the state level, as has been the practice in Kerala, arguably the most advanced state in local self-government?

The failure to ask and answer these questions has vitiated the election process in most states, leading to the exercise of political muscle power and widespread misuse of money power in panchayat elections, inevitably resulting in high levels of corruption and nepotism.

The key question to which the PM had an unambiguous answer was that law and order must vest in the district magistrate and not be devolved to the panchayats. The panchayats must have devolved powers only in respect of planning, economic development, and social justice. Moreover, the process of devolution was left to be decided and determined by state governments, subject only to the constitutional fiat that on all subjects devolved, the process of devolution must be such as to render the panchayats 'units of self-government', not mere implementation agencies of state governments. (Article 243G is the heart of the amendment and, as such, is reproduced in the note.[26])

Finalizing the Draft

The drafting group's tentative answers to questions were transmitted to and from the PM by me. Among other directives, he instructed us to look carefully at the proposed devolution list in L.M. Singhvi's annex to the 1979 Asoka Mehta Report; the 13th Amendment to the Sri Lanka Constitution that detailed the subjects for devolution to the Tamil provinces; and the devolution list in the Darjeeling Accord. He also told us to consult Dr Balakrishnan, legal counsel to the home ministry, who had prepared the famous Annexure C to the accord negotiated by Indira Gandhi's special envoy, G. Parthasarathi, with Sri Lanka (later rejected by Sri Lanka).

---

[26] 243G. Powers, Authority and Responsibilities of Panchayats: Subject to the provisions of this Constitution, the Legislature of a State may, by law, endow the panchayats with such powers and authority as may be necessary to enable them to function as institutions of self-government and such law may contain provisions for the devolution of powers and responsibilities upon panchayats at the appropriate level, subject to such conditions as may be specified therein, with respect to –
    (a)   the preparation of plans for economic development and social justice;
    (b)   the implementation of schemes for economic development and social justice as may be entrusted to them including those in relation to the matters listed in the Eleventh Schedule.

When we were at the penultimate stage of our endeavours, he called in the group to look at the draft Eleventh Schedule which illustratively listed the subjects for devolution to the panchayats. We entered the PM's room fairly confident that we had got it right. I do not think anyone expected RG to go through the list with as fine a toothcomb as he did, weighing every word and every line as if he were weighing diamonds to determine their carat value! When he came to 'bridges', the PM asked, 'Why only bridges? Aren't culverts even more important in villages?' I saw Rural Development Secretary Vinod Pande's eyes open wide with wonderment. That, I think, was the moment when Vinod, who was very close to V.P. Singh and Murali Manohar Joshi of the BJP, began to see merit in Rajiv Gandhi.

The text was eventually ready to the PM's satisfaction by mid-April 1989 after undergoing 120 drafts (as estimated by Law Secretary P.C. Rao who, with Legal Secretary Rama Devi, did the legal drafting)![27]

In consultation with the Lok Sabha speaker, RG fixed 15 May as the date for the introduction of the bill. He decided to convene the Chief Ministers of all states at a conclave in Delhi a week in advance of 15 May to try to bring them all on board. Most accepted; a few sent their representatives. The Congress CMs had been asked to come a day earlier so as to be prepared to respond to their more recalcitrant non-Congress counterparts. They gathered in Krishi Bhawan under the chairmanship of the minister of agriculture and rural development, Bhajan Lal. Bhajan Lal soon yielded the floor to me, and I proceeded to outline the main features of the draft and explain the reasons why the PM regarded this

---

[27] Scholars and others interested are invited to go through the entire proceedings of the Panchayati Raj section (pp. 1–82) of the second volume ('Economics') of the Golden Jubilee retrospective subtitled *People in Democracy and Development*. Unfortunately, the publishers, UBSPD, have wound up their firm and so the four volumes are available only at the Rajiv Gandhi Foundation, Jawahar Bhawan, New Delhi (website: www.rgfindia.org) or in select libraries.

bill as his government's most important legislation. Once I finished, almost everyone thanked me and rose to go.

There was one exception: Sharad Pawar, chief minister of Maharashtra. He said that while he was satisfied with the briefing, he would like to know what arguments were likely to be raised against it by non-Congress chief ministers. I flagged such possible arguments. Sharad was not through. He asked me to provide the counterarguments to rebut the points I had mentioned. I obliged as best as I could. Very courteously, he thanked me for a comprehensive briefing and took his leave. Bhajan Lal was left beaming.

Next morning, the plenary of all CMs was held in Vigyan Bhawan. Once everyone was seated, the PM said he wanted a freewheeling discussion, not the reading of prepared speeches. I was told to gather all the prepared speeches, including the PM's own, while the CMs were assured that all their pre-prepared interventions would be brought on record.

While the oral discussions proceeded, I rifled through the prepared speeches and was horrified to find that the one Congress CM adamantly opposed to the Panchayat Raj constitutional amendment bill was none other than Sharad Pawar! I slipped up to him and asked whether he would want to substitute his speech with another as it went completely contrary to the PM's line. He shook his head and said those were his true views and nothing he had heard had persuaded him to change them. At the lunch break, I took the PM aside to forewarn him. He merely smiled and said he had been expecting Pawar to take this stand. Also, did I not think this would help convince non-Congress CMs that this was really a meeting to ascertain diverse views and not a military *patti parade* (Hindi for the fallout at a military parade)?

Another major development at the CMs' meeting was RG's prompt acceptance of UP CM Narayan Dutt Tiwari's proposal that as half the Indian population was likely to be urban early in the twenty-first century, something should be done to bring urban local bodies under the umbrella of a similar system as the rural panchayats. With the PM's vigorous efforts, the 65th Amendment (which eventually became the 74th Amendment) was drafted within a few weeks and introduced in the Lok Sabha at the start of the monsoon session in July 1989 by Mohsina Kidwai, urban development minister. A detailed (and at times hilarious account) of how that bill came to be drafted (and my role in it) has been provided by K.C. Sivaramakrishnan, urban development secretary, in his memoir.[28]

It was now time to draft the PM's speech for Parliament. It had seen in some ways a smoother passage than many other set speeches – largely, I suspect, because the IAS officers involved were not 'merchants of words' like their IFS counterparts. But the PM was pernickety as ever. In the afternoons, when he was supposed to be taking a break for lunch and a siesta, he would call me on the RAX (the secret phone used for inter-office connection at the highest levels of government) and, taking one sentence or two at a time, tell me why it did not exactly convey what he wanted to say. Sometimes whole passages would have to be rewritten; others deleted; yet others written in. I think this was not merely a matter of getting sentences right but also of absorbing the thoughts. At the end of this exercise, he would have so internalized the speech as to make it truly *his* speech.

As I explained in my memoirs, it was about 2 a.m. on the intervening night of 14–15 May when he finally signed off on his speech. I continued sitting in the 7 RCR conference room transferring the speech on to prompt cards, as was the usual practice, marking with a slash in pencil where it might be best to pause and with a yellow highlighter the word that, in my view, he should emphasize. Then, the internal phone rang. Normally, the faithful V. George would pick it up. But he was not

---

[28] *Power to the People? The Progress and Politics of Decentralization*, Sage, New Delhi, 2000.

immediately available. So, I picked it up and said, 'Yes, sir?' Astonished that I was still around, Rajiv asked, 'What are you doing here so late?' It was my golden opportunity. Gravely I intoned: 'While the world sleeps, India awakes to life and freedom!'

He laughed and ordered me to bed.

Let me briefly outline the principal points of the bill:

- Making it constitutionally mandatory to have a democratically elected three-tier panchayat system responsible to gram sabhas comprising the entire adult population in a village-level panchayat.
- Securing 30 per cent reservations for women at all three levels of the panchayats – village; intermediate (block/taluka); and district (later raised to a third).
- Ensuring reservations for SCs and STs (and sub-quotas for women of these social categories) in accordance with their share of the population at each of the three levels.
- Complementing this for STs with a provision for the governors of states with tribal Fifth Schedule areas to modify state conformity legislation after consulting tribal representatives on any matter of special concern (later converted into central legislation for Panchayat Raj in tribal areas – PESA Act, 1996).
- Exempting Sixth Schedule states (that is, states with overwhelming tribal majorities) with their own traditional systems of local self-government, unless they opted in of their own volition (as Arunachal Pradesh did).
- Guaranteeing regular, timely elections to panchayats, organized by an independent, qualified, statutory State Election Commission guided by the Central Election Commission (later the Central Election Commission was dropped).
- Ending arbitrary suspensions and dissolutions of local bodies and their members by state governments by ensuring that by-elections

for any suspended body or member would be held within six months of dissolution/dismissal.
- Exponentially increasing the number of elected representatives relative to the size of the electorate with a view to bridging the gap between the elected and the electors, thus bringing governance to the grassroots, the better to ensure inclusive growth through inclusive governance.
- Listing illustratively in the Eleventh Schedule the possible subjects for devolution to PRIs.
- Detailing by law and administrative orders the responsibilities of the different tiers of PRIs.
- Widening and deepening, through laws passed by state legislatures, opportunities for the deployment of India's vast human resources by empowering panchayats to function as 'institutions of self-government', *not mere self-governance*, in regard to the 'preparation of plans for economic development and social justice' (bottom-up planning) and for 'implementing schemes ... as may be entrusted to them'.[29]
- Linking economic development to social justice, particularly with a view to meeting concerns of elite capture of PRIs.
- Establishing district planning committees, with the chair automatically entrusted to the president of the zila (district) panchayat (this was brought in through the 65th Amendment on nagarpalikas – or urban local bodies).
- Securing the 'sound finance of the Panchayats' through State Finance Commissions, to determine the apportionment of state revenues between the state and its panchayats; the assignation of sources of revenue to the panchayats, including those that may be 'appropriated'

---

[29] Article 243G, the core of the legislation. The language of the Constitution amendments being very legalistic, an attempt has been made in this section to explain key points in ordinary English, interspersed with quotations taken from the text of the amendment.

by the panchayats for their own use; and 'grants-in-aid to the Panchayats from the Consolidated Funds of the State'.
- Subjecting the panchayats to social audit through the gram sabhas and NGO facilitation in gram sabha meetings besides formal audit under the overall aegis of the Centre's CAG (the latter provision was ultimately dropped, to the great detriment of fiscal propriety in the panchayats).

The constitutional amendment for urban local bodies – initially 65th, later 74th – was on similar lines with some modifications, particularly on spatial planning and metropolitan corporations. Unfortunately, the Parliamentary Select Committee, set up after Rajiv Gandhi's death to examine the 65th Amendment bill, dropped the original provision that district planning committees should invariably be headed by the zila panchayat president. This has materially affected the independent choice of panchayats on their planning priorities, especially as the local MP/MLA or even the local district minister [appointed by the state government to be in charge of a district] has been made chair of the district planning committee, thereby significantly eroding the autonomy of the local bodies in planning their own economic development and plans for social justice.

On 15 May 1989, the PM introduced the bill in the Lok Sabha. I was in ecstasy as I took my place in the officers' gallery with everyone making place for me as the star of the show. I was, at the same time, anxious, wondering how it would all go down with the members. But, above all, I felt I was at our second 'tryst with destiny', as this was, in my view, the single most historic amendment to the Constitution – and I had been part and parcel of this momentous development.

In a long speech,[30] the PM covered all the specifics of the bill, describing 'devolution and sound finance' as 'the heart of the matter'. He finished with a rousing peroration: 'We trust the people. We have faith in the people. It is the people who must determine their own destinies . . . To the people of India, let us ensure Maximum Democracy and Maximum Devolution. Let there be an end to the power-brokers. Let us give power to the people.'

The speech was heard out in unusual silence, with few of the standard disruptions. The huge Congress majority held. I received my share of the plaudits. But the Rajya Sabha was the real hurdle to be cleared.

Between the introduction of the bill on the last day of the budget session and the start of the monsoon session in July at which the bill was to be debated and passed, there occurred the deliberate and engineered leakage of the report of the CAG on the acquisition of the Bofors gun.[31] The Opposition made the CAG report the excuse to walk out of the Lok Sabha on the eve of what was to be the last monsoon session of Parliament, although they clung, as RG said, 'like limpets' to their chairs in the Rajya Sabha. (There was a howl of protest, that continues to this day, for my having suggested the simile to PM. It was not mine but pinched from P.G. Wodehouse!) This gave easy passage to the bill in the Lok Sabha but pointed to the difficulties that might be encountered in the Rajya Sabha where the Congress did not enjoy what the Opposition called a 'brute majority' as in the Lok Sabha.

The decision to make Panchayati Raj the campaign theme for the next general elections had been taken when P. Chidambaram and I were with

---

[30] Major extracts from the speech, essential reading for anyone interested in the subject, are included in the website https://www.rajivmisunderstood.com, which can be accessed by scanning the QR code at the end of the chapter, or by looking up his speech in his *Selected Speeches and Writings*, Vol. V, put out by the Publications Division, pp. 167–77.

[31] Covered in detail in the section on Bofors in chapter 2: 'The Controversies'.

the PM on the flight to and from Manipur on 2 April 1988 to attend the third DMs workshop in Imphal. When, later in 1988, RG decided to shift the responsibility for drafting the constitutional amendment from the Department of Personnel to the Department of Rural Development, that is, from Chidambaram to Bhajan Lal, I got the impression that PC was somewhat miffed. Certainly, he complained to me on seeing the draft amendment that this was no way to write an amendment to the Constitution – as if it were municipal law rather than constitutional law (a point also made by Law Minister Shiv Shankar). I carried PC's argument to the PM who dismissed it saying there had been plenty of time for PC to have raised the issue with him earlier and it was now too late to recommence the drafting exercise. I did not want to get into the crossfire and so just dropped the subject.

The Denouement

Now that the bill had crossed the first hurdle, the PM decided the Rajya Sabha vote would be called by 14 August, win or lose, so that he could use the platform on Independence Day to either laud the passage of the bills, or to regret their non-passage, as decided in the Rajya Sabha, and promise that after the next election, the two bills would be taken up again for implementation or passage by Parliament, as the case may be, in the expectation that people were keen on their own empowerment. Panchayati Raj was thus to be made the central issue in the forthcoming general elections. In anticipation of the vote in the Rajya Sabha, I had been instructed to work with the ministers concerned (Margaret Alva in Women and Child Development and my old boss, H.K.L. Bhagat in I&B) to bring to Delhi a large number of Anganwadi workers from all over the country who would be seated right in front of the PM; the VIP enclosure would not be up front as usual, but shifted to the side for the VIPs/diplomatic corps to be accommodated elsewhere. Media cameras would be perched to the side of the vanguard of the crowd, so as to not be in the way of a clear view for the anganwadi workers of the ramparts from where the PM would be delivering his Independence Day address.

Meanwhile, the PM's principal political advisers, R.K. Dhawan and M.L. Fotedar, busied themselves suborning these arrangements. They argued the PM's prestige would suffer if he were to lose the Rajya Sabha vote and, therefore, sought to expel from the Rajya Sabha V.P. Singh's supporters, led by Satyapal Malik, who were transgressing the anti-defection provisions of the Tenth Schedule by refusing the Congress whip. Most unfortunately – in my view (that counted for nothing) – Dhawan and Fotedar succeeded in persuading Rajiv Gandhi to postpone the Rajya Sabha vote until after the defectors had been replaced by loyalists in by-elections. They also contacted, or were contacted by, an AIADMK dissident from Tamil Nadu, Valampuri John, who apparently promised five Dravidian votes in favour of the amendments, enough, the PM's political advisers calculated, to enable the bills to inch their way past the Rajya Sabha.

A mundane Independence Day address followed, leaving the anganwadi workers puzzled but proud at having been invited to Delhi. Instead of carrying the message of Panchayati Raj to the people, they spent their time in Delhi seeking additional remuneration for themselves.

The Rajya Sabha began debating the proposed 64th and 65th amendments together on 18 August and, after the Rajya Sabha was reconvened after a break, the debate spread over three days, 11–13 October. The auguries were not happy. The Opposition were opening up with all their guns blazing. They only had to secure a third of the votes to defeat the amendments and it was clear the decision rested on a razor's edge.

The principal arguments of the Opposition were summed up in Sivaramakrishnan's book: decentralization was not a matter of 'constitutional amendment but of political will and political leadership'

(M.S. Gurpadaswamy); devolution to the local bodies needs to be 'preceded, or at least accompanied by devolution from the Centre to the states' (P. Upendra); the amendments reflected a lack of trust in state governments, 'many of which had done a good job in promoting Panchayati Raj' (also Upendra); the exercise was 'nothing more than an election gimmick' designed 'to correct the declining image of the Prime Minister' (L.K. Advani); the bills were the declaration 'of a "virtual war" on states' (Murasoli Maran); 'the philosophy behind the measures is undesirable, the timing and motivation highly objectionable', and the manner of presentation and projection 'almost obscene' (Ram Jethmalani); the bills 'pass on all the responsibilities to the states but curtail their rights' (Chitta Basu); 'setting up State Finance Commissions without a provision of devolution from the Consolidated Fund of India is meaningless' (Chaturanand Mishra).[32]

In the Rajya Sabha, the PM did his best to address every issue that had been raised.[33] He began with a sentence whose full import has become evident only as constitutional Panchayati Raj evolved over the decades: 'By and large, it appears to me there is general acceptance of the need for Maximum Democracy and Maximum Devolution.'

I don't think any of us realized this was to be his most enduring legacy: 'the general acceptance' of the need for constitutional provisions to protect and promote Panchayati Raj through 'maximum democracy and maximum devolution'. This filled the most gaping lacuna in the Constitution by reconciling Gandhiji's 'romantic' view of India's villages with Dr Ambedkar's 'realistic' view of our villages as 'a sink of localism, a den of ignorance and communalism' that 'has the effect of making the Scheduled Castes slaves of the caste Hindu'.

---

[32] I am grateful to K.C. Sivaramakrishnan, *op. cit.*, for providing the leads to these quotes.
[33] From pp. 212–25, Vol. V of *Selected Speeches and Writings*, Publications Division. Most essential reading for scholars and those interested and, therefore, reproduced in extenso on the website https://rajivmisunderstood.com that can be accessed by scanning the QR code at the end of the chapter.

It was to be his last speech as prime minister. The vote was called at a few minutes past midnight (marking the end of my last day as a civil servant and the beginning of my first day as a politician). When the electronic counting board displayed the outcome, I raised my arms in joy, but Rajiv Gandhi shook his head and, after the correction slips had been collected, the chair announced that the Ayes were 157 and the Noes 83 so the motion was negatived as it fell short by three votes of a majority of two-thirds of members present and voting, as required for constitutional amendments.

Vinod Pande, in particular, seemed utterly distraught. To comfort him, I told him not to worry for when we returned to office after the elections, I would persuade the PM to name him a Member of the Planning Commission in charge of Panchayati Raj and we would have five years to get the bills passed. Pat came his reply: he only needed to be named a Planning Commission Member until 10 July 1993. Asked why he was citing such a specific date, he replied that he had cast his own horoscope and found that he would die on that date! For the record, I visited him on 10 July 1993 and ribbed him on finding him fit as a fiddle. He solemnly explained that a close relative of his had, in fact, died on that date and he must have mixed up the identities! Vinod Pande survived until February 2005.

The story of how Panchayati Raj eventually made it to the Constitution in December 1992, a year and a half after Rajiv Gandhi's assassination, will be told in the sequel to these memoirs (Vol. II: *A Half-Life in Politics*) at the appropriate point in the narrative. A detailed evaluation of how Panchayati Raj has worked out in actual practice on the ground was undertaken in 2011–13 by an expert group constituted under my chairmanship by the government of Dr Manmohan Singh. But as readers might want to get a feel of how the legislative process actually translated into practice, a summary is appended at this point.

Panchayat Raj in Practice: An Assessment

Despite the involvement of the highest in and across the land in the legislation that led to constitutional Panchayat Raj, it cannot be denied that thirty years on, Panchayat Raj in operation has made little impression on our polity and public perceptions of grassroots democracy. Genuine grassroots democracy would mark our journey from what is essentially a 'bourgeois democracy', which disproportionately benefits only our upper and middle classes, to a just and people-oriented democracy that works for the lowest and most downtrodden and does so with the full participation of the depressed segments that most need inclusive growth through inclusive governance. That goal remains, but, like most idealistic aims, still has a long way to go.[34]

Now to a general, broad sweep assessment.

First, the successes: thanks to the relevant provisions in Part IX of the Constitution, Panchayat Raj, as noted earlier, become ineluctable, irreversible, and irremovable. Over the last three decades, a three-tier system of panchayats has come to stay in all states where constitutional Panchayati Raj is applicable. All such states have also passed state conformity laws that faithfully reflect the constitutional provisions, thus making Panchayati Raj justiciable in legislative, if not constitutional terms. Unfortunately, NGOs and even panchayat associations have not gone to courts in sufficient numbers to secure enforcement of the conformity laws passed by state assemblies. Their efforts have been piecemeal. They are nervous of the effect on their own political future of mounting a full-scale assault on their state governments in the courts on what is being denied them despite being clearly available in the state legislation, based on the 'may' provisions of the Constitution. This has

---

[34] A SWOT analysis I have prepared of the state of Panchayati Raj in May 2023 may be seen at this book's website that can be accessed by scanning the QR code given at the end of the chapter.

more or less blocked the road to judicial correction of administrative and political lapses.

Reservation provisions for SC/ST, OBC and, above all, women, have been arguably the single biggest success story of Panchayati Raj, as indicated earlier, in reconciling Mahatma Gandhi's vision and Dr Ambedkar's contradictory views on local self-government in village India, on the one hand, and, on the other, in electing more women to local bodies in India alone than in the rest of the world put together. Indeed, so successful has been women's reservation that as against 30 per cent reservation for women conceived by Rajiv Gandhi, twenty-one states (up until September 2022) have reached 50 per cent. In actual practice, women generally have a few percentage points more than the legislative provision for seats in the panchayats because they also win in general unreserved seats. This appears to be particularly true of SC/ST women.

It has been argued that this may be true in terms of 'representation' but hardly in terms of 'effective participation'. But is this not also true of MLAs and MPs? And have the processes of devolution left men panchs more empowered than their female counterparts? And is there not more effective participation as women learn the ropes? Certainly, even in the 2006 study I commissioned as minister, one of the more unexpected findings was that by bringing women into the public sphere, the panchayat system has had the spin-off effect of empowering women in their family lives. Also, defeated women candidates often function as a kind of opposition to the current panchayat establishment in meetings of the gram sabha.

To my mind, the most definitive proof of the effectiveness of women in the panchayats, in a roundabout way, is what happened when the Haryana government in 2015 took the retrogressive step of imposing educational and financial conditions on women's candidacies. It resulted in 85 per cent of the women elected in the previous panchayat elections not even being able to stand in the next round. To a very telling extent, their places were taken by women from more elite families, who had not won when these restrictive conditions had not been imposed. This, to my mind, showed that when women are encouraged to stand in panchayat elections, poor women from weaker sections of society tend to win because their workplaces have made them more familiar with men-dominated social conditions. More importantly, the electorate recognizes that the poorer the woman, the more accessible will she be; elite women would not be so accessible and would tend to spend more time away from the village than women of lesser means.[35]

By and large, elections have been held on time as provided for in the Constitution and the state high courts have intervened when there have been delays. Although accounts are being kept and state audit authorities check panchayat accounts, under the overall aegis of the CAG, there remains considerable scope to improve the recording and maintenance of accounts. Unfortunately, a proposal made years ago by the Institute of Public Accountants of India to deploy chartered accountants to check panchayat records remains unimplemented to this day.

State Finance Commissions have been constituted with fair regularity and many – but not all – of their recommendations have been fully or partially accepted. The Central Finance Commission has emerged as the single most important source of funds for the panchayats. Their generous untied grants have made the village panchayats flush with untied funds. I would particularly commend the Fifteenth Finance Commission, chaired by my college friend, Nand Kishore Singh, for substantially augmenting untied grants to the panchayats from the divisible pool of the resources available. The downside is that as the panchayats are yet to be made effective units of local self-government – in the absence of

---

[35] The Modi government has now commissioned an updated a report on the status of women in the local bodies by my former senior research officer in the minister's office, Dr Nupur Tiwary.

effective devolution – the generous grants from the Central Finance Commission are transforming panchayats into agencies for patronage and privilege; this is spurring huge expenditure in panchayat elections and corruption in panchayat operations. Perhaps the answer lies in linking the disbursement of Central Finance Commission grants to the Devolution Index.[36] This would incentivize states to undertake more devolution and greater resort to district planning, and also promote transparency in panchayat transactions.

I would sum up the successes by saying that Panchayati Raj has come to stay, thanks principally to Rajiv Gandhi having determined to give local self-government the constitutional status, sanction, sanctity, and safeguards that the system lacked otherwise. Where governance was once confined to the approximately 5,000 MPs and the state assemblies, we now have a massive 32 lakh elected participants in governance, thus moving our democracy one rung up from being merely representative to becoming participatory. Progress is being made in all states – substantial in many, at snail's pace in some – but even the laggard states are slowly, if not steadily, improving their functioning. The ranking of states in effective Panchayat Raj has remained much the same over the past three decades: Karnataka and Kerala rivalling each other in the top category; Maharashtra, Gujarat, Tamil Nadu, Madhya Pradesh, Rajasthan, Haryana and Bihar in the next category; hill states like Himachal, Uttarakhand, Tripura and, above all, Sikkim, in a commendable category of their own, along with small states like Goa and Puducherry. Laggards are led by UP; the other states, like Assam, West Bengal, Andhra Pradesh, and Telangana, fall in between. Regrettably, despite having several villages on its outskirts, the National Capital Region of Delhi has no Panchayat Raj, their governance being the responsibility of municipal authorities This is

---

[36] An index, developed by the Indian Institute of Public Administration during my time as minister, which, on different key parameters, measures the degree of devolution to the PRIs achieved by the state concerned.

my categorization. Other observers may have a different categorization and I am open to correction.

In short, the mandatory provisions of Part IX of the Constitution are being observed. The problems really arise when we come to the recommendatory provisions of the constitutional legislation. The relationship between the mandatory and recommendatory provisions is akin to that between the shell and the substance. The Constitution mandates how the panchayats are to be structured; the state conformity legislation lays down the parameters of implementing the substance of devolution to secure 'power to the people'. Here the record is mixed.

As the essence of Panchayati Raj is effective devolution of power for economic development and social justice, it is essential that the three Fs – functions, finances, functionaries – be synchronized in the process of devolution through what is technically called 'activity mapping'. This technical issue was elaborated at length in the report of the Expert Group on Leveraging Panchayat Raj Institutions for the More Effective Delivery of Public Goods and Services (2012–13) which I chaired. Karnataka has recently made commendable progress in this direction. In other states, it is still not recognized that otherwise panchayats cannot function as 'units of local self-government' as mandated in the Constitution (Article 243G). While state legislation has largely followed the Eleventh Schedule in identifying the subjects for devolution, and in many cases added subjects in an enlightened manner, the government orders issued to implement the state legislation have, almost everywhere, fallen woefully short of the objective of simultaneously devolving the three Fs. State governments cling (like limpets!) to their powers and at most allow panchayats to operate as agencies for government programmes, not as 'units of self-government'.

This is compounded by the failure to proceed with the letter and spirit of district planning as envisaged in the Constitution. While funds in large quantities reach the district level, something like 90 per cent of the available funds from the state and central governments are credited to, and disbursed by, the district collector and his/her officers, not the three-tier panchayat system.[37] In the absence of clear knowledge of what funds are to be made available to the panchayats at each of the three levels of the system, the planning system proposed in the Constitution has generally been observed only in the breach. And this despite excellent guidelines for effective district planning from the village panchayat level through the intermediate and district levels to the district planning committee sent out by the Planning Commission nearly two decades ago. The political class and the bureaucracy collaborate to make devolution symbolic and not real or effective. Thus, panchayats exist but function as arms of the state, not as autonomous entities empowered to respond to the people's wishes. This has leached the panchayat system of a meaningful role in rural development.

The exception to the generally woeful state of district planning is Kerala where the People's Planning movement led by Thomas Isaac, CPI(M) leader and former finance minister, has galvanized local communities into planning their own future development. More than anything else, it is People's Planning combined with the Kudumbashree programme – for women's participation in village-level micro economic activities – that has propelled Kerala to the top, although the state would do well to look at the new gram swaraj legislation and 'activity mapping' in Karnataka based on three decades of field experience in running the Panchayat Raj system.

The other major lacuna in the operation of the system is that while

---

[37] I have recently learned that departmental grants for the maintenance of assets are being almost entirely devolved to the panchayats in Kerala. This is a development of great importance that deserves emulation in other states.

measures are taken to convene meetings of the gram sabha, almost no state has issued binding guidelines for the functioning of this entity aimed at making the local panchayat truly responsible to, and responsive to, the people. In the absence of meaningful action on public requirements through the gram sabha, interest in participating in meetings declines. This gives the state bureaucracy the excuse to say people are not interested in attending meetings. Moreover, as it is the officials more than the elected representatives who are actually conceiving and running programmes of economic and social development, the elected panchayat office bearers helplessly point to the officials (who are not accountable to the gram sabha) when complaints are made in gram sabha meetings.

All this has been gone into in (painful) detail over the last two decades of the operation of the central ministry of Panchayati Raj and solutions suggested for each identified problem, but because the ministry can only suggest solutions and the state governments are free to ignore or reject such suggestions, there has been little progress (other than in the states identified above) in making devolution effective and meaningful. The five-volume report of the expert group submitted a decade ago gathers dust even as the solutions suggested to identified problems wither in anonymous cupboards.

Basically, what this means is that although panchayats are here to stay, unless they take the political initiative to make MLAs dependent on their favour rather than the other way round, as is the case now, Panchayati Raj will flourish only as a shell, without any real substance. Hope lies only in panchayat representatives clubbing together in associations and confronting state governments and going to court rather than, as regretfully at present, in panchayats acquiescing meekly in whatever comes their way. The Karnataka State Gram Panchayat Association has blazed the trail. Others should follow, for power has been constitutionally devolved to the people but, in large measure, the people are still to grab the opportunities being offered them. To them, I say, paraphrasing Karl Marx's famous call in *The Communist Manifesto* of 1848: 'Panchayats of India, unite. You have nothing to lose but your chains. You have a world to gain!'

See detailed footnotes and endnotes by scanning the QR code above.

6

Rajiv Gandhi – The Man and His Office: A Brief Evaluation

Rajiv Gandhi's brief five-year stewardship of the nation, followed by eighteen months as leader of the Opposition before he was cruelly assassinated, is but a wink in historical time. I have dealt in detail in this book with the accords he signed, the controversies he waded through, his foreign policy initiatives, and his innovative domestic initiatives, above all, Panchayati Raj. I propose in this concluding chapter to sum up the main points of the events of his time, in and out office, and my impressions of the man himself.

It was a period of turbulence in politics combined, contrarily, with steady progress in nation-building. While several new beginnings were signalled in his first term of office, had RG been destined for further terms as prime minister many of his dreams for the nation would have been more fully realized. As it was, the political atmosphere was polluted by media baiting that was speculative at best and defamatory at worst,[1]

---

[1] The media attack was so vicious that it was proposed that an Anti-Defamation Bill be brought into Parliament. After we had returned from an unusually strenuous tour at well past midnight, I was unexpectedly and unprecedentedly instructed to join a late-night policy meeting at 7 RCR to discuss the bill. As far as I remember, many of us in the meeting, including myself, requested him to not proceed with the bill. This appeared to

especially relating to the Shah Bano case and the Bofors affair – for both of which he was vindicated by the courts years after he was no more. Unfortunately, justice delayed is justice denied.

On Sri Lanka and the IPKF, the high aims and objectives of Rajiv Gandhi's Sri Lanka policy were undermined by bad advice from virtually every quarter – diplomatic, military and intelligence (as High Commissioner J.N. Dixit contritely concludes). On Operation Brasstacks, he was quite simply betrayed but recovered in time to re-establish personal control over the army and his erstwhile friend, the minister of state for defence, Arun ('Roon') Singh. On A.P. Venkateswaran's dismissal, he had good reason to dismiss the errant foreign secretary but did so in the worst way possible. On nuclear disarmament, I commend his initiative which is now bearing fruit through the 2017 UN-backed Treaty on the Prohibition of Nuclear Weapons – long after he presented his Action Plan in 1988. He was not wrong, just way ahead of his time.

On the other hand, RG's path-breaking visits to China and Pakistan were well timed and could have led to more fruitful outcomes had destiny not snatched him away when he was not quite forty-seven years old. His intervention in the Maldives was hailed at the time but, in my minority view, presaged an undesirable change in the national mood towards hegemonism in South Asia. His initiating steps that a decade later led to India's emergence as a nuclear weapons power has received general praise but, in my maverick view, was a retrograde if inevitable reaction to the prospect of a Pakistan bomb. It took but three weeks for Pakistan to demonstrate its nuclear weapons.

On the domestic front, he will be remembered less for the wholly bogus but widely bruited allegation that he was surrounded by 'computer

---

accord with the PM's own view that the bill should not be proceeded with. It was dropped. This shows that although RG and his office were the principal target of the media, he was too much of a democrat to let insult and injury to himself take away his belief in the freedom of the press.

boys' than for his Technology Missions entrusted to an NRI he discovered in Chicago: Sam Pitroda. RG's principal legacy to the nation was the constitutional imperative of Panchayati Raj that would by now have blossomed had he remained at the helm of the nation for a few more decades. In his lifetime, he was most hailed for capturing the nation's imagination with his vision of 'taking India into the twenty-first century'. As the memory of him drifts into a little-remembered past, his most enduring image will be that of the prime minister who prepared the nation for the economic reforms that followed in the aftermath of his sudden absence.

On the Babri Masjid–Ram Janmabhoomi dispute, Rajiv Gandhi listed to the wrong side in the middle of the 1989 general election but then course-corrected when in Opposition. But by then, it was perhaps too late. His secular credentials were often challenged but, as I have tried to show, he always emerged true to the Gandhian–Nehruvian values to which he was heir. Perhaps the best of his expressions of secular beliefs was his opening lines in a Lok Sabha debate on secularism that he himself had initiated just as the Babri Masjid controversy was emerging as a principal electoral platform of the opposition to him: 'A secular India alone can survive. Perhaps, an India that is not secular does not deserve to survive.'[2]

He went on: 'A patriotic Indian is a secular Indian. A nationalist Indian is a secular Indian.'[3]

It was an oration that deserves more attention in these troubled times when the three 'principles' of secularism he underlined are being suborned. The three principles he espoused were: one, that 'our secularism is not anti-religious or irreligious'; two, 'we respect all religions equally'; three,

---

[2] *Rajiv Gandhi: Selected Speeches and Writings*, Vol. V, Publications Division, Ministry of Information and Broadcasting, New Delhi, 1991, p. 32. The full speech at pp. 32–37 is reproduced on this book's website, https://rajivmisunderstood.com, which may be accessed by scanning the QR code at the end of the chapter.

[3] *Ibid.*, p. 34.

'religion has high value but must remain in the sphere of private and personal life' since 'mixing religion with politics is against the traditions of our civilization, the canons of our Constitution and the survival of the State'. Presciently, he concluded:

> The challenge to secularism is not from one quarter, but from fanatics of all faiths, stirring trouble in various ways. There are those who ignore our composite culture and project to their followers a distorted and motivated picture of India's history, creating grievances where there are none, making political capital out of distressed religious sentiment.[4]

Tragically, these very elements have been in power for the past nine years. They were brought into the mainstream of our national polity from the wilderness into which they had been driven in 1984 when some of RG's party colleagues joined hands with the saffron forces to defeat him because he repeatedly sacrificed party interest to national interest and refused to touch tainted funds from suspect sources. In a more enlightened time, he might have been hailed for doing so. He wasn't.

Overall, three decades after he was snatched from us, his term of office and its aftermath are a fading memory. As one who had the opportunity of seeing him in action from the ringside and the sidelines, I think it is fitting that I leave behind my memories of him as well as this analysis of RG as a leader: what motivated him, the values he cherished, the reasons – right and wrong – for what he did and thought. He was a human being unexpectedly elevated to the highest office in the land when he was barely forty and after a preparatory period of political probation that lasted only two to three years. Given that, I think he did pretty well.

Personally, I found him most personable. He had a ready smile, an ability to laugh with others and at himself. He ran a harmonious office.

---

[4] *Ibid.*, p. 36.

While entitlement sometimes lent him an aura of arrogance, he was basically a humane, compassionate man dedicated to improving the lot of the poor and unempowered and taking our nation to the highest heights. He had ideas of his own that he discussed with exuberance and pursued with zeal. But as setbacks occurred, he accepted advice from those with longer political experience. Unfortunately, these 'expert' political advisers often led him up the garden path – but, of course, he had only himself to blame for accepting their advice. He had little guile and no deception in his dealings with political colleagues and opponents. He was intelligent, intellectually alive, tireless, and dedicated to improving the moral tone of our democracy. Essentially, a good man, a decent man, a trusting human being, honest with a high sense of probity and integrity.

Ironically, he was felled by allegations of financial corruption that were negated by court findings, but, alas, a decade after his death. By then, there was little public interest left in his exculpation.

He was also betrayed by some of friends and party colleagues, and a few of those he appointed. Arun Nehru had mobilized the party leadership to propose him as PM to succeed his assassinated mother but, in hindsight, it is clear that Nehru did so because he considered Rajiv a dilettante who could be easily manipulated. It was only because Arun Nehru wanted to be the sole 'Power behind the Throne' that he pressed for and secured a dynastic succession. When, very soon thereafter, once the electorate had overwhelmingly endorsed the party leadership's choice, RG showed himself to be his own man and no one's puppet, with a mind and will of his own, and endowed with a quite different vision for India than the anything-goes, power-lusting Arun Nehru, that Nehru began to realize his error in thinking RG would be his puppet. It was then that Arun Nehru began to see he had made the wrong choice. This worsened when RG discovered Arun Nehru to have been the hand behind the opening of the locks at the Babri Masjid (which, had he been asked or informed, the PM would never have countenanced) that he began doubting the wisdom of retaining the man as a powerful party boss and minister. Above all, it was Arun Nehru's dubious dealings in the Bofors affair, that he dropped Arun Nehru – a cousin by blood – from the inner circle and Council of Ministers. This, in turn, sparked a revolt within the party led by Arun Nehru and his cohort, which eventually resulted in V.P. Singh of the National Front becoming a very short-lived PM after the 1989 election. RG was also severely let down by a school friend he wrongly trusted as minister of state for defence and an undisciplined chief of army staff. Perhaps RG lacked the deviousness that makes for a long-lasting prime minister but his only fault was that he was too good a man to see in time the machinations of others.

Cynics will think this shows a good man makes a bad PM. But for the nation to remain a democracy and progress to its due heights, morality needs to be the seed from which the nation flourishes. Mahatma Gandhi and Jawaharlal Nehru tried to lay that seed and nurture it. When the Emergency killed the nascent plant, RG – who had never aspired to be PM – decided to use his high office to restore the nation to its foundational values. He failed because allegations were incessantly hurled at him by a decimated Opposition and a biased media that the courts, a decade and more later, were to dismiss as not containing a 'scintilla of evidence'.[5] As that had always been my view, through thick and thin of

---

[5] See Delhi High Court Justice J.D. Kapoor, *op. cit.*, who stated at para 77 of his judgment (p. 729), 'so far as Public Servants viz. late Shri Rajiv Gandhi and Late Sh. S.K. Bhatnagar are concerned sixteen long years of investigation by a premier agency of the country viz CBI could not unearth a scintilla of evidence against them for having accepted bribe/ illegal gratification, in awarding the contract'.

Earlier, at para 9 (p. 697): 'After hogging publicity and holding the person guilty in the eyes of the public, police and CBI go into soporific slumber and take years in filing the chargesheet and thereafter several years are taken in the trial.'

At para 7 (p. 696), the Hon'ble Justice has remarked: 'This case is a nefarious example which manifestly demonstrates how the trial and justice by the media can cause irreparable, irreversible and incalculable harm to the reputation of a person and shunning of his family,

my working closely with a good man, I have availed of this opportunity, in the evening of my life, to recount the truth as it surfaced through the judicial process.

As Laertes said of Hamlet in Shakespeare's immortal words:
'Good night, sweet prince, and flights of angels sing thee to thy rest.'

See detailed footnotes and endnotes by
scanning the QR code above.

---

relatives and friends. He is ostracized, humiliated and convicted without a trial. All this puts at grave risk due administration of justice'.

RG might have been assassinated by a human bomb but his reputation was assassinated by a partisan media.

Index

Aaberg, Carl, 119
Aam Aadmi Party, 17
Abdullah, Farooq, 29, 31–32, 34–35, 38
Accords, 15
   Assam, 22, 27
   Darjeeling, 47, 226
   J&K, 29–30, 33
   Mizoram, 24, 26–27
   Punjab, 15–18, 21, 27
   Sri Lanka, 77, 81, 85
Acts,
   Evidence Act, 138
   Commission of Inquiry Act, 70
   Muslim Women (Protection of Rights on Divorce) Act, 5, 10–11, 50, 55–58
   PESA Act, 210–11, 230
   Prevention of Corruption Act, 138
Advani, L.K., 178, 236
AE Services, 5–8, 92, 110, 117–21, 123–24

AFRICA Fund, 179
Agarwal, Deoki Nandan, 66
Ahluwalia, Montek Singh, 173, 199–200
Ahluwalia, V.K., 113
Ahuja, Anil, 113
Akali Dal, 10, 18
Akbar, M.J., 52
All-Assam Students Union (AASU), 22
All India Anna Dravida Munnetra Kazhagam (AIADMK), 235
All-India Muslim League, 50
All-India Panchayat Parishad, 214
All India Radio (AIR), 36, 195
Alva, Margaret, 234
Ambedkar, Dr B.R., 61–62, 203, 209, 236, 239
Anderssòn, Bo G., 119–22, 126
Ansari, Hamid, 211
Ansari, Ziaur Rahman, 60–61
Apna Utsav, 147, 183, 186–87, 189–91

Index

Ardbo, Martin, 7–8, 92, 117–20, 122, 124, 126, 128
Arora, Gopi, 3, 9, 92–93, 103–04, 154, 159, 181, 200
Aruna, Aladi, 106
Arunachal Pradesh, 158–60, 212, 220
Asom Gana Parishad (AGP), 22
Asoka Mehta Report, 226
Assam, 12, 22
Assam Rifles, 16
Athulathmudali, Lalith, 80
Atomic Energy Commission, 153
Aurora, General Jagjit Singh, 113
Ayodhya, 66
Azad, Ghulam Nabi, 9

Babri Masjid, 3, 5–6, 11–12, 49, 58, 65–66, 70–71, 178, 249, 251
Bachchan, Ajitabh, 131–33
Bachchan, Amitabh, 131–33
Bajpai, Girija Shankar, 167
Balakrishnan, Dr, 79, 226
Balakrishnan, K.P., 135
Banatwala, G.M., 50, 56, 61
Bandyopadhyaya, D., 205
Bangladesh, 27, 169
Barnala, Sardar Surjit Singh, 16, 18
Basu, Chitta, 236
Basu, Comrade Jyoti, 46, 218, 224
Bhabha Atomic Centre, 149, 154
Bhagat, H.K.L., 234
Bharatiya Janata Party (BJP), 23, 33–35, 43, 52, 59, 65–66, 110, 178, 227
Bhatia, Madan, 223–24
Bhatnagar, S.K., 11, 117, 140–42
Bhuria, Dilip, 210
Bhushan, Prashant, 110, 117, 124, 134
Bhutan, 165
Bhutto, Benazir, 33, 174–75, 177–78
Bofors controversy, 3, 5, 11–12, 49, 75, 91–116, 120–24, 127–45, 220, 248, 252
    Joint Parliamentary Committee (JPC), 105–08, 110–12, 114, 116, 125
Paris Tribunal, 97–98, 100
Swiss bank payouts, 95, 125–26
Bohr, Niels, 155
Border Security Force (BSF), 39
Bose, Sumantra, 30
Burma, 24, 28

CPI (M), 37–39, 50
Chadha, Win, 120, 126, 128, 140–41
Chandigarh, 15–17
Chari, P.R., 74
Chaturvedi, T.N., 107, 109, 115
Chawla, Justice M.K., 135
Chawla, Prabhu, 123
Chidambaram, P., 116, 233–34
China, 12, 146, 158–75, 248
    Treaty on Peace and Tranquility, 171
Chowdhury, H.S., 135
Chowdhury, Saifuddin, 50

Index

Colombo, 78–81
communal violence, 21, 42–43
  on Muslims, 22
  on Sikhs, 2
Confederation of Indian Industries, 197
Congress government, 5, 27, 34
Congress Party, 29–30, 38–39, 41, 65, 67
  Avadi Congress, 198
  centenary session, 214
  electoral defeat, 192
  Karachi Congress, 198
  Rajiv Gandhi Panchayat Raj Sangathan, 206
  Working Committee (CWC), 92–93, 222
Constitution of India, 57–58, 63, 70, 79, 203–05, 208, 217–18, 223, 238, 240–43
  amendment, 232, 234
  draft, 203

Dandavate, Madhu, 10
Darjeeling Gorkha Hills Council, 44
Dasgupta, Biplab, 39
Davies, Mr Justice, 132
Deb, Alok, 113
Deng Xiaoping, 159–62, 172, 199
Deo, K.P. Singh, 186
Desai, Justice D.A., 16
Desai, Morarji, 204
Devi, Rama, 227
Devolution Index, 241

Dhawan, Dr Satish, 154
Dhawan, R.K., 20, 235
Dikshit, Uma Shankar, 45
Dixit, High Commissioner 'Mani', 83–85, 87–91, 248
Doordarshan, 36, 39, 41–42, 83, 195
Dravida Munnetra Kazhagam (DMK), 109
Dubey, Muchkund, 150, 156–57

Economic Strategy for the 80s, 199
Edelstram, Axel, 123
Emergency, 199, 223, 252
Eradi, Justice Balakrishna, 17
Ershad, General H.M., 27

Fernandes, George, 35, 42
Fernandes, Oscar, 9
Food Corporation of India, 196
Fotedar, Makhan Lal, 7, 56, 67–68, 235

Gandhi, Prime Minister Indira, 2, 8, 21–22, 25, 79, 81–82, 115, 159, 186, 191, 194, 223, 227
Gandhi, Mahatma, 65, 203, 205, 209, 217, 236, 239, 252
Gandhi, Priyanka, 191
Gandhi, Rahul, 186, 191, 206
Gandhi, Rajiv, 1
  and Accords, 26, 29–30, 44–46
  and Africa, 179

and Babri Masjid, 69–71, 249, 251
and Bofors, 5, 7–8, 11–12, 49, 75, 91–116, 120–45, 248, 252
and Darjeeling, 44–46
and nuclear disarmament, 6, 13, 149–53, 155, 157–58, 248
and Operation Brasstacks, 71–72, 74–77, 149, 248
and Pakistan, 73–74, 149, 153, 174–78, 248
and secularism, 249–50
and sustainability, 192–93
death, 4, 13
drought-proofing, 195–97
electoral defeat, 70
in China, 170–73, 248
Indian Airlines pilot, 2
Jawaharlal Nehru centenary speech, 155–57
opinions, 50–55, 58, 61–65
political strategy, 23, 28
Science Congress, 183–84, 191
Technology Missions, 183–85, 195, 249
workshops with DMs, 216–20, 234
Zakir Husain Memorial Lecture, 188
Gandhi, Sanjay, 2
Gandhi, Sonia, 2, 26, 64, 175, 192, 205–06
Gauffin, Rolf, 121–22, 126
Gavai, P.G., 2
Gayoom, President, 180

George, Vincent, 34, 155, 158, 229
Gharekhan, Chinmay, 154
Ghisingh, Subhash, 44–46
Gill, K.P.S., 20–21
Gogoi, Ranjan, 142
Gogoi, Tarun, 9
Golden Temple, 20
Gorbachev, Mikhail, 164
Gorkha National Liberation Front (GNLF), 44–46
Grewal, Sarla, 75, 104
Gupta, Hemant, 142
Gurpadaswamy, M.S., 236
Guru Gobind Singh, 194

Habibullah, Wajahat, 10, 30–31, 64, 67, 113, 194
Handoo, P.L., 36, 38–39
Haq, General Zia-ul, 73–74, 174–75
Hegde, Ramakrishna, 218, 224
Hinduja, Srichand, 142
Hindujas, 126, 140, 142
Hirohito, Emperor, 191
Hoon, Lieutenant General P.N., 72
Husain, Zakir, 188

Inderjit, 45
India,
 Central Reserve Police Force (CRPF), 16
 Consolidated Funds of the State, 232, 236
 Constituent Assembly, 204

Index

Department of Rural Development, 221, 234
Election Commissions, 230
Emergency, 199, 223, 252
Finance Commissions, 231, 236, 240–41
Intelligence Bureau (IB), 35
Ministry of External Affairs (MEA), 85, 101, 159, 167
Muslim Personal Law, 7, 10–11, 49–55, 60–64
Planning Commission, 221, 225, 237, 243
Prime Minister's Office (PMO), 4, 13, 52, 64, 69, 75, 82, 85, 104, 155, 159, 175, 186, 194, 197, 220
India Today, 8, 68, 114, 123, 134
Indian Air Force, 180
Indian Army, 71–72, 83, 90
Indian Council for Cultural Relations (ICCR), 186
Indian National Congress, *See* Congress Party
Indian Peace-Keeping Force (IPKF), 6, 12–13, 49, 81, 83–84, 86–91, 180–81, 248
Indira Gandhi Institute of Development Research, 200
Indus Waters Treaty, 17
International Court at The Hague, 97
Isaac, Thomas, 243
Island Development Authority (IDA), 193–94
Islands of the Marigold Sun, 194

JKLF (Jammu Kashmir Liberation Front), 30, 36, 38
Jaffna, 77, 83, 86, 88–90
Jagmohan, Governor, 32–37, 41–44
Jaitley, Arun, 128–31, 133, 137, 211
Janata Party, 25
Jayakar, Pupul, 189, 191
Jayawardene, President, 6, 77, 80–82, 91
Jethmalani, Ram, 140, 236
Jha, L.K., 199
Jilani, Salim Abbas, 178–79
Joseph, K.M., 142
Joshi, Murali Manohar, 227
Junejo, Mohammed Khan, 72–73, 76

Kakodkar, Dr A.K., 154
Kalha, Geetika, 187
Kalkat, Amarjit Singh, 89–90
Kanimozhi, 109
Kapoor, Coomi, 121
Kapoor, J.D., 104, 125, 138–40, 142
Kargil war, 12, 112–14, 131
Kashmir, 29–31, 40–42
  conflict, 12, 32–35, 174
  evacuation of Pandits, 33, 39–40, 42–43
Kashmir Files, 43
Katju, Justice Shiv Nath, 66
Kaul, B.M., 167
Keeler, Trevor, 158

Index

Kerala Planning Board, 225
Khan, A.Q., 149
Khan, Ambassador Humayun, 74
Khan, Arif Mohammed, 3, 9, 12, 27, 50–52, 56, 60, 65
Khan, Ayub, 99
Khan, Dr A.Q., 74
Khosla, Romesh (Romi), 193–94
Khurshid, Salman, 51–52
Kidwai, Mohsina, 229
Krishnamurthy, V., 201
Kumaratunga, Chandrika Bandaranaike, 77

LTTE (Liberation Tigers of Tamil Eelam), 78–79, 83–91
    Pulendran, 88
    Thileepan, 88
Ladakh, 31, 161, 209, 211
Lal, Bhajan, 227–28, 234
Lal, Devi, 34, 37, 40
Laldenga, 25, 27
Lalthanhawla, 25
Lambah, Sati, 176, 179
Latifi, Danial, 56–57, 59
Lindstrom, Sten, 120–21, 132–34
Line of Actual Control, 161, 165–66
Line of Control with J&K, 166
Longowal, Sant Harchand Singh, 15, 21

Mahanta, Prafulla, 23
Maldives, 146, 149, 180–81, 248
Malik, Satyapal, 235

Mandal Commission, 130
Mandela, Nelson, 180
Manipur, 29, 218, 234
Maran, Murasoli, 236
Marwah, Ved, 37
Mathew, Justice K.K., 15–16
Mathur, Kaushal Kumar, 194
Mehmood, Jamil, 90
Mehta, Ashok, 89–90
Mehta, Asoka, 204–05, 217
Mehta, Balvantray, 204–05, 217
Menon, Krishna, 167
Mishra, Chaturanand, 236
Mitra, Aloke, 26
Mitterand, President François, 117
Mizo National Front (MNF), 25, 27
Mizoram, 12, 19, 24–28, 45, 158–59
Modi, Prime Minister Narendra, 11, 29, 142, 155, 172, 206
Muslim United Front (MUF), 29–31
Muslims, 7, 10–11, 22–23, 29, 39, 43, 51–52, 61–62
    remarriage of divorced women, 54
My Frozen Turbulence in Kashmir, 44

Nagaland, 24, 45, 195, 212
Nandy, Pritish, 76, 134
National Conference (NC), 29–31, 36, 38–39
National Front, 8, 33, 59, 62, 109–10, 134, 146, 252
National Institute of Rural

Index

Development and Panchayati Raj, 216
Nayyar, Dr Deepak, 201
Nayar, Kuldip, 74, 149
Nehru, Arun, 3, 6–9, 12, 27, 65, 67–68, 119, 121–24, 126, 146, 251–52
Nehru, Jawaharlal, 24, 61, 65, 99, 155–56, 164–65, 167–70, 175, 197–98, 200, 204–05, 217, 252
Nepal, 44
Non-Aligned Movement Summit, 179

Operation Black Thunder II, 20–21
Operation Blue Star, 101, 115
Operation Brasstacks, 5, 49, 71–72, 74–77, 101, 149, 248
Operation Pawan, 89, 101

Padgaonkar, Dileep, 189
Pakistan, 13, 17, 32, 41, 71–76, 99, 110–12, 146, 149, 152–53, 155, 164–66, 167, 169, 174–79, 192, 248
Palekar, Amol, 189
Palme, Prime Minister Olof, 100, 118
Panchayati Raj, 12, 79, 147, 181, 183, 185, 187, 195, 203–25, 228–30, 233–44, 247, 249
 reservations, 208–10, 212–13, 221–22, 230, 239
 and women, 239–40

Panchayati Raj Institutions, 231, 242
Pande, Vinod, 221, 227, 237
Pandian, S.R., 135
Pant, K.C., 116
Parliament of India, 205, 207–08, 233
Parliamentary Select Committee, 231–32
Parthasarathi, G., 79, 82, 226
Parthasarathy, G., 172
Partition of India, 51
 riots, 2
Patel, Ahmed, 9
Patel, Sardar, 167
Paul, Swraj, 124, 126
Pawar, Sharad, 228
People's League, 38–39
People's Planning movement, 243
Pitroda, Sam, 183, 249
Prabhakaran, Velupillai, 78, 80, 83–91
Pradhan, R.D., 22, 159
Prasad, H.Y. Sharada, 186–87
Prasad, Mahesh, 222
Pratap, Anita, 84–85
Premadasa, Prime Minister, 80
Puniyani, Ram, 43
Punjab, 12
 terrorist activities, 20–21, 23, 32–33
Puri, Hardeep Singh, 85
Puri, Mohinder Singh, 113
Purie, Aroon, 8
Putin, Vladimir, 158

Quattrocchi, 124, 126, 140–42

Raja, A., 109
Rajiv Gandhi Foundation, 205
Ram Lalla, 66
Ram Janmabhoomi, 6, 67, 70–72, 249
Rama Rao, N.T. (NTR), 218, 224
Ramachandran, V., 225
Ramesh, Jairam, 183, 185
Ranganathan, C.V., 172–73
Rao, K.V. Krishna, 34
Rao, Nirupama, 165
Rao, P.C., 223–24, 227
Rao, P.V. Narasimha, 2, 80, 178, 186
Rashtriya Jan Parishad, 135
Ray, Siddharth Shankar, 70
Reddy, K.J., 135
Reserve Bank of India, 200
Ruati, Van Lal, 26

SAARC (South Asian Association for Regional Cooperation) summit, 72, 75–76, 174–75, 177
Sahib, Abdul Nazir, 218
Sahni, Kedar Nath, 39
Sampantham, 77
Sangh Parivar, 65–66
Sanghvi, Vir, 19, 73, 117
Saravanamuttu, Pakiasothy, 77
Sarkaria Commission, 223
Saikia, Hiteswar, 22
Sailo, Brigadier, 25

Sarin, Ritu, 19
Sarkar, Aveek, 26, 73
Sarkaria, Ranjit Singh, 223
Sayeed, Mufti Mohammad, 33
Schmid, Dr Pierre, 129
Sen, Asoke, 11, 55–56
Sen, Ronen, 145, 154, 175
Sen Gupta, Alok, 140
Seshan, T.N., 82
Sethi, Rajiv, 189
Sethna, Dr Homi Nusserwanji, 74
Shah, Ghulam Mohiuddin, 30
Shah, Mohammad Yusuf, 30
Shah, Shabbir, 38–39
Shah Bano controversy, 5, 7, 10–12, 49, 51, 53, 57–59, 62–65, 248
Shahabuddin, Ambassador Syed, 69
Shankar, Meera, 82
Shankar, P. Shiv, 39, 190–91, 234
Shankaranand, B., 106
Shekhar, Chandra, 70–71
Shivaiah, Dr M., 217
Shourie, Arun, 12, 19–20, 145
Sibal, Kapil, 140
Sikhs, 19–21
 separatist movement, 21
Singh, Ajay, 115
Singh, Amarinder, 16
Singh, Arun 'Roon', 3, 9, 11, 71–72, 74, 76, 96, 99–100, 102–03, 105, 114–15, 117, 120, 130–31, 144, 159, 248
Singh, Balbir, 215
Singh, Buta, 46, 69, 191
Singh, Dinesh, 172, 221–22

Index

Singh, Dr Manmohan, 154, 199, 201, 206, 211, 237
Singh, General Depinder, 86–88
Singh, Giani Zail, 9, 12, 18–20, 146
Singh, Jaswant, 34–35, 112, 125
Singh, K.C., 9
Singh, K. Natwar, 154
Singh, Major General Harkirat, 87–89
Singh, Nand Kishore, 240
Singh, Ramesh Inder, 20
Singh, Raminder, 114, 117
Singh, S.K., 149
Singh, T.P., 115
Singh, V.P., 3, 8–9, 12–13, 27, 32–34, 41, 43, 59, 65, 93–96, 103, 109, 116, 122, 124, 127–28, 130–33, 136, 146, 186, 227, 235, 252
Singh, Veer Bahadur, 6, 66, 68
Singhvi, L.M., 205, 217, 226
Sivaramakrishnan, K.C., 229, 235
Sodhi, R.S., 142
Sofma, 8, 106–08, 110–12, 114–17, 119–20
Sri Lanka, 12–13, 77–91, 146, 180, 248
Constitution, 226
Subramanian, Arjun, 113
Subramanian, Chitra, 8, 120–21, 124–25, 128–29, 132–34, 136
Sundarji, General Krishnaswamy, 3, 9, 11, 71–72, 74, 76, 89, 97, 99–102, 104–05, 110–12, 114–15, 117, 119, 130–31

Sunday, 19, 44, 73, 84, 103–04, 117, 174
Supreme Court, 5, 7, 11, 49, 52, 56–59, 61–64, 66, 69–71, 135, 142
Swamy, Narayan, 85
Swedish National Audit Bureau (SNAB), 92, 95–96
Swedish National Bureau of Investigation, 120

Tamil Eelam, 77, 79, 80, 84, 86, 91
Tamil militants, 78–79
Tamil Nadu, 78, 87, 235
Thapar, P.N., 167
The Fractured Himalaya, 165
The Hindu, 125, 134
The Illustrated Weekly of India, 76, 121, 134
The Indian Express, 19, 120, 125, 134
The Telegraph, 26, 134
Thungon, P.K., 220
Tibet, 167–69
Tiwari, Narayan Dutt, 228
Trudeau, Justin, 98

Uniform Civil Code (UCC), 51, 59–61, 66
United Liberation Front of Asom (ULFA), 23
United Nations (UN), 6, 13, 44, 212
Comprehensive Test Ban Treaty (CTBT), 151

Conference on Disarmament, 150, 153
General Assembly, 118, 157
United Nations Development Programme (UNDP), 208
United States of Soviet Socialist Russia (USSR), 164
Upendra, P., 236

Vajpayee, Atal Bihari, 130, 153
Vanlalvawna, 28
Vasudevan, R., 75–76
Venkateswaran, A.P., 75–77, 248
Venkataraman, President, 41
Venkataramiah, E.S., 16

Venkatraman, N., 4
Vishva Hindu Parishad (VHP), 66
Vohra, N.N., 178

Waqf Board, 54, 57, 63, 69
Westander, Henrik, 121
Wilson, 'Bob', 92, 118, 120–21, 126
Working with Rajiv Gandhi, 22
World War II, 72

Zaiwalla, Sarosh, 132
Zhou Enlai, 170
Zonal Cultural Centres (ZCCs), 186–92

Acknowledgements

I have acknowledged the contribution to my memoirs to several of those without whom the first volume could not have been written. I avail this opportunity to thank a few who got left out by error and added several others whose contribution to this volume is immeasurable:

Govind Dhar, editor of the Doon School alumni magazine, who was most cooperative and conscientious about answering my numerous queries.

Mrs A. Qizilbash, the Doon School archivist who fished out a number of articles published in the fifties that enlivened my chapter on my school days.

Mrs Sangeeta Kain, principal of Welham Boys School, for discovering my first-ever printed article, published in 1950 or 1951, on a school picnic.

General A.S. Kalkat for clarifying a number of things about our ill-fated IPKF in Sri Lanka.

Major General Ashok Kumar Mehta for his insights into the IPKF.

Shri N.N. Vohra, then Defence Secretary, for filling me in on the reasons for the collapse of the Siachen Agreement after it was ready for signature.

Janab Salim Abbas Jilani, Shri Vohra's Pakistani counterpart, who confirmed Shri Vohra's version and very discreetly added insights of his own.

Acknowledgements

Ronen Sen, who, notwithstanding his obsession with secrecy over 'old, unhappy far-off things and battles long ago', has vouchsafed me, and attempted to correct me, on a number of foreign policy events related to Prime Minister Rajiv Gandhi.

Meera Shankar for clarifying a great deal about Sri Lanka.

Neena Gopal, who allowed me to play around with the order of her sentences in her eyewitness account of Rajiv Gandhi's assassination.

Air Vice Marshal A.V. Subramanian, who spoke to me over the telephone about technical features of the Bofors gun.

Wajahat Habibullah, who was ready with word and written word to clarify any number of questions in my mind about Rajiv Gandhi, his controversies, particularly over the Shah Bano and Bofors issues, as also Kashmir, on which he is an authority, and especially the Island Development Authority, a concept the PM developed with Wajahat.

Rajeev Sethi, a cultural genius and Rajiv's favourite, about the Apna Utsav and the Zonal Cultural Centres.

Sam Pitroda, who taught my brain that is half-dead on scientific and technological issues all about the Technology Missions with which he was entrusted by Prime Minister Rajiv Gandhi,

and, perhaps above all,

Gopi Arora, who for all our differences was a firm and fast friend, far more knowledgeable about the intricacies of Indian politics than I could ever have been.

Mani Shankar Aiyar
G-43, Jangpura Extension,
New Delhi-110014

14 November 2023
(Jawaharlal Nehru's 134th birth anniversary)

A Note on the Author

Although the author and Rajiv Gandhi overlapped at the Doon School and Cambridge, Mani Shankar Aiyar was far too senior to Rajiv at school and far too impecunious at Cambridge to have more than a nodding acquaintance with the future prime minister. Even though Rajiv Gandhi invited him into the PMO in March 1985, and put him in charge of the PM's tour programmes, speech writing, and his cultural and Panchayati Raj initiatives, Aiyar was firmly excluded from all other political and policy matters! Nevertheless, despite never having been Rajiv Gandhi's confidante, a bond between them grew to the point where the PM – albeit with considerable reluctance – permitted Aiyar to resign from the IFS for an alternative career in politics with the Congress Party. This book is thus the outcome of the author's research and reflections on Rajiv Gandhi as the PM and as a person, written some three decades after his brutal assassination.

Excerpt from Mani Shankar Aiyar's
Memoirs of a Maverick

12

The Transition from PMO to CPO

Taking the plunge

After the prime minister's colourless Independence Day address on 15 August 1989, when he should have been proclaiming Panchayat Raj as his banner for the next election but did not, he flew out to Karnataka on 17 August and to Andhra Pradesh on the 18th. I travelled with him. It struck me that this was a golden opportunity to discuss my personal future. If I spoke to him on the flight from Karnataka to Andhra Pradesh, when politicians from either state were not in the helicopter, I would get a clean hour and a half to talk to him without interruption – a rare window.

As we flew from Haasan to Mysore on the 17th, I walked up to him and said I would like to talk to him about something important the next day. He was intrigued and asked why not now. I replied I would rather wait until the morrow. He was so intrigued that when the day's events were over, the SPG knocked on my door and said the PM was awaiting me. Rajiv Gandhi once again enquired what it was that I wanted to talk about. I once again demurred because I was trying to make up my mind whether to consult my wife. The PM let it go, and I spent much of the night wrestling with myself over whether or not to sound out Suneet, then decided it would only complicate my resolve if she were to ask me to think it over.

Next morning, at first light, we got into the helicopter and the PM motioned me to the seat next to him even before we quite took off. But before our conversation began, I first had to fulfil my usual role of acting as the prime minister's right hand – literally – as I was required to wave from the window across the aisle at the cheering crowd (without showing my face) while RG handled the crowd from the window next to him.

Immediately after take-off, the PM looked at me enquiringly. I cleared my throat and began by saying I wanted to quit the IFS to join him in politics. Rajiv Gandhi looked stunned. Why on earth did I want to leave an assured job in which I was doing very well for the uncertainties of politics? I reminded him of our Cambridge days when I had run for president of the union. I said ever since I was in school, my dream had been to enter politics, but I had no constituency, nor the required linguistic skills, nor my own resources. I wanted to leverage this opportunity to make the transition. Rajiv looked sceptical.

He himself believed, I continued, that he would win the coming election and I certainly hoped he would, but everyone I knew – including my wife who was running a journal, *India Speaks* that furnished English translations of language journals – was convinced that the Congress would lose. So my request was to hitch my star to his wagon, win or lose, and this appeared to be the right time. He did not reply immediately. Either he did not agree with me or he wondered why he should take me on as an additional political burden. In any case, he asked me to think things over. But as far as I was concerned, the die was cast.

I then turned to another consideration that I regarded as germane. I said I knew he was on the target list of assassins. There was always that danger. But I did not think anyone would get him in Delhi where he was well protected; things were more uncertain when he was on the move.

'However, as I am always in the open jeep that travels ahead of you, any assassin would mow me down before they get you.' He listened sombrely.

We landed at Cuddapah (now Kadapa) without a decision. On the way from Cuddapah to Delhi, he did not resume the conversation, and from then on, I found him deliberately avoiding my eye. I decided to bide my time.

I then broached the subject with my family. Suneet, always my support, immediately fell in with my plans. The children looked concerned when I said it might be difficult to finance their higher education if things went wrong. My brother, Jam, stepped into the breach. He pledged to take care of their college education in the event of my coming a cropper. His worry, he said, was altogether different. He was certain that Rajiv Gandhi would be jailed after losing the election; so why did I want to go to Tihar when I had not benefitted by even one *khota paisa*[1] from Bofors? I brushed off the question.

Finding that I was sticking to my guns, the PM waited for over a month and then asked his principal secretary, B.G. Deshmukh, to take me in hand. Deshmukh discovered I was impervious to argument and, moreover, I had the backing of my family. I had thought through the entire issue and my mind was made up. I was finally ushered into the PM's presence on 10 October, Suneet's birthday.

RG began by saying he would never be able to make me a minister. As I had heard that Dhawan was telling anyone who cared to listen that my ambition was so overweening that I would not be satisfied being made foreign secretary and was aspiring to be foreign minister, I took this opening gambit in my stride. I said I was ready to never be made a minister.

The PM then emphasized that the 'system' would never accept me, just as it had accepted neither 'Roon [Arun Singh] nor even Arun

---

[1] 'Not even a brass farthing' would, I think, be the right English translation.

[Nehru]'. (I have sometimes wondered whether he was also thinking of himself as 'not having been accepted by the system'.) I nodded, saying that while I entertained no false hopes of a ministership, I did hope he would be able to fulfil my lifelong desire to be an MP. He said he had been reflecting on that and had come to the conclusion that he could get me into the Rajya Sabha from one of the three seats available to the moribund Municipal Corporation of Delhi (MCD). Although this would be equivalent to being born out of the womb of a corpse, I gratefully accepted the prospect. (This was never fulfilled because immediately after the Lok Sabha elections, the MCD was deservedly put to sleep and a new Delhi legislative assembly was put in its place; however, very few Congress MLAs were elected.)

Having clarified matters, he agreed that I might put in my papers and, after my voluntary retirement was agreed to by the government, I could join the Congress. He then said he required something else from me. He wanted me to continue with him in the PMO as an officer on special duty even after resigning. I promptly agreed, but he seemed to think further explanation was needed.

'I want you with me because you never come back to me on any task that I assign to you except to say the task is done. And you often seem to comprehend my thoughts better than I do.' What greater compliment could I receive? I walked out of his study floating on cloud nine.

On Foreign Minister P.V. Narasimha Rao's instructions, the paperwork at the MEA took virtually no time. On the afternoon of 13 October, I handed over to the PM my letter of resignation and asked him to sign it. Is that necessary, he asked? I said, 'No – but for me it would be a historical record.' He smiled and appended his signature.

R.K. Dhawan, who was present, asked whether I would be prepared to take the Congress ticket from New Delhi to contest against Lal Krishna Advani! I immediately recognized the ploy as a subtle attempt to ground me before take-off. Dhawan made one more attempt to nobble me. I asked Rajiv Gandhi whether I might designate myself 'Special Assistant to the Congress President' but Dhawan wanted to know why I needed a designation at all. Fortunately, Rajiv Gandhi overruled him and said I could call myself his special assistant. No one else ever called me that!

My kids were appalled that I had chosen for my transition to politics the inauspicious date of Friday the 13th. I dismissed their apprehensions as superstition – but there is no denying that, at least in hindsight, it was a very bad start.

The news of my voluntary retirement from the IFS to pursue an alternative career in politics caused a mild flutter. Ajoy Bose, the journalist, was to tell me later that my former classmate Arun Shourie, editor of the *Indian Express* and a vitriolic critic of Rajiv's, scoffed when Ajoy handed him his copy, 'Don't you guys have anything better to write about than Mani Shankar, Mani Shankar...!'

Pritish Nandy, editor of the *Illustrated Weekly of India*, had me on the cover, following Rajiv at a pre-election meeting in Kizhakkarai, Tamil Nadu, with a bundle of petitions under my arm, and the heading 'Mani Friday'. Within was a long interview with me introduced by Nandy and laced with his hallmark sarcasm:

> The Tamilian brahmin with the odd sense of wit first came into prominence when, within weeks of his joining the prime minister's office, he had a brush with the press in Washington, DC... Aiyar never lived down that confrontation, and the Indian press... found in him an excellent opportunity for target practice...[2]

Then came the rather perceptive assessment that I understood what my PMO colleagues had not, that is, Rajiv Gandhi's priorities, and that

---

[2] Pritish Nandy, 'Mani Friday', *The Illustrated Weekly of India*, 29 October–4 November 1989.

I took my work seriously, 'despite the silly witticisms for which he is best known'.

Nandy went on to explain that although I had 'harmed' the PM's image with the speeches I wrote becoming 'more and more provocative' and 'facetious', yet when I 'teamed up' with rural development secretary Vinod Pande, I presented the PM with 'two of his finest political weapons, the Panchayat Raj Bill and the Jawahar Rozgar Yojana, followed by the Nagarpalika bill'. Granting that 'Aiyar's contribution towards the schemes were brilliantly conceived, a fact which no one seemed to notice since the air was too thick with Bofors and HDW', he ended by asserting that 'Aiyar's contribution towards drafting the bill(s) remains the single biggest achievement of his bureaucratic career'.

It was, I think, on the whole a fair assessment of my time in the PMO.

Lok Sabha elections, 1989

To my astonishment and that of most people, Rajiv Gandhi announced the next general election on 16 October – three days after I had quit the IFS.

I got down to the task of drafting the Congress manifesto – which came to be called the Mani-Festo, not in praise but in denigration of me, many journalists delighting in the comeuppance that was about to be delivered to the Congress.

I then travelled with the PM to Haldia, Narora and Trivandrum. He had tentatively enquired, at the start of the journey, whether instead of accompanying him on the election tour, I would prefer to man the press room along with M.J. Akbar. I baulked at this suggestion. In any case, the idea came to an abrupt end when Akbar was given the Congress ticket to contest from Kishanganj in Bihar. 'Watch out,' counselled Akbar, 'Dhawan is trying to shaft both of us.'

RG was busy with fraught discussions involving the allocation of

542 tickets for Lok Sabha seats to Congress candidates. Aspirants were legion, many getting their applications and biodata typed out by the itinerant typists who had set up shop at 24, Akbar Road, the Congress headquarters. One enterprising entrepreneur, who had an electronic typewriter, advertised his services by claiming that applications typed on manual typewriters could not be fed into computers. He was literally besieged!

My first 'political charge'

One night at about 2 a.m., when RG's office at 7, Race Course Road was still buzzing, he phoned to say he was entrusting me with a delicate task. There were two women from Andhra Pradesh, Geeta Reddy and Uma Gajapati Raju, to whom he had promised tickets, but he was facing heavy opposition in the Congress Parliamentary Board (CPB). Would I call and persuade the women to choose any assembly segment in their proposed parliamentary constituencies and he would ensure that they were at least allotted the assembly segments of their preference?

I rang Geeta Reddy who burst into tears but told me the segment she desired, even as she sobbed uncontrollably (she went on to win it and became a state minister several times over). Uma was a different proposition. She had a large vocabulary of colourful abuse and, when I gave her RG's message, she used it to shattering effect. She adamantly refused the PM's offer of a seat in the state assembly and, cursing him in language worthy of a stevedore, turned her ire on me. She continued calling me through the night – much to Suneet's annoyance – blasting her stream of off-colour expressions.

I returned to Race Course Road at 5 a.m. to be told the PM had gone to bed only a few minutes earlier. His diligent private secretary, V. George, having been up all night, looked a little dishevelled, unlike his normal dapper self, and took himself off. I picked up an atlas and, covering myself with it, put up my legs and went to sleep.

I woke to hear Makhan Lal Fotedar, Rajiv's political adviser, confidentially whispering to George that the ticket for Visakhapatnam had been awarded to a well-known Andhra industrialist. Fotedar was worried. As steel minister, he had ordered an enquiry into the business baron's affairs. Hence, the award of a Congress ticket to a man under formal investigation might reflect adversely on him. I went still behind my atlas. I came out from behind it only after Fotedar had left and, going to the lawn, stationed myself at a point RG would have to pass on his way from an early morning meeting on the lawns to the conference room.

As RG walked up to me with a questioning look, I whispered that I needed a moment to inform him of the reaction of the two Andhra ladies and what I had overheard Fotedar saying this morning; I thought it gave the PM an opportunity to fulfil his pledge to Uma. He told me to get it in writing from Fotedar, which I did, and Uma fought and won the seat.

The 'Ram Rajya' plank

On moving out of the PMO to the Congress President's Office (CPO) in mid-October 1989, I was immersed in working out the complexities of the PM's election tour itinerary with its intricate logistics. The tour, as decided months earlier, was scheduled to kick off in Nagaur, Rajasthan, where Jawaharlal Nehru had gone on Gandhi Jayanti, 1959, to inaugurate his version of Panchayat Raj – the principal proposed plank of our campaign.

I was discussing the tour programme with the PM when Sheila Dikshit, his minister of state, entered the room and said she had come on behalf of her colleagues; they wanted her to emphasize that Panchayat Raj could not be the main issue as all attention was fixed on the Ram Janmabhoomi–Babri Masjid controversy. She and her colleagues wanted him to begin his campaign in Faizabad on the outskirts of Ayodhya. She also said the PM should stop driving his own vehicle on these tours.

After she bustled out, I reminded him that when Margaret Thatcher won an unexpected election victory after the Falklands war, he (RG) had presented me with the book *Campaign!* by Rodney Tyler; my main learning from it was that no campaign must be fought on a turf of the Opposition's choosing. I was, therefore, of the view that we should stick to our long-planned intention of making this election about Panchayat Raj, not fall into the trap of making the BJP's principal issue our issue. He nodded but made no comment.

RG later sent me a message saying that the first meeting of the election campaign on 3 November 1989 should be in Faizabad. Nagaur could come later. At the Faizabad airfield, I busied myself on the hotline with arrangements for the next stop. I was, therefore, not on the platform when Rajiv Gandhi mentioned 'Ram Rajya' in his first election speech, which the Opposition later made into a whiplash to lacerate the sitting PM's campaign, portraying him as an opportunist hunting with the hounds and running with the hares to appeal to the Hindu vote while appeasing the Muslim vote.

I knew that 'Ram Rajya' was not included in his speaking notes, and he had not asked for it to be included. So somebody on the stage must have asked him to refer to it. I have, therefore, studied the news reports to unravel what happened. Here are my findings.

The Hindi-language *Hindustan* (4 November 1989) had the most detailed report. It does not even mention the words 'Ram Rajya', whereas the Calcutta *Statesman* of the same date headlined its brief report 'PM pledges Ram Rajya' and ran a story that claimed his 'promise was greeted with cries of "*Har, Har Mahadev*", "*Bajrang Bali ki Jai*" and "*Jai Bharat Mata*". The *Statesman* correspondent appears to have been the only one to have heard these BJP/VHP-associated slogans. I certainly had not – and no other report I found mentioned this.

The mystery was cleared by the following day's *Economic Times* which reported that 'Leaders of the National Front and BJP, at simultaneous evening briefings, ridiculed the Prime Minister's claim for [*sic*] bringing about a "Ram Rajya"'. Obviously, the Opposition had cottoned on to the phrase often used by Mahatma Gandhi to run their campaign of calumny.

I think it was there and then that Rajiv Gandhi lost the election. If only he had stuck to his two-year resolve to make Panchayat Raj the main plank of his platform, perhaps the margin of defeat might have been narrowed. Nevertheless, his campaign for re-election was going quite well when unmitigated disaster struck a week later.

As I have noted earlier, his political advisers, led by Dhawan and Fotedar, had persuaded the PM to facilitate the *shilanyas* of a new Ram temple on the land identified by Home Minister Buta Singh as 'undisputed'. This was a gross misrepresentation on Buta Singh's part because a piece of the so-called 'undisputed' land was in fact part of the dispute. On the basis of the Buta Singh report, Rajiv Gandhi's political advisers were able to persuade the PM that not only should he authorize the *shilanyas*, but he should also schedule it within the election period, not before or after, and, to that end, suddenly announce elections to squeeze the maximum political benefit out of the ritual.

I was not part of this discussion and was, therefore, startled to hear this sudden call to elections. The Dhawan–Fotedar belief appeared to be that such a dramatic announcement would not only take the wind out of the sails of an increasingly belligerent Opposition, it would also enable Rajiv Gandhi to make the building of the Ram temple (along with the physical preservation of the Babri Masjid) his main election platform. This cynical, unprincipled, opportunistic strategy was put in play.

The very idea of playing off both sides – guaranteeing the continued existence of the Babri Masjid to the Muslims while offering the Hindus the prospect of a grand Ram Mandir –appalled me. But there was little I could do as I had entered politics only a few days earlier. In any case, I was still imbued with a strong belief that Panchayat Raj, not Ram Janmabhoomi, was going to be our key issue.

The shilanyas and its consequences

On the day of the *shilanyas*, I was told to cancel his scheduled tour programme for him to stay in Delhi to monitor developments. By the late afternoon it appeared that there had been no negative fallout of the event, so I was asked to immediately arrange for him to fly to a Jammu rally that evening and to route him from there to Goa at night. The following day, he was due to campaign in coastal Karnataka before returning to Delhi and heading for the Fursatganj airfield, from where he would travel by helicopter to Sultanpur, the district headquarters of his own Amethi constituency. I slotted three hours for his road journey from the Sultanpur election rally to Tatarpur, where he was to spend the night, to give time to the cheering crowds expected to line the road.

When we reached Chikmagalur, next stop Udipi where Oscar Fernandes was contesting, the PM received a call that all hell had broken loose in Sultanpur district, and it would be advisable to return at once to Delhi. It fell to my lot to call Oscar and inform him of this. I must say he took this last-minute cancellation well.

Back in Delhi, Rajiv Gandhi listened to the bad news of communal riots in his own constituency in the thick of election season and decided to proceed to his election meeting in Sultanpur. As dusk had fallen, we could not take the chopper from Fursatganj airport to Sultanpur and reached the election meeting ground by road hours behind schedule. It was all but empty. I counted an audience of about 186 people. Nevertheless, RG delivered a full speech.

We then drove to Tatarpur in darkness. It took us less than forty-five minutes compared to the three hours I had set aside. The roadside was empty. For the first time in my five years with him, he was silent, withdrawn, his brow furrowed with worry, his famous smile wiped off his face. At the Tatarpur rest house, I busied myself with reorganizing the next day's programme while RG, Dhawan and Fotedar gathered in the garden outside and plunged into earnest conversation at which my presence was obviously not desired.

Next day, we helicoptered to rallies in Hardoi, Sitapur, Pilibhit, Mau, Jaunpur and finally Allahabad, reaching Allahabad before sunset. RG had heard that the BBC were repeatedly reporting the unfounded rumour that the Babri Masjid had been razed to the ground. So, at each stop, he urged the Congress candidate to hire a bus and take local Muslim leaders to see for themselves that the masjid was standing where it had for the past 500 years, untouched and as stolid as ever. The only one to follow his advice was Kalp Nath Rai in Mau. He was one of the two Congress candidates to win from the many hundred constituencies scattered between Amethi and the Bangladesh border. (M.J. Akbar was the other, from Kishanganj.)

The Nehru centenary address

In the Allahabad circuit house that bleak evening, RG pulled out his laptop and opened the first page of the draft I had prepared for his Nehru centenary address in Vigyan Bhawan on 13 November. The source of the draft was a memo of thirty pages, translated into Russian and hand-delivered to Gorbachev in response to a request made by Gorbachev to RG to explain how such a diverse country as India, beset by separatist movements, had been held together.

To Gorbachev, this seemed a miracle and he wanted to know how. It was obvious that Gorbachev was feeling the stresses that were to bring the Red Revolution to a close a few months down the road. The PM was flattered at his request. He handed over the responsibility of preparing the draft to his intelligence chief, M.K. Narayanan. Narayanan did a thorough policeman's job of it. Rajiv read through it, called me in and asked, 'Is this the way we have held the country together?' Of course, it was a policeman's report and comprehensive and thoroughgoing as far as it went. But it talked of no dimension other than thumbscrews on the nails of rebels!

My instructions were to prepare another draft to which Narayanan's contribution was to be attached as an annex, to give a fuller picture of how we had ensured the unity of India. I had never before penned a more detailed or lengthy account of the 'miracle' of India's unity in diversity. The PM had my draft loaded on to his computer and for about a month or more travelled with it everywhere, availing of every spare second to peruse the draft with a toothcomb to make or suggest the changes he wanted. It was only when he was fully satisfied the draft included everything important that final clearance was given. The official translator was summoned from our embassy in Moscow to render the memo into the Russian language, so that we could control the version that Gorbachev would read in his native tongue.

Soon after the memo to Gorbachev had been dispatched, the question of who was to be invited to deliver the Nehru centenary lecture in Vigyan Bhawan, New Delhi, was raised. I insisted that it could not be anyone other than the prime minister of India. 'Who, me?' was RG's response. 'But I am the man's grandson. Would this not stink of nepotism?' It took me a while to persuade him that it would be absurd to call a foreign dignitary to speak on this historic centenary. I reminded him that there were no living persons of adequate distinction who had worked with Panditji or who could be described as Nehru's comrades-in-arms. (I had in mind the precedent of Khan Abdul Ghaffar Khan having been invited as chief guest for Mahatma Gandhi's centenary in 1969.) Even though he was the grandson, I believed the prime minister – none other – should pay this tribute.

Rajiv Gandhi must have consulted others. But I prevailed when I said the draft Nehru centenary speech was ready. What did I mean, he asked? The memo to Gorbachev, I replied. He himself had spent so much time on it that it could be considered his contemporary interpretation of Jawaharlal Nehru's idea of India. What could be more befitting than a modified version of that memo as his draft centenary address? I think that persuaded him. The draft of the address was readied and he once again uploaded it on to his personal laptop and kept fiddling with it whenever he was undisturbed.

After dinner that night, I sat with him in his suite, and we went through the draft, as modified by him, word by word and phrase by phrase. My memory is that we finished in the early hours, around 2 or 3 a.m.

It turned out to be his last public speech as PM. There was one remaining hitch. Ronen Sen had objected to a phrase scoring the atrocities inflicted on Red Indians (now more correctly called 'Native Americans'). I was adamant that the phrase was necessary to make the point at which we were driving. Ronen felt it gave needless cause for complaint. RG gave no decision on the question. So Ronen and I waited tensely as the PM approached that part of the address. He used it! In the event, the speech made no impact as Rajiv Gandhi was to be ousted a few days later.

Defeat looms

Our hurtling towards defeat was greatly aggravated by Sanjay Singh – the raja of Amethi who was a principal aide to Rajmohan Gandhi, Rajiv Gandhi's main opponent in his constituency – becoming the target of an assassination attempt. Sanjay Singh had been brought to a Lucknow hospital by his wife, Garima, and RG put aside the campaign programme to make an unscheduled visit to the Lucknow Raj Bhawan to meet Garima. We waited a long time, but Garima did not turn up and we overheard stories that she had refused to come to the Raj Bhawan because she and her husband's supporters believed Rajiv Gandhi or his associates were complicit in the assassination attempt. There was not an iota of truth to that rumour but no one was looking for the truth.

The only thing left to do was to fly to Gorakhpur airport (which had night-landing facilities) and proceed to Gopalganj in Bihar by road. It was way beyond midnight when we reached the almost empty and very cold Gopalganj election meeting venue. We then went on a futile road journey to Patna with almost no one on the road or at meetings. It did not take a pollster or soothsayer to see the end was nigh.

As the campaign was winding its way to a conclusion, we found Gopi Arora, M.K. Narayanan and B.G. Deshmukh waiting to board the PM's plane at Calcutta. They had not been summoned but had come to Calcutta of their own volition. They went into a huddle to tell him the only way of saving the election was for him to announce that no place of worship would ever be demolished for whatever reason. I was told later that RG's argument was that even in Saudi Arabia shrines had been demolished to make way for highways, so how could he in all conscience make the statement they had come all the way to Calcutta to plead him to make. (I did not then, and do not now, believe that such a statement would have made any difference to the outcome.)

On the very last day of the campaign, we flew back to Delhi from Varanasi. All of us were aware, I think, that this was the last of the hundreds of journeys we had made in that aircraft.

The following evening, I was at a reception hosted by K.K. Sharma, correspondent of the London *Financial Times*, in his very elegant Chanakyapuri home, to discuss election prospects. Yashwant Sinha was among the guests. I had known him for decades because we had both served in Delhi on trade matters and, later, he was consul general in Frankfurt reporting on European Community issues to our common boss, Ambassador K.B. Lall in Brussels. He drew me aside to confide that his incoming government would allow Rajiv and Sonia to go to Italy, if they were so inclined. I was livid. Whatever made him think they were planning to flee to Italy? Rajiv Gandhi knew he could answer all the bogus charges levelled against him by V.P. Singh and his cohort. He and his wife were not going anywhere, they were staying put!

The results came in sluggishly. There could be no doubt that a majority, however reduced, eluded Rajiv. In the end, the number of Congress seats was slashed by over half from over 400 to under 200. Yet, the Congress was the single largest party. I was unable to see Rajiv or learn his intentions despite leaving messages with his staff.

My phone rang. It was a very indignant Aroon Purie of *India Today* who had been at school, indeed, in the same class, as Rajiv: the two had tied at a low second-class position in their school-leaving examination. Purie demanded to know why Rajiv Gandhi was going to Rashtrapati Bhavan to meet the president when he had quite evidently lost the election. By what right was he staking his claim to cobble together a government? I heard him out until he calmed down.

Then I asked, 'You know everyone at school stole compasses from other students' geometry boxes. Did Rajiv ever steal your compass – or anyone else's?' Rajiv Gandhi, I said, was going to the top of Raisina Hill only to tell the president that as he had lost the election fair and square, he would not be asking to be invited, as head of the largest single party, to form the government. He would be content to sit in the Opposition. I did not know this for sure. I was only guessing from what I knew of the man's innate integrity. I guessed right!

I was summoned to the PM's office in South Block one last time. He was back to his usual cheerful self. We got on with recording his farewell message. From there, we went straight to Central Hall, where a meeting of the Congress Parliamentary Party had been convened. We marched in, me right behind RG, to the thunderous sound of Arjun Singh leading the thumping of desks. I proudly stood by Rajiv Gandhi's side and slightly to his rear, as he delivered his extempore address to his defeated colleagues. There was nothing tearful about the event. It was an expression of determination.

It marked the end of one of the most decisive phases of my life, and it was the start of a whole new chapter.

Special assistant to the Congress president (1989–91) and a columnist

Elections over, much of that first month in the Opposition was filled with setbacks for me. Far from grooming me as his V.K. Krishna Menon, as I had hoped, I hardly got to see RG as he was very busy personally conducting an introspection process with Congress leaders. I was pointedly excluded. Suman Dubey tells me it was perhaps at this juncture that I remarked to him, 'I am the only rat I know that has jumped on to a sinking ship!'

One day, on a now rare private moment, just as we were boarding an aircraft, RG suddenly asked, 'Am I arrogant?' I replied, 'I don't think so, but people resent your having been born with a silver spoon in your mouth that you have turned to gold.' Obviously, there was a great deal of churning going on in his head, heart and soul.

Left on my own, I scouted around for something to do. It was Vir Sanghvi, editor of the Calcutta-based *Sunday* magazine, who inducted me into an altogether new vocation as a columnist. In a *Sunday* box item during the elections (he was certain Rajiv Gandhi would be defeated), Vir famously predicted that Captain Satish Sharma would find himself 'unemployed and unemployable'! As for me, his prediction was that I would become a *Sunday* columnist, although I had given him no hint I was interested.

I leave the rest to him by reproducing this passage from an introduction he wrote for a book I published a couple of years later:

> I still remember his first column for *Sunday*. Published . . . when the media were singing the praises of V.P. Singh, it accurately presaged the end of the Janata Dal government. . .
>
> Abusive letters from Disgusted of Jabalpur and Hysterical of Bangalore poured in. Many readers threatened to cancel their subscriptions. . .

At *Sunday*, we were stunned by the response. The anger of some of our readers did not surprise us – Mani went out of his way to provoke them. What staggered us was first, the large number of letters and second, that to be provoked by Mani you had to first read him. Clearly, all those who loathed his column nevertheless turned to it as soon as their copies of *Sunday* arrived to find new reasons to hate it. He was probably the most widely read columnist in the history of *Sunday*.[3]

Although my first piece, which caused such a furore, was a 'guest column', Vir's boss, Aveek Sarkar, quickly moved to make me a regular with a most generous remuneration, along with permission to place the column, after initial publication, wherever I liked. Within a few months, I had secured publication in many journals – in English, Hindi, Tamil, Gujarati, Marathi and others – that would take my income well above my last government salary. I remain astonished that I was not taken to court, for not only did the column display an astonishing chutzpah in not taking the electoral defeat lying down but it also dripped with sarcasm and often contained an abusive strain in its critique of personalities and policies.

One incident remains in my memory. Pinki Virani was at Bombay's *Mid-Day* evening paper which carried my column after publication in *Sunday*. One day, I found the column in *Mid-Day* had been cut off arbitrarily in full flow before going to the end. I rang in high dudgeon to complain. Pinki answered. After listening to my rant, she patiently explained, 'I am sorry, Mr Aiyar, but half our subeditors hate your column and half of them love it. One of the former must have been on duty when your column was aborted.' I think that neatly illustrates the public reception to my writing.

My college friend, IFS colleague and keen phrase maker, Shekhar

---

[3] Mani Shankar Aiyar, *In Rajiv's Footprints: One Year in Parliament*, Konark, New Delhi, 1993, pp. x–xi. For the full article, please scan the QR code on p. 362.

Dasgupta suggested the standard disclaimer at the end of the column be amended to read, 'The views expressed in this column are not even those of the author'! Another good friend, Steve Weisman of the *New York Times*, who had been transferred from New Delhi to Tokyo, wrote back to say I had 'an amazing talent to abuse and amuse'. That, I think, was the column's USP. It was also the same USP that led to many arrows being shot into my back.

My wife Suneet was annoyed with some of my columns where she thought I was being petulant. So when I ended my second column with the news account of L.K. Advani asking his taxi driver to take him to the PM's residence and the driver bringing him to the doorstep of RG's home, I quipped that it showed who the ordinary people of India thought the real PM still was. She called Vir and insisted that the punchline be deleted. To keep the peace, Vir assented.

An IFS colleague, Jitendra Daulet Singh, asked me bluntly to stop making a fool of myself and gracefully accept defeat. Others, such as S.S. Ahluwalia, were also gunning for me. Just as I was despairing, Vir told me to hang in there, as in a few months I would be hailed as a prophet who had foretold the demise of the V.P. Singh regime. That, indeed, is what happened. Yet, I thought it prudent to check with Rajiv Gandhi whether I might persist. He replied that he had not read any of the columns, but Rahul had and said they were fine. Thus, Rahul Gandhi at age nineteen became the patron saint of *Mani-Talk*!

If finding a regular source of income was my first concern, finding suitable private accommodation was my second. As a retired government servant, I was entitled to six months' continued occupation of my government house. However, I sneered at Urban Development Minister Murasoli Maran in one of my columns saying his 'government that works' functioned so inefficiently that months after my resignation, his ministry had not got around to sending me an eviction notice. He promptly sent it. My mother-in-law had a couple of rooms to spare in her Defence

Colony residence. We stayed with her, in extremely cramped conditions that interfered with the children's studies, until my fortunes changed.

In the meanwhile, Suranya, my eldest, went to St Stephen's and the other two, Yamini and Sana, quickly adjusted themselves to the changed circumstances. Indeed, Suranya got so involved with the anti-Mandal students' agitation that she and Yamini were detained at the Parliament House police station. That did not faze them so much as the prospect of confessing to their parents that they had been in police detention. When I heard that Suranya had achieved at seventeen what I was to still achieve at nearly fifty – police detention – I quite startled her by enthusiastically congratulating her on her achievement. It somewhat melted the ice that had grown between her and her parents in her early adolescence – one of my most painful personal memories.

Failed attempts at Rajya Sabha membership

As I have mentioned, RG's promise to get me into the Rajya Sabha from Delhi had gone awry with the incoming government dissolving the moribund MCD (whose members constituted the electorate) and upgrading it to a regular elected state assembly. I had also lost the opportunity of coming in from Uttar Pradesh, which the state's chief minister Narayan Datt Tiwari had arranged for me, when RG delayed accepting my resignation from the IFS to the very eve of the general elections. I decided to try my luck from Pondicherry, but that too was ruled out by Jayalalithaa. I was left with little option but to rely on Jayalalithaa's benevolence to come in from Tamil Nadu. This seemed on the cards for a while and RG deputed my old boss, Dinesh Singh, to persuade her to let us have the seat in exchange for support we were extending to her in Pondicherry. But this fizzled out. RG encouraged me to try my luck in Arunachal Pradesh but that too proved illusory. I was on my own, stranded and without any prospects.

I moved into my tiny office in the AICC where I was given a small room adjacent to the ladies' toilet. The smell was unbearable. I made the mistake of mentioning this at a dinner party and soon enough the story had wended its way to the media who greatly enjoyed me getting my comeuppuance.

What rescued me was a poor joke I cracked at a Congress demonstration where I remarked that it was clear to me that RG had not taken the Bofors money for my room did not even have an AC. Pritish Nandy published this remark in his gossip column at the *Illustrated Weekly of India*, adding that my lack of an AC was not because RG had not taken the Bofors money but because I had ceased to matter. To my surprise, the Congress treasurer, Sitaram Kesari, barged unannounced into my office demanding to know where the AC was to be installed. It seems Nandy's article had been shown to RG and he had ordered the treasurer to rectify matters without delay. If I did not melt in the heat of that summer, it is only because Nandy, as was his nasty wont, had decided to take a swipe at me!

Convention against communalism

Under the Jammu and Kashmir rubric of my companion volume, I have described at length my involvement from end January to mid-March 1990 in RG's concerns over the alarmingly deteriorating situation in the Kashmir Valley. After our return from Srinagar, RG concentrated on organizing an AICC 'Convention against Communalism' in May 1990, and on measures to whip a demoralized Congress back into shape.

The convention, to be held in Talkatora Stadium, was scheduled for 19 May, about five and a half months after the electoral reverse. The newly elected Congress MP for Kishanganj in Bihar, M.J. Akbar, and I were asked to prepare the draft theme paper. We were asked to meet the senior leaders P.V. Narasimha Rao and V.N. Gadgil before putting pen to paper.

When we arrived for the meeting, I, for one, was quite taken aback by both Rao and Gadgil being not only unenthusiastic about the idea, but just barely stopping short of opposing it. Rao had scraped through the 1989 elections, standing from Ramtek in Vidarbha, Maharashtra. Gadgil had, in fact, lost in Pune.

After Akbar and I briefed the two veterans on the course we had planned, they began, almost offensively, denigrating the traditional Congress line on secularism, saying people were not interested in listening to standard cliches. They were seeking answers to questions about the *tushtikaran* (appeasement) of the Muslim minority. They listed the questions they had faced in their respective campaigns and asked us how we proposed to answer these.

I took down the questions and said we would return with draft answers. Akbar seemed a little shaken and, to the best of my memory, took little further part. A sampling of the questions:

- Why should we not have a uniform civil code?
- What justification was there for negating the Shah Bano judgment by an Act of Parliament?
- What is the logic of persisting with Article 370?
- Why should Hindus adopt family planning when Muslims resist it?
- Why build a Haj Manzil in Bombay for Muslim pilgrims embarking for Jeddah when there is nothing similar for Hindu pilgrims proceeding to Nepal?
- Why does the Government of India subsidize Hajis when it does not similarly subsidize Hindu pilgrims?
- Why should we make such a hue and cry over secularism when no Muslim country practises it?
- Does not a religion which talks of '*kafir*' (non-believer) and '*jihad*' (holy war) pose a special threat?
- Why do Indian Muslims cheer Pakistani teams at sports events?
- Does not the demand for *azadi* on the part of Kashmiri Muslims show that a Muslim can never be a patriotic Indian?

- Why are Indian Muslims so worried about the Al Aqsa mosque when there are so many dilapidated mosques in India?
- There have been cases of Muslim shrines being shifted to other locations in Islamic countries such as Saudi Arabia. Why not in India?
- Why do Muslims object to singing the national song 'Vande Mataram'?
- Why do Muslims seek a separate identity in India when they do not do so in countries like Indonesia?
- Why do foreign missionaries proselytize in India?
- Why should we permit Christian missionary activity?

When I took my draft answers to these questions to Narasimha Rao, he pouted and, without reading the draft, enquired whether these were the official views of the Congress. I stuttered, saying I did not know, I was only providing tentative answers to the questions he and Gadgil had asked. I was dismissed. It was my introduction to the mind of the person, P.V. Narasimha Rao who, as prime minister, was to facilitate the dismantling of the Babri Masjid. I seem to remember the convention being held without a theme paper. But I was not done and so titled my paper 'Secular Answers to Communal Questions: A Catechism for Communalists' and sent it off to Pritish Nandy who happily published it in the *Illustrated Weekly of India*.[4]

The success of the convention, and my startled discovery of opposition to it in the top echelons of the party, led me to accept an invitation I received from Iqbal Hasnain, a professor of geology at Jawaharlal Nehru University, to become president of an organization he proposed to set up, called the Society for Secularism.

With plenty of time to spare, I travelled to west Uttar Pradesh – Bijnor, Saharanpur, Muzaffarnagar, Moradabad, Meerut, Bulandshahr, Kanpur, Fatehpur (V.P. Singh's constituency), Aligarh (town and university),

---

[4] The text is included in my book, *Confessions of a Secular Fundamentalist* (Penguin Viking, New Delhi, 2004).

Ghaziabad – and farther afield in Haryana (Panipat, Kaithal, Faridabad); Indore and Jabalpur in Madhya Pradesh; Pilani and Churu in Rajasthan; Bangalore, coastal Andhra Pradesh (Guntur), Hyderabad city and Trichy (Tamil Nadu) in the south – spreading the message of secularism, largely based on the paper Rao had rejected.

The Uma Shankar Dikshit report

Meanwhile, Rajiv Gandhi, synthesizing all he had learnt from older, more experienced colleagues, decided the answer to revitalizing the party lay in a report prepared at his instance by a veteran Congressman, the octogenarian Uma Shankar Dikshit, which stressed the imperative of organizational elections at all levels within the party. So the Congress president set about convening an 'extended' meeting of the CWC, which meant that besides the twenty full-time members, Congress chief ministers, PCC presidents and other senior Congress leaders, including general secretaries and other office bearers, would be invited. I too was slipped in.

The gravamen of the proceedings was the adoption of the Dikshit report and the resolve to implement its recommendations. (Extraordinarily, no copy of the report could be found in the Congress archives at 24, Akbar Road, despite Priyanka Gandhi Vadra's attempts on my behalf at tracing a copy. Not even Sandeep Dikshit, the grandson of the author, has been able to locate a copy in the family's personal papers. Viswajit Prithvijit Singh was reported to have possessed a personal copy. But his wife, a retired IFS officer, has, at my request, searched and reported back negatively. That, I think, reflects the state of the party now.)

It was decided to convene a plenary meeting of the AICC to debate and endorse the extended CWC's resolution. They convened in July 1990 in Mavlankar Hall and passed, after debate, the required resolution. Just over six months of his electoral defeat, RG had found a consensual road to the rehabilitation of the party – through the Uma Shankar Dikshit report. Thirty years later, as the Congress struggles to find its feet after two resounding electoral reverses, in the ninth year of Modi Raj, the most useful lesson the party could learn from Rajiv Gandhi's brief leadership was the speed and conviction with which he moved to resurrect and rejuvenate the party.

The descent and fall of V.P. Singh

Alas, the recommendations of the Uma Shankar Dikshit report were never implemented. The principal reason for this was that within weeks of the Mavlankar Hall AICC session, V.P. Singh, who described himself as a master 'manager of contradictions', destabilized his own government by announcing his acceptance of the long-pending recommendations of the Mandal Commission on reservations for OBCs.

Singh found himself caught in the claws of the worst contradictions within his own government. On the one hand, there was the internal pressure to act on the Mandal Commission recommendations for OBC reservations in educational institutions, government employment and representation in the panchayats – which could result in deepening fault lines along caste contours in Hindu society. On the other hand, the BJP sought to thwart such salami slicing of the Hindu community by promoting, as the alternative, the vicious 'othering' of the minority Muslim community as the basis on which to unite the majority.

Rajiv Gandhi initially took a hard line, based on the stands taken by his grandfather, Jawaharlal Nehru, and mother, Indira Gandhi, on, respectively, the Kakasaheb Kelkar report (1956) and the Mandal Commission recommendations (1980) on reservations for OBCs. He felt, like his predecessors, that any implementation would not only prove deeply divisive but would privilege the freezing of caste over its dismantlement.

But several of his advisers, led by Arjun Singh, persuaded RG to moderate his opposition. So, while Advani got on with organizing his '*rath yatra*', the country was consumed in the double fire of communalism and the fierce opposition against reservations for OBCs, including self-immolation by a student.

From the day V.P. Singh made this announcement in Parliament on 7 August 1990, his government began to totter. It fell when Advani's *rath* was stopped at Samastipur in Bihar by Chief Minister Lalu Prasad Yadav, one of the central government's supporters, for spreading communalism in a state that had a substantial Muslim population. The BJP reacted by withdrawing their outside support from the central government and V.P. Singh's government was left dangling in mid-air. It lost a vote of confidence on 7 November 1990, eleven months after it was sworn in. Attention then focused on whether to call another general election or to try to cobble together an alternative government.

I wrongly thought RG would plump for a general election. By then, I had concluded that the Rajya Sabha option was closed, and I should try my luck in open electoral contest. I went to see President Venkataraman on my own, banking on his having known my parents when he was a member of the Constituent Assembly. I wanted to leverage this family connection to secure a ticket to contest from the president's former constituency of Thanjavur, which is also where my ancestral village lies. He was totally unsympathetic (I later learnt that he had in mind his former constituency right-hand man, Tulasiah Vandiyar). I was sternly rebuked that we were a poor country and could not afford frequent general elections. Leave alone endorsing my electoral ambitions, it was essential, he said, that an election be altogether avoided. I was out on my ear within minutes of being ushered into his august presence!

Instead of pressing for another election to return to power, RG chose the alternative of extending the Congress party's outside support to a government led by Chandra Shekhar – a classic case of the tail wagging the dog.

The erosion of secularism

I was disappointed at this development, but much more distressed at the impact of Advani's *rath yatra* on the Congress mind. Staunch Congressmen of the ilk of Narayan Datt Tiwari – who had just lost his chief ministership to long-term opponent Mulayam Singh Yadav of the Samajwadi Party, a hard-line Mandal proponent – were looking at the Ayodhya (read Hindu) card as the road back to power despite their left-wing orientation (socialist, secular). Dinesh Singh too seemed to be drifting in the same direction, telling me in some wonderment that food was not being cooked in Lucknow households because the womenfolk were out on the streets beating pots and pans to voice their support for a Ram temple to replace the Babri Masjid. I had earlier experienced the reactions of P.V. Narasimha Rao and V.N. Gadgil.

I, therefore, took myself off to the Nehru Memorial Museum and Library to research how Nehru had stared down a similar challenge to his unflinching secularism when religion-based prejudice raised its ugly head within the party back in 1949–51. The flagbearer of that revolt was Purushottam Das Tandon, who contested and won the September 1950 Congress party leadership election at Nasik, with the support of Sardar Vallabhbhai Patel, against the much-respected Gandhian, Acharya J.B. Kripalani. In 1950 there were a number of other factors pulling the Congress away from its anchoring in Gandhi–Nehru secular values, including intra-party opposition to the Nehru–Liaquat pact on the treatment of minorities in India and Pakistan. There was also the controversy over the president, Dr Rajendra Prasad, wanting to be officially present at the inauguration of the rebuilt Somnath temple; Nehru and his cabinet opposed this as being incompatible with the constitutional requirement that the State must be above all religions and not demonstrate affinity with particular faiths.

My research led to the discovery that Nehru had succeeded in ridding the party of Tandon by the expedient of getting members of the CWC to resign, thus forcing Tandon's hand. Jawaharlal Nehru then took up the presidency of the party and, in a memorable address at Ramlila Ground on Gandhi Jayanti, 2 October 1951, proclaimed: 'If any person raises his hand against another on the ground of religion, I shall fight him till the last breath of my life, both as the head of the government and from outside.'[5]

A fortnight later, Syama Prasad Mookerjee founded the Jana Sangh.

I wrote up my research and sent it for publication in the *Hindustan Times*. When it was printed, I took it to RG and said this was a private letter to him published in the guise of a public article to warn him against those in his own ranks who had lost trust in the bonding adhesive of secularism. I warned him that the main threat secularism faced was from within, not without the party. RG told me not to worry. He would remain true to his basic beliefs. I was not entirely reassured.

My apprehensions were soon put to the test. RG thought up the novel idea of leading a *padayatra* (journey on foot) from Allahabad to Ayodhya as a way of publicly demonstrating the contrast between the methodology and objectives of Advani's *rath yatra* and the proposed Congress *yatra*. He went deep into the details, and summoned the PCC chiefs to discuss arrangements and fix dates. Asking me to brief the PCC presidents, he sat with his senior colleagues. I was feeling very buoyed at being put in charge of conveying RG's plans to the PCC chiefs in the conference room at 24, Akbar Road, little knowing that in the higher-level meeting RG had convened next door at 10, Janpath, he was being persuaded, perhaps even pressurized, to abandon his plans as needlessly provocative and potentially counterproductive.

So, when I emerged from the meeting I was chairing, I was informed in a whisper by Murli Deora that I had been wasting my time and those

---

[5] N.L. Gupta (ed.), *Nehru on Communalism*, Hope India Publications, New Delhi, 1965, p. 217.

of his colleagues as it had been decided at 10, Janpath, not to go ahead with the counter *yatra*. The Congress was fleeing the field of battle.

Rajiv Gandhi's Sadbhavana Yatra

Then Rajiv Gandhi, reverting to type, decided on a 'Sadbhavana Yatra' (communal harmony journey – literally 'pilgrimage') as the alternative. The *yatra* began at Rajghat, Mahatma Gandhi's samadhi, on his birth anniversary, 2 October, with a pledge in Jawaharlal Nehru's words: 'to dedicate myself to building a secular India, where every religion and belief has full freedom and equal honour, where every citizen has equal liberty and equal opportunity'.[6] Instructions were sent to the PCCs to repeat the pledge at exactly the same time and in the same words by knots of Congress workers and party sympathizers in each of the 5 to 6 lakh villages. The yatris then set out for Delhi Gate and down Daryaganj before wheeling left into the teeming lanes of Shahjahanabad that housed a concentration of Delhi's Muslim citizens.

Over the next three weeks, I walked in the wake of Rajiv Gandhi through Fatehpur and Faizabad; down the narrow *gali*s of Ayodhya; in the by-lanes of Ghaziabad and Modinagar; late through the night past the crowded tenements of Hashimpura – scene of some of the worst communal atrocities in 1987 in Meerut; from the famed Charminar in the old city of Hyderabad to Gandhiji's statue in the twin city of Secunderabad. I was in a procession that took seven hours to wind past him and Jayalalithaa taking the salute, as it were, at Spencer's Point in Madras; and then accompanied him on a deeply evocative pilgrimage to the temple of Vaikom in Kerala, where Gandhiji had thrown open the temple doors to Harijans.

Further *yatra*s by Rajiv Gandhi included going from Bhagalpur in

---

[6] *Independence and After: A Collection of the More Important Speeches of Jawaharlal Nehru from September 1946 to May 1949*, Publications Division, New Delhi, 1949, p. 36.

Bihar, site of the horrendous rioting on the eve of the 1989 general elections, to Dhubri in Assam; then Calcutta and Bhubaneswar; from Raipur by train through Chhattisgarh and Mahakoshal to Bhopal; by the Garib Nawaz Express to Ajmer and Pushkar; then on to Ahmedabad and Bombay. Everywhere he went, there was love in the air in sharp contrast to the hate spewed through Advani's near simultaneous *rath yatra* leaving a trail of scores of lost lives and hundreds injured. To the multitudes that thronged his addresses, Rajiv Gandhi's message was of harmony and peace, of the ending of strife and the binding of wounds, of our unity in diversity.

The slogans that rent the air were:

Hindustan ke char sipahi:
Hindu, Muslim, Sikh, Isai

Hindustan ka yeh hai nara:
Hindu hamara, Muslim hamara

Awaz do:
Ham ek hain.[7]

Alas, the sounds of hate drowned out the sounds of love.

Search for solutions

On the question of the masjid/temple at Ayodhya, Rajiv Gandhi closeted himself with a cabal of advisers to work out an alternative plan for dealing with the Ram Janmabhoomi–Babri Masjid crisis. Siddhartha Shankar Ray, the statesman-jurist, was the strongest voice of those making the

---

[7] The English translation would be something along the lines of 'Four soldiers of Hindustan / Hindu, Muslim, Sikh, Christian / This is the slogan of Hindustan / Hindus are ours, Muslim are ours / Raise your voices / We are one'.

argument that the crux of the issue lay in determining whether Babar's general, Mir Baqi, had, in fact, destroyed an extant Ram temple to erect the Babri Masjid or whether he had only built the mosque on unused land that was now being claimed as the birthplace of Lord Ram. He suggested that it be left to the Supreme Court to pronounce its view on this limited but crucial question after hearing the historical and archaeological evidence from respected experts.

Siddhartha Ray further argued that there were two ways of securing the Supreme Court view on this 'key question': either under Article 142 or 143. Under Article 142, the Supreme Court view would be expressed in court as an order that 'shall be enforceable throughout the territory of India'.[8] If raised before the Supreme Court as a presidential reference under Article 143, the court's finding would be a non-binding 'opinion' addressed to the president. Ray preferred raising the issue in the Supreme Court under Article 142 as that would result in a 'binding' order.

Another alternative that was considered related to requesting the Supreme Court to convoke a commission of inquiry under Section 3 of the Commission of Inquiry Act, 1952, comprising five sitting judges of the Supreme Court, selected by the chief justice of India, to determine the question of fact as to whether, at the site of the dispute, a Ram mandir was in fact destroyed to build a masjid in its place. If it was held that such a commission could not be established owing to the same question pending before the Allahabad High Court, an ordinance or law might be passed under Article 138 enlarging the jurisdiction of the Supreme Court.

These alternatives were put to PM Chandra Shekhar by Rajiv Gandhi in writing and others were conveyed orally. Chandra Shekhar finally decided on Article 143, a non-binding opinion on a presidential reference.

---

[8] 'Part V: Article 142', Constitution of India. https://www.constitutionofindia.net/articles/article-142-enforcement-of-decrees-and-orders-of-supreme-court-and-orders-as-to-discovery-etc/.

That could not, by definition, have definitively ended the matter. This caused RG considerable annoyance.

The invasion of Iraq

Another thing that caused him annoyance was the approval accorded by PM Chandra Shekhar to the US to refuel American warplanes en route to Iraq on bombing missions without full UN sanction and certainly without an approving vote from India. I was in Fatehpur for my Society for Secularism when the news broke. I was summoned back by V. George. When I protested that I was, in any case, scheduled to return the next day, George said nothing doing; RG wanted me back the same evening. So I was driven helter-skelter to Lucknow airport with barely minutes to spare for boarding the flight. I rushed to 10, Janpath, to find a somewhat distraught RG indignant that such a major decision had been taken by PM Chandra Shekhar without consultation with the principal party supporting the government.

Saddam Hussein was not only a leading member of the NAM, he was also a staunch friend of India. The firm championing of non-intervention by a military superpower, which had been a core principle of NAM, had been violated and the 'coalition of the willing' put together by the US was outside the pale of international law. Moreover, I was told by RG that at the intervention of RG's great friend, the crown prince of Jordan, Saddam had agreed to withdraw from his unwarranted intrusion into Kuwait and it was only the US military intervention that had stalled his voluntary withdrawal of forces.[9]

At this stage, another favourite of RG's, Ronen Sen (who had continued as principal foreign policy adviser in the PMO to both V.P. Singh and Chandra Shekhar), drew RG's attention to the standing instructions

---

[9] See also Chinmaya R. Gharekhan, *Centres of Power: My Years in the Prime Ministers Office and Security Council*, Rupa, New Delhi, 2023, p. 209–210.

that any military aircraft overflying India (unless the passengers included heads of state/government and, sometimes, foreign ministers) had perforce to land in India. They were also entitled to refuel before taking off. These were instructions which RG himself had endorsed.

Ronen contended PM Chandra Shekhar was only following standing operating procedure in agreeing to let US military aircraft refuel at Indian airports. Ronen also strongly felt that our self-interest would be affected if India withdrew permission to the American military aircraft to overfly or refuel in India as we might be denied overfly rights by Pakistan and others as a consequence; this would disrupt the frequent sorties that our Air Force undertook to Soviet destinations to pick up munitions, spares and equipment. He apprehended that this would jeopardize our relations with the West and other members of 'the coalition of the willing'. (I countered that our Air Force could easily cross the Pamirs into Kazakhstan, then part of the Soviet Union, without overflying Pakistan, but I made the argument to Ronen long after the Iraq war was over.)

Ronen was also not sure that banning US military overflights on their way to bombing Iraq with whom we had no quarrel would be adequately appreciated or endorsed in either the UN or even NAM. Finally, he had no doubt that US and Soviet intelligence agencies were closely monitoring developments, perhaps even in touch with each other, so that no US military step caught the Soviet Union off guard. I have learnt all this from Ronen Sen only decades later; neither RG nor anyone else in Congress circles (like Natwar or Romesh Bhandari, my erstwhile senior IFS colleagues) told me about these arguments.

My guess is that RG continued to denounce Chandra Shekhar's approval to US warplanes refuelling in India because RG had agreed to such landing and refuelling of military aircraft in peacetime, not in a time of war where India would implicitly become a collaborator in US aggression. Ronen does not agree. We have agreed to disagree.

A Lok Sabha opening for me

In the aftermath of the dust-up between RG and Chandra Shekhar over Iraq, my attention was distracted by a potentially life-changing occurrence in the last days of January 1991. I had been invited to a joint meeting of all Rotary Clubs of the Bangalore region to speak on secularism. I had to return post-haste next morning to Delhi by the first flight from Madras, but the usual road route to Madras from Bangalore had been blocked at the call of a *hartal*[10] by Jayalalithaa of the All India Anna Dravida Munnetra Kazhagam (AIADMK), then in the Opposition. So I had to find my long way around via Andhra Pradesh in the middle of the night, which meant running the gauntlet of dacoits. The chief minister, S. Bangarappa, provided me a police escort and we fetched up at Madras airport at about 5 a.m. to catch the 6 a.m. red-eye to Delhi. At the airport, we found that the flight to Delhi had been delayed until the evening. So I dossed down at the nearby apartment of one of the party and slept until late in the morning.

On awakening and opening the *Hindu*, I discovered that the serving Congress MP for Mayiladuthurai, E.S.M. Packeer Mohamed,[11] had passed away the previous night. This presented an opportunity of finding a seat in Parliament through the by-election this would necessitate. I rang my cousin in my ancestral village of Kargudi and ordered him to carry the biggest wreath he could find to the hospital to express my condolences.

On reaching Delhi, I made a beeline for RG's office. I told him I wanted to fill the Tamil Nadu vacancy that had arisen. Rajiv looked quite startled. He remarked it would mean my fighting an election. Of course, it would – but that was just the point. I would, I told him, much rather be in the Lok Sabha than the Rajya Sabha and was confident I could win

---

[10] Stoppage of all work and movement; a common form of protest in India.

[11] In the Tamil script, 'F' does not exist, and 'P' is substituted in its place. The pronunciation of the late MP's name would have been 'Faqir Mohamed'.

if I were given the ticket. He enquired if my ancestral village, which he had visited three years earlier, lay within the constituency. I said it didn't but lay only 15 kilometres from the western edge. 'Near enough,' Rajiv said and seemed ready to go along with the suggestion. I floated on air. This was why I had quit the foreign service.

RG seeks to end the Iraq war

Meanwhile, RG was wondering if a direct appeal from India to Saddam might not result in a compromise that ended armed hostilities and spared Iraqi civilians the horrors of war. He decided to make his way to Baghdad via Moscow and Tehran to meet Saddam. I was included, along with Natwar Singh and Bhandari, in the accompanying team.

In Moscow, RG asked me to accompany him to the Kremlin for his pre-dinner meeting with Gorbachev. He wanted me to be at hand when the conversation turned to the thirty-page letter he had sent Gorbachev in response to Gorbachev's query as to how the Government of India had kept together a country even more diverse than the USSR. Rajiv Gandhi went into Gorbachev's chambers and I sat in the anteroom, awaiting the call to join them. However, within just a few minutes of going in, RG and Gorbachev walked out, RG signalling me to come up to him. He whispered that I should go back to the dacha and await him.

I went back somewhat disconsolate and accepted the invitation from our chargé d'affaires, Alfred Gonsalves, for a spin around town to catch a glimpse of Moscow by night. I was astonished to see a long queue outside the Baskin-Robbins outlet because the Russians used to be inordinately proud of their ice cream. Why then were they queuing up to eat American ice cream? Alfred said it was a symbol of the crumbling Soviet system. The Russians waiting patiently in line for their Baskin-Robbins ice cream were demonstrating their disenchantment with the Soviet regime. He gave another example. Apparently, no one referred to

Leningrad by that name any more. They were not quite ready to revert to the Czarist name, St Petersburg, but were content to call it 'Peter's'.

When Rajiv returned to the dacha, he was frustrated on two counts. One, Gorbachev had not even glanced at the letter over which RG had toiled so hard. Moreover, while agreeing with RG that his permanent representative at the UN, Vorontsov, should take a strong stand on Iraq, Gorbachev had requested Rajiv to instruct Vorontsov as he, Gorbachev, was not in a position to do so! After all, Gorbachev pleaded, Vorontsov had been a long-serving Soviet ambassador in Delhi and would, therefore, heed any advice tendered by India at a sufficiently high level. Nothing could have more effectively evidenced Gorbachev's crumbling hold over his country. And next morning, when it proved impossible for the former PM to get through to the current PM in his country retreat of Bhondsi, because if the Indian PM's communications network was so poor, it was also clear that Chandra Shekhar's hold over his administration was as tenuous as Gorbachev's. In RG's time as PM, the hotline, as I well knew, never failed even from the remotest regions.

We proceeded to Frankfurt to catch our connection to Tehran. In the lounge at Frankfurt airport, we saw the television coverage of the end of Operation Desert Storm as the US road-roller swept through the disputed oil-rich desert dividing north Kuwait from south Iraq, burying alive the elite of Saddam's formidable army and the Revolutionary Guards. It was evident that Saddam had lost the 'mother of all battles' and little purpose would be served by Rajiv Gandhi driving out to meet him in his hideout.

We landed in Dubai preparatory to proceeding to Tehran. Royal protocol were waiting at the bottom of the front ramp to receive their distinguished visitor, even if he was no longer a serving head of government. They fell into utter confusion as Rajiv, Sonia and the entire delegation descended from the rear ramp, as we had all been booked in economy!

We landed about an hour later in Tehran. The next morning, RG asked me to accompany him to his meeting with President Ali Akbar Hashemi Rafsanjani. I trotted along. RG opened the discussion by asking, 'After Saddam, who?' Rafsanjani came up with a startling answer: 'Saddam.' Rajiv was certain there had been a mistranslation somewhere. He began patiently explaining that what he meant was that as Saddam had been abjectly defeated on the battlefield, who did Rafsanjani think would succeed Saddam?

With equal patience, Rafsanjani explained that he had fully understood the question the first time round and his answer remained the same: 'Saddam would succeed Saddam.' He went on to explain that the Kurdish problem was common to Turkey, Iraq and Iran. As Turkey had the largest number of Kurds, this NATO ally could not brook any secession and so the Americans had to keep Saddam in office because he was the only one of the three (Iran, Iraq and Turkey) who had the ruthlessness to keep the Kurds in check. He freely confessed that Iran could not do more. And so, the Kurdish problem would require Saddam remaining the president of Iraq, notwithstanding his crushing defeat at American hands, to serve US long-term interests in keeping the Turks – who guarded the underbelly of the Soviet Union – satisfied.

Saddam, in fact, remained president, and rained chemical weapons on the Kurds, until President George H.W. Bush's son invaded Iraq a second time about twelve years later. But along with Saddam, US sanctions also remained, leading to half a million Iraqi infants and children dying of starvation, malnutrition and hunger-related diseases. It was the kind of callousness I had seen first-hand in Vietnam.

After that conversation, there was a somewhat romantic interlude. It was RG's and Sonia's wedding anniversary and they had not been allowed by their personal security detail to eat out together since one outing in London at the start of his premiership. The Iranians said they would handle the security (and, by God, they did!) and so Rajiv and Sonia (for the last time, as it turned out) were able to visit a restaurant together to celebrate twenty-three years of marital bliss.

The following day, we landed in Dubai and found that Shaikh Zayed, the ruler of Abu Dhabi and head of the United Arab Emirates (UAE), horrified at the prospect of his distinguished guest flying out of the UAE in economy, had placed his personal plane at RG's disposal to return to Delhi. It was the only time I washed my hands under taps made of solid gold!

The mess in the economy

Soon after our return from Tehran, I called on an old friend, Deepak Nayyar, chief economic adviser in the finance ministry, to get some statistical information for an article I was writing comparing wholesale prices of foodstuff in 1947 with prevailing wholesale prices. The required data was furnished soon enough but Deepak motioned me to continue sitting. He then filled me in on the details of the economic crisis facing the country, particularly in respect of the balance of payments tottering in the wake of Gulf remittances having dried up. There was a great deal else also wrong with the economy.

I rushed to 10, Janpath, to apprise Rajiv Gandhi and found that he was about to join a CWC meeting that was just starting. I made bold to request him to spare me a moment before the meeting commenced and he obliged by walking to the window on the far side of the room for me to speak to him in confidence. After hearing me out for a few minutes, he interrupted to say I should be informing the whole of the CWC about this impending disaster and invited me to address the senior leaders present.

I did so as briefly as I could. RG then asked me to wait in the anteroom until the CWC meeting ended. The meeting was soon over and, when I returned, he laughed, saying that virtually no one had understood the gravity of my disclosure. He wanted me to immediately visit Dr Manmohan Singh, who was then serving as chairman of the University Grants Commission, to request him to come by and see him.

I drove over to Manmohan Singh's Pandara Road residence and asked to meet the good doctor. His wife, Gursharan Kaur, came out to say Dr Singh was very ill with some kind of flu and could my message wait? I replied that I had come from the former prime minister with an urgent message to be delivered personally. Could I, therefore, be permitted to meet doctor sahib? All I needed was a nod. With great reluctance, Gursharanji let me in. Doctor sahib was lying prone, obviously drained of energy. I conveyed my message to him as succinctly as I could and asked him only to indicate by a shake of the head if he would be prepared to meet RG when he was better. Dr Manmohan Singh pulled my head down towards himself and whispered hoarsely in my ear that he would call on RG as soon as he felt a little better. That was enough, and I took my leave. This call was to have profound consequences, unforeseen by any of us at the time.

Intimations of assassination plots

In early February, Ramesh Dalal, a social activist and trade union leader from Haryana, called on RG to say that Chandra Shekhar had sent one Mahant Sewa Dass to London, all expenses paid, to contact Jagjit Singh Chauhan – who was coordinating the different militant factions of the Khalistan movement – apparently to persuade Chauhan to call off the Khalistanis. To combat the London cold, Chandra Shekhar even loaned the mahant his personal overcoat.

The mahant had told Ramesh Dalal that in London he soon found himself caught up in a plot being hatched by representatives of the Babbar Khalsa, JKLF, ULFA and LTTE gathering together under Chauhan's tutelage to coordinate the assassination of Rajiv Gandhi. Not wanting any further part in these murky goings-on, the mahant had returned post-haste to India and informed Prime Minister Chandra Shekhar, but the PM dismissed him and seemed disinclined to take the threat seriously. Therefore, Ramesh Dalal had sought an appointment with RG to apprise him of the plot.[12] I ran into Dalal outside RG's office and found him somewhat down at the mouth. He said he had told RG of the plot, but RG had shot back that there was nothing he could do about it. It was for PM Chandra Shekhar to take the required steps.

RG was right. He had personally conceived the SPG and empowered it to overrule even the local district magistrate, if necessary, to provide the required level of security. Unfortunately, despite lacunae in the legislation being pointed out to the minister of internal security, P. Chidambaram, in the debate on the SPG Bill, no steps had been taken to provide for SPG cover in the event of the person protected ceasing to be prime minister without any diminution in his threat perception.

V.P. Singh had, therefore, withdrawn the SPG from RG saying only serving PMs were entitled to that kind of security. In RG's view, it was only that level of security that could provide an iron-clad guarantee of his life. However, as Chandra Shekhar had not seen fit to restore SPG cover to RG, he knew his life hung by a thread. But he refused to be intimidated, or to curtail his tour programmes, or his RG-to-people contacts.

Intimations of my first election

Within days of our return from Iran, two Haryana constables, Prem Singh of CID Narnaul and Raj Singh of CID Rohtak, were caught maintaining vigil at the edge of the Congress office at 24, Akbar Road, overlooking RG's residence at 10, Janpath, next door, ostensibly 'to keep a watch on terrorist

---

[12] See Ramesh Dalal, *Rajiv Gandhi's Assassination: The Mystery Unfolds*, UBSPD, New Delhi, 2001.

activities at 10, Janpath/24, Akbar Road'. RG was furious that the very government that was dependent on his goodwill for existence should have had the gall to set spies on him. He demanded the chief minister of Haryana be asked to resign; Chandra Shekhar, who relied heavily on Haryana chief minister Chautala, would not agree.

Accordingly, the Congress withdrew its support from Chandra Shekhar on 6 March 1991, the day the budget was to be presented. The prime minister tendered his resignation that evening to the president but was asked to continue as head of an interim government.

For me, this meant, I would be fighting in Mayiladuthurai in a general election, not a by-election. I expected to win, both because of the past record of Congress wins in the constituency but also because Jayalalithaa had signalled to me her enthusiastic support – *if I got the ticket*. This latter condition surprised me as I thought that with the support of RG, getting the ticket might be taken for granted. But she was clearly on to something that had missed my eye.

The principal opponent to my Congress candidacy for Mayiladuthurai, I found, was none other than G.K. Moopanar, the strongman of the Congress in Tamil Nadu. I thought I had built an excellent rapport with him in the thirteen gruelling road journeys RG had undertaken in Tamil Nadu during the run-up to the state's assembly elections in January 1989. I particularly prided myself at having persuaded the Congress president to name Moopanar as our chief minister-designate at a public rally in Madras. There was a much-photographed moment when I hugged Moopanar on the sands of Marina Beach as RG broke the tension by making the announcement. That Moopanar had been utterly wrong in predicting a win for the Congress if we were to go it alone after MGR's death was another matter, but throughout the thirteen long months of that campaign, I had stood shoulder to shoulder with Moopanar to ensure that every detail of every tour was worked out to his entire satisfaction.

What I did not know was that two of Moopanar's three principal homes were in the Mayiladuthurai constituency and that the great kingmaker could not abide the thought of anyone other than a designated puppet representing the constituency. Hostilities were initiated when I attended a buffet lunch hosted by Moopanar in Delhi for RG and the host refused to greet me as I entered the venue and studiously ignored me throughout.

His antennae were alerted when I made a special trip to Kumbakonam (the main town of the constituency) in February 1991 with the excuse that I was paying my condolences to the bereaved family of the deceased MP when it was perfectly clear to everyone that I was casing out the constituency. I had even used the cover of my Society for Secularism to address a public meeting in Kumbakonam.

My most challenging moment there came in the Q&A session when a girl dressed in the standard black of the Dravidar Kazhagam asked how I dare speak on secularism when my caste was emblazoned in my surname. Sometimes, spontaneity comes to one's rescue. Instead of being fazed by her question, I told her that the first time my name had been printed in the newspapers was when I stood first in Delhi University in the Economics Hons exam. I then slyly added that if there had not been an 'Aiyar' dangling at the end of my name, the credit would have gone to Uttar Pradesh – where 'Mani Shankar' was a common enough name! I stressed the 'Aiyar' in my surname was not a caste name in the north where I had been raised, but an identity tag pointing to my Tamil origins.

The problem of the division of the Cauvery waters between Tamil Nadu and the upper riparian state, Karnataka, came to the fore at this time. The three-man commission to resolve the dispute was visiting the Cauvery delta and their tour was scheduled to begin near my ancestral village. When I joined the members of the commission, they seemed relieved to have an English speaker among them. We journeyed in a cavalcade from the banks of the Cauvery near my ancestral village to my hoped-for future constituency.

My first political engagement was at the village of Govindapuram, about midway between Kumbakonam and Mayiladuthurai, where the commission broke journey for their first interaction with the farmers of the delta. I had written the Tamil equivalents of some of the technical terms on a prompt card and, after briefly making my points in Tamil, referring frequently to my prompt card, I said I would explain what I was saying in English as the members of the commission did not speak Tamil. This led to my principal DMK opponent-designate mistakenly campaigning on the theme that I knew 'no Tamil at all'. This redounded to my benefit because the electorate were pleasantly surprised to discover that, however halting and incorrect my pidgin Tamil, it was untrue to say I knew no Tamil at all. The tour also gave me the opportunity to join a public demonstration at Sirkazhi, in the far north-east of the constituency, to demonstrate my solidarity on the Cauvery waters issue with the delta farmers who constituted four-fifths, if not more, of the electorate.

It was in the CPB that final decisions were taken on the distribution of tickets. Dinesh Singh, a member of the board, filled me in on the details of the CPB proceedings. Moopanar had vigorously opposed my candidature for the Mayiladuthurai constituency. RG had then remarked that if Moopanar did not want me to have the ticket, would he contest the constituency himself? Moopanar, who had barely scraped through the assembly election, threw up his hands in horror and refused point-blank. 'Then why,' enquired Rajiv, 'are you so opposed to Mani being given the ticket?' Moopanar shot back, 'Because he'll lose.' At that point, P.V. Narasimha Rao intervened to say, 'Then let him lose. After all, in politics, you have to learn to both win and lose. Let him learn by losing first.'

And, thus, on the assurance that I would be defeated, I was selected as the MP candidate for Mayiladuthurai (which means the 'bank of the river on which the peacock dances' – a reference to a legend that Lord Shiva had arrived in the guise of a peacock to dance with the other peacocks on the banks of the Cauvery river). But Moopanar made the condition that my candidacy would not be officially announced until candidates for all our twenty-nine Tamil Nadu seats (out of a total of thirty-nine, ten of which would go the AIADMK) had been decided.

This left me biting my fingernails when I came to know that Jayalalithaa would be campaigning in Mayiladuthurai on 22 April. It was imperative that my candidacy be officially announced by then as I would not otherwise be able to legitimately join her on her campaign trail. As it turned out, the official spokesman, Janardan Dwivedi, persuaded All India Radio to announce my name in its 10 p.m. broadcast on the evening of 21 April. I caught the evening flight to Madras and the overnight train to Mayiladuthurai to reach the constituency before Jayalalithaa.

Before leaving Delhi, I paid one last call on Rajiv. Brushing past others waiting to go in to see him, I told him I was leaving for the election campaign, but I did need to tell him that my colleagues in the local Congress insisted on referring to me as RG's *'iniya nanbar'* (close or dear friend). I thought it necessary to warn him before he fetched up in the constituency. He smiled and replied, 'Are you not my friend?' Those, as it turned out, were the last words he spoke to me.

Electioneering in Mayiladuthurai

That same evening, I stood on the side of the highway hoping Jayalalithaa would recognize me and stop her vehicle. But her car-cade rushed past me at high speed. And that is when S. Rajakumar, an ordinary Congress worker, then twenty-three, demonstrated his presence of mind and quick reflexes that eventually led to his becoming my principal aide in the constituency. He rushed to the open jeep that followed which was carrying the candidates and shouted to them that the MP candidate was waiting to be picked up. They stopped and, at the first halt, I clambered on to the stage. In acknowledgement of my presence, Jayalalithaa gave me a curt nod.

I was dreading the prospect of being asked to speak, but that, I was relieved to find, was not on the agenda. My fellow MLA candidate signalled to me that all I was expected to do was stand at the rear of the platform and keep my head down and my arms crossed over my chest in prayerful respect to the Leader and to only put my hands together in a *'vanakkam'* (greeting in Tamil, respectful) when she mentioned my name as the Lok Sabha candidate.

First lesson learnt, we moved to the next stop. A police constable was precariously perched on the step at the rear of the jeep on which I was travelling. Suddenly, our jeep braked to let a pig amble past. The vehicle right behind us screeched to a halt but not before it smashed into the constable. I shall never forget the spectacle of his ankle dangling from the edge of his leg or the acute pain etched on his face. We continued in the car-cade as the constable was taken first to the local hospital, then to Thanjavur and finally to Madras; sadly, he died there the same night. (I caught a return flight from Trichy to Madras and back the next day to condole with, and give some money to, the old grief-stricken parents.)

In the wake of 'Amma' (Mother) – as Jayalalithaa liked to be called – we covered the entire constituency, east to west, stopping at every town on the way, the throngs of people on both sides of the road only increasing as we continued the journey. I learnt that in Tamil Nadu, candidates were not expected to wave but to bow in the direction of the audience with hands folded.

One major problem I had to deal with was that my *veshti* (equivalent to a 'dhoti' in Hindi but differently worn), which I had wrongly tied across my potbelly, kept slipping and I had to frantically stop my assets from being fully revealed to the voting public! I learnt to tie the knot at my waist and to keep the top of the *veshti* well above my heaving stomach at just under chest level. The other problem was language. The structure of my mother tongue had been built into my mind by my mother. But my vocabulary was limited. However, I was endowed with a quick ear and soon started picking up the words and sonorous alliterations used by the 'orator' who kept up a steady commentary on my varied virtues and those of our alliance from the front seat of the jeep as we drove through the constituency.

What I found almost impossibly difficult to cope with was the burning heat of the sun. I tried to overcome that by asking that my tour programmes start as soon after dawn as possible and take a break at noon until the afternoon sun became bearable around 4 p.m. My colleagues, who had no difficulty with the scorching temperatures and high humidity, were a little puzzled but soon adjusted themselves to what they saw as my weird timings. But as there were no Seshan-imposed restrictions[13] on the closing time of the campaign, my fellow MLA candidates would keep the vehicles moving till well past midnight. I feared I would die of exhaustion before the results came in!

I also found my mood oscillating between wild optimism and, more realistically, deepening despair, as the campaign gathered steam. The optimism sprang from the growing realization that the electorate wanted Jayalalithaa to form the next government; my pessimism from my obvious inadequacies in an unfamiliar milieu, a strange land, among people with whom I had just got acquainted and speaking a language I barely knew. What kept me going was the assurance from almost everyone that once Rajiv Gandhi arrived and spoke, I could consider the election sealed and delivered.

---

[13] T.N. Seshan was the chief election commissioner who earned a nationwide name for himself for bringing in various restrictions on candidates that the chattering classes highly approved of. Sadly, Seshan destroyed his reputation for integrity by standing as the Shiv Sena candidate for the post of president of India – which, of course, he lost.

In the meantime, I received the endorsements of Muhammad Ali, the nawab of Arcot (important, I thought wrongly, to tie up the 15 per cent minority vote); Maragatham Chandrashekhar who had earlier represented the constituency (important, I thought wrongly, to tie up the 20–25 per cent SC vote); Tamil Nadu Congress Committee (TNCC) president Vazhapadi Ramamurthy; and, most important of all, G.K. Moopanar who, I was told, had been sternly warned by Rajiv Gandhi that he would be held personally responsible if I were to be defeated. I must say Moopanar was his charming old self and soon whipped his many followers into at least not publicly displaying their hostility to my candidature. There were, besides, a few AIADMK leaders who came canvassing, including R.M. Veerappan, the cine moghul.

Moreover, my shaking legs slowly found the stamina to put up with the strain. My self-confidence grew as I got to know my fellow campaigners better. And as I progressively found my voice, I even tried out a couple of jokes. I had been a month on the road without a break. Rajiv's visit would be at the cusp of the election campaign and the vote. Overall, the signs were encouraging.

The assassination of Rajiv Gandhi

Rajiv Gandhi's visit was first announced for 19 May but soon postponed to the 22nd at the somewhat awkward time (for crowd gathering) of 9.20 a.m. I spent most of 21 May writing up a draft speech for RG and converting it into speaking points. I then faxed it to S.V. Pillai, an assistant and stenographer in RG's office, who, in turn, sent it to the TNCC president, Ramamurthy. At Madras airport, Rajiv put the speaking notes in his pocket and set out for Sriperumbudur, beckoning to Neena Gopal of *Gulf News* to get into his vehicle.

She poignantly recounts his last moments:

There was a sea of flags fluttering . . . it was just open ground with a few hundred people milling about within the bamboo barricades. The lighting was poor.

In my mind's eye, I can still see Rajiv Gandhi's gentle smile that showed not the slightest irritation . . . Stepping out from the front seat, Rajiv Gandhi had said, 'Come, come, follow me,' ... A suicide bomber, let alone the first female suicide bomber on Indian soil, was the last thing on anyone's mind as Rajiv Gandhi plunged into the crowd of supporters.

But as the huge explosion went off a few minutes later and I, standing about ten steps away, felt what I later realized was blood and gore from the victim splatter all over my arms and my white sari, a nameless dread took hold – something terrible had happened . . . The heat, searing, singeing, knocked me back with its strength.[14]

The bomb went off at 10.21 p.m. At 10.21 p.m., I was making up for time lost in drafting Rajiv Gandhi's never-to-be-delivered speech and supervising arrangements for the rally the next morning. I went in the late evening to remote villages in the Kuttalam assembly segment to garner a few last-minute votes, finishing the campaigning well past midnight.

We clambered out of our jeeps and threw our exhausted limbs into the chairs laid out in a semicircle in a friend's coconut grove under the star-spangled sky. Talk turned inevitably towards the morrow's great event. Pon. Govindarajan asked me how long it had been since I had last seen Rajiv. I counted. 'Thirty days,' I said. 'That's the longest I haven't seen him since I joined the PMO in March 1985.'

We finished our fresh tender coconut water and stood up to leave. I asked the driver to take me straight to our election office in the city bazaar. Waiting for me in the bazaar was the teenaged son of one of my

---

[14] Neena Gopal, *The Assassination of Rajiv Gandhi*, Penguin/Viking, New Delhi, 2016. (I have rearranged the sentences to give coherence to this eyewitness story, which has been accepted by the author vide email dated 23 May 2023.)

principal campaign managers. Stumbling over his sentences, he conveyed the news: Rajiv Gandhi had been assassinated a few hours earlier in Sriperumbudur.

I couldn't believe my ears. I rushed to the rally grounds. There, in the dark, I thought the workers were busy putting up the stage, the sound system, the barricades. (They were, in fact, dismantling them.) I turned around thinking to myself that this was a silly, thoughtless, cruel rumour being spread.

I arrived home. Suneet, who had accompanied me to the campaign along with our three daughters, met me at the doorstep. Sawani, superintendent of police, Thanjavur, and previously on Rajiv's SPG detail, had been on the phone to her. The news was confirmed. I went to one of our fleet of campaign cars that was fitted with a car radio and asked for the BBC to be switched on. And over the radio waves came the information that would not be denied: Rajiv Gandhi was, indeed, no more.

We woke the children and told them to get ready. We had to leave for Trichy almost immediately as it was generally believed that Pattali Makkal Katchi (PMK) workers would soon begin their protests in the usual way: cutting down trees and laying them across the roads to block all traffic. From Trichy, we could catch the overnight train to Madras and from there fly to Delhi.

We arrived in Delhi and, while the family went home, I set out for Teen Murti Bhavan to say my last farewell to my friend, patron and mentor. Sitting stoically beside the casket was Sonia Gandhi. When we were told in whispers to get up to make place for the myriad others who wanted to pay their last respects, Sonia signalled to security to let me be. It was a gesture of compassion I have never forgotten.

The following day I went to 10, Janpath, and a new guard asked me in stentorian terms, '*Aap hain kaun aur aapka kaam kya hain?*' (Who are you and what is your business?) Other security personnel on duty recognized me and hustled me past the entrance. But, clearly, a new age had begun.

At the funeral, I sat apart. Vir Sanghvi came up to me as the rituals were drawing to a close to ask if I would do a special column for *Sunday* by noon the next day. I woke at 5 a.m. and began to write. As I arrived at the last paragraph, the emotional dam burst:

> In my mind's eye, I see Vazhapadi Ramamurthy handing over the fax message to Rajiv at Meenambakkam airport. I see Rajiv glancing at it, tucking it into his shirt pocket. I see it travelling with him as delirious crowds wave him on through Villivakkam and Poonamallee to his tryst with destiny at Sriperumbudur. I see the woman with the garland bending down to touch his feet as Nathuram Godse did to Mahatma Gandhi. And I hear the deafening explosion that carries Rajiv and my speech away to eternity.
>
> Goodbye, Sir. We'll meet up again, up there. I'll never forget what you've meant to me. Goodbye, Sir. 'Good night, sweet prince.'

And the tears coursed down my cheeks to stain the paper on which I had written.

My first election victory

I returned to the constituency. It was apparent that the shock of Rajiv's assassination – and that too on the sacred soil of Tamil Nadu – had altered the entire milieu. I shall never forget one old woman on a distant village road coming up to my jeep and, putting her head on a poster of Rajiv's, crying her eyes out. Victory was certain. The only question was the margin. I was hoping against hope for 35,000; the actual margin was over 1,50,000.

Fittingly, the results were declared on 17 June, my late mother's eighty-first birth anniversary. If it had not been for her drilling Tamil into my unwilling ears, this moment would have never come. I, therefore, dedicate my parliamentary life of nearly a quarter century to her memory. And to my father, whom I called Appa, I say: 'It was because of your Brahmin identity that you had to leave the banks of the Cauvery. Now, sixty-five years later, I have brought the family back.'

There was an analysis done in 2007 of my dark horse election win by Professor M.M.S. Pandian of the Centre for the Study of Developing Societies, New Delhi. In his magnum opus, *Brahmin and Non-Brahmin*, he presented an interesting take on how I became one of the very few Brahmins in at least a generation to win a Lok Sabha seat from rural Tamil Nadu:

> As we have seen, Brahmins were steadfastly preoccupied with authenticity during the colonial period and claimed the Brahminic as the national. In the 1990s, the political context had so dramatically changed that the chances of a Brahmin's political survival hinged on his denial of his Brahmin identity ... Mani Shankar Aiyar was carefully demonstrating in public that his Brahmin identity was essentially false.[15]

That is true. I was born a Brahmin, but since my early adolescence I had denied my 'twice-born' caste. It is that denial which enabled me to make it to Parliament.

I found myself in a confused state of mind and emotion. On the one hand, I had fulfilled my life's ambition of making it to Parliament. On the other, my benefactor who had wrought this miracle was dead. I did not know how much further I could get without his patronage. At the same time, I was determined to make the most of this opportunity. That

---

[15] M.M.S. Pandian, *Brahmin and Non-Brahmin: Genealogies of the Tamil Political Present*, Permanent Black, New Delhi, 2007, p. 235.

I was on my own from now was a challenge; there was no one to help if I stumbled. I knew there were very many in my party who considered me an upstart. At the same time, I knew the aura of having been closely associated with Rajiv Gandhi would be my biggest asset. I also knew Sonia Gandhi would be around to help me *in extremis*. I had the self-confidence to expect that I would make it. It was thus for me 'the best of times and the worst of times'.

Meanwhile, I must hoe the field my father had been compelled to abandon. I had to work towards my mother's earnest hope that I would learn the Tamil language that she had loved. I also had before me the example of the times without number I had seen Rajiv Gandhi trudging the rural roads and interacting empathetically with villagers and farmers, prioritizing solutions to their problems over his own comfort or convenience.

I could perhaps use these memories as a beacon to signal my own way forward in this still unfamiliar rural milieu in a language in which I was woefully deficient and with a people I knew only as voters. I had now to rediscover them as living, breathing human beings with problems that I barely understood and had certainly not lived through, and do what I could to alleviate their suffering. Above all, I had to replicate the sincerity, honesty and integrity I had seen and experienced in RG. So long as I kept in mind his example, I would not walk alone.

I also knew Suneet would always be there, and so would my hugely talented daughters, Suranya, Yamini and Sana.[16] More than anything else, it was this which gave me the confidence to soldier on.

I had just turned fifty. Apart from about twenty years as an infant and then a student, I had been a diplomat for a quarter century. I was now embarking on a new, unfamiliar path for which I had no training, no experience. I knew I had to succeed, if only to get my daughters educated

---

[16] Suranya, in a recent social media post, has written: 'Mani Shankar Aiyar does not have three daughters. He has three lionesses!' Never was a truer word said.

at Oxbridge and beyond, and my own and Suneet's life steadied and on an even keel. I little anticipated the roller-coaster ride that lay ahead. I took what came in my stride and hoped it would all work out.

What actually happened, my rising and falling like a wave in a stormy sea, is the story of the rest of my life. I call it a 'half-life' in politics, much like the radioactive half-life discovered by Ernest Rutherford, the father of atomic physics – that is, the phenomenon of radioactivity growing for a while and then slowly petering out. In a similar way, my life in politics rose in spurts to its highs and then spluttered out to the point where I find myself sidelined by Rajiv Gandhi's heirs and marginalized even in the party. But that is another story for another book.

See detailed footnotes and endnotes by
scanning the QR code above.